LIVE FOR TODAY!

PLAN FOR TOMORROW

FOURTH EDITION

Robert Montague
Certified Financial Planner

Order this book online at www.trafford.com
or email orders@trafford.com

Most Trafford titles are also available at major online book retailers.

Print information available on the last page.

ISBN: 978-1-4907-7922-5 (sc)
ISBN: 978-1-4907-7924-9 (hc)
ISBN: 978-1-4907-7923-2 (e)

Finance, Personal-Canada
Retirement Planning
Investing
Life Planning

Library of Congress Control Number: 2016920427

Live For Today! Plan For Tomorrow
Published by Trafford Publishing 2007, 2008 and 2009

Trafford rev. 02/11/2017

 www.trafford.com

North America & international
toll-free: 1 888 232 4444 (USA & Canada)
fax: 812 355 4082

To my loving wife Margo Montague,
You have stood by my side for over 30 years.
For your unwavering support and unconditional love,
my heart belongs to you.
&
To my daughter Carley Montague,
a precious miracle in my life.
Your adventurous spirit, strength and
determination are a constant inspiration.

I love you both!

TABLE OF CONTENTS

PREFACE

"The most dangerous risk of all – The risk of spending your life not doing what you want on the bet you can buy yourself the freedom to do it later."
Anonymous

After seven years and numerous historic events since the publishing of the third edition in 2010, I felt compelled to provide updated information, for the fourth edition. In this fourth edition, my goal is to clarify and simplify a number of industry concepts. If I can explain complex principles in non-technical language then you will be better prepared when you interview and ultimately work with an Investment Advisor or Financial Planner. I have kept to my original premise to promote living every day to its fullest while planning for a long life and comfortable retirement. I have updated many statistics, originally retrieved from a variety of sources, such as Statistics Canada and World Health Organization and The Investment Funds Institute of Canada. Several new sections highlight the topics of the day, such as Climate Change, Income Inequality and historic low interest rates. All of these issues affect us directly or indirectly in ways that we do not yet fully understand. I have updated the rules and regulations of the Financial and Investment Industry as it has gone through immense changes, since the Financial Crisis in 2008. Many of these regulatory changes have improved transparency and the full and plane disclosures to investors. The disclosures should minimize or eliminate misunderstandings and the possibility of conflicts of interest, which can arise between advisors and their clients. Similarly, these changes will have both positive and negative affects on investors, big and small, as well as thousands of Portfolio Managers, Financial Planners, Investment Advisors, and Insurance Representatives.

Quite interesting that I would discover the quote above, eight years after I wrote the first edition of Live For Today! Plan For Tomorrow. It sums up the entire philosophy underlying this book. As an Investment Advisor, my clients are some of the wealthiest top 10 percent living in our society. The World Wealth Report conducted a study and found the number of millionaires in Canada climbed to 320,000, in 2013 (The Star.com, June 28 2014). A millionaire defined as having at least $1 million in financial assets, excluding their residence. The number of billionaires in the world climbed to 2,473 in 2015. The incredible statistic reported by wealth4billionaires.com claims their combined income for 2015, $7.7 trillion of a total $17 trillion globally. These numbers reveal the astronomical gap between the superrich and the rest of the population. It also reveals the incomprehensible need to acquire more and more. Contrast that concept with the fact that far too many individuals live way beyond their means, while the wealthiest top 1-10 percent ironically chooses to live within or well below their means. It seems to be a catch 22, in order to become wealthy you must live modestly, if not significantly below a level of income that would assume a more extravagant lifestyle.

However, in line with the premise of this book, I am often witness to those savers and investors building their wealth and sacrificing for tomorrow at the expense of the many daily conveniences available to them today. Much more troubling, I have seen those same individuals postpone their true desires for travel, owning a boat, cottage or even buying a new fridge until it is too late. Their health fails, they die or their spouse dies and they can no longer enjoy the wealth they worked so hard to create. This is tragic and it is the impetus for writing this story.

The primary purpose of this book is to highlight a variety of ways to have a more balanced, meaningful and contented life. A common thread found throughout the pages reveals how money and investing plays a role in the process. Understanding and developing your personal and financial goals are the first steps in life and more specifically financial planning. Once you have established goals, it becomes essential that you develop a clear path to achieving them. I am not suggesting that you develop an obsessive desire to achieve your goals. Rather, find a balance that fits for you.

Clearly, there is an innate desire in humans to build, create and achieve and that should never be stifled, otherwise, we return to living in caves. From multiple years of formal education to having a family, a career, social and leisure activities and retirement, I attempt to highlight strategies to help you enjoy each of these major parts of life. Although there is a philosophical slant to my writing, this is a financial planning book, so I will always circle back to tie these issues to your financial life. Through a better knowledge of money, the economy, financial markets and prudent investing you can more easily enjoy the other parts of your life.

I find it fitting to explain the Yin and Yang symbol at the top of the first chapter heading. It is the Chinese "symbol for Tai Chi, or Supreme Ultimate". "Yin and Yang represent a dynamic balance of forces in the natural world, a form of evening things out...Yin and Yang forces are constantly trying to overwhelm each other, but in truth one cannot *occur* (italics added) without the other..." (Forstater, 2003). This book, as it will become clear, is about balance and moderation. It is about the concepts of saving and spending, work and play, pain and pleasure as well as safety and growth investing.

* Excess and Moderation *
* Saving and Spending *
* Work and Play *
* Pleasure and Pain *
* Safety and Growth *
* Buy and Sell *
* Active and Passive *
* Bull and Bear *
* Needs and Wants *

"Yin and Yang are not about opposites but of complementary forces throughout the cosmos. Their meaning is obtained *from* each other, and they find their completion *through* each other." (Lee, 1999). For example, we need the passion, strength and perseverance to live for today, while simultaneously having the foresight to plan for tomorrow. Without experiencing loss, pain or deep sadness we cannot fully appreciate all the physical and emotional pleasures life provides us.

Intuitively, we know that one of the primary stressors in our lives is money. In fact, a survey conducted by the Financial Planning Standards Council (FPSC) in 2014, found that 42% of Canadians site money as their greatest source of stress. There are many others, such as work, personal health and relationships, especially for people living in the developing world, but I will focus on western society and personal finances here. For those who have already attained wealth, the stress comes from thoughts of loss. For others, stress comes from never having enough. Working and striving to make money, acquire assets like dream homes, sports cars, luxury yachts and more stuff is neither healthy nor unhealthy as long as there is a balance. It is my belief that effectively managing your day-to-day responsibilities and finances while learning alternative ways to put meaning into your life in addition to pursuing success are the keys to happiness. Moreover, I would add that if working long hours and focusing on a project or goal brings you happiness without hurting yourself or others, then go for it!

Developing personal and financial goals, without neurotic attachment will give you balance, direction and happiness. Without goals or a sense of purpose, you may not have the motivation or vision to move forward in a positive way, as you age. Over two hundred years ago, an English Poet, William Blake said, "Happiness is something to love, something to do and something to hope for". It was a fitting statement then and equally poignant today. Owning a bigger home full of material goods, another new car in the driveway or making more and more money every year without understanding why you need them has become a terrible habit. Earning money to purchase modern conveniences of our world is understandable, but *things* will never provide you with lasting happiness.

* Constant striving triggers stress and anxiety *
* Personal and financial goals provide balance *
* Educate yourself about health and finances *

Having nice things is neither good nor bad. Rather, it is the happiness or unhappiness and the anxiety that comes with having or not having them that is distressing. Not having material things or obsessively striving to obtain them brings with it a whole list of physical and psychological ailments. The American Institute of Stress lists over 50 signs and symptoms of stress. They claim stress will trigger everything from headaches, backaches, nausea, chest pain and palpitations, nasty colds and infections due to reduced immunities, heart burn, anxiety and depression to name a few. I suspect a majority of Doctors' appointments are psychosomatic in nature. In other words, the physical examination shows no physical basis for the aches, pain, or illness that requires any medical treatment. Reducing stress is the only remedy. If we were better educated about money and what it can and cannot do, as well as learning healthy ways of eating a nutritious diet and exercising daily, we would have less stress and fewer medical ailments. The number of visits to the doctor would drop dramatically and we would all be enjoying life to its fullest. Unfortunately, it may all be in your head.

An epidemic of alcohol, prescription and non-prescription drug use and addictions are the norm. A society plagued by obesity and heart disease are the result of lifestyle choices. There are no magic pills out there to cure you of your physical and psychological troubles, other than changing your lifestyle. You have the choice and the power to make the necessary changes. Eating properly, exercising and having balance in your life is the simple answer. Live within your financial and emotional means. Stop taking those high stress promotions and projects to increase your income and status, and sit back and smell the roses. I would dare to say that poorly performing managers and executives were promoted to their personal level of incompetence. This statement may strike you as somewhat funny if you ever worked for a manager that simply should not be in the position, but I say it in all seriousness. Be secure in your own self-worth as a whole and complete person, just as you are, without the need for 1 more promotion to obtain more stuff. It is all too clear that life is precious and is a tragedy if wasted on unhappiness.

Giving a little thought to personal and financial goals will serve you immediately as well as over the entire span of your life. I provide ideas for helping you to determine what you really want in the chapters on goals, the meaning of life, and living for today. In the chapter on The Meaning of Life, I emphasize the many options we have available to us. We do not have to blindly, conform to the norms of the day. We can think, ask questions and we have choices to make change. With change, sacrifices will also become apparent, as there will always be a price for the freedom to be happy.

* Financial independence, Capital Preservation *
* Protection and financial security *

The title of the book, Live for Today, Plan for Tomorrow, speaks volumes about the premise of this book. Working as a Financial Planner for over 20 years, I have observed several persistent goals and dreams of my clients. Many of the people I have had the privilege of working with are looking for financial independence, capital preservation, tax minimization, protection in case of death or disability and most importantly a sense of financial security. All of these goals represent a means to a more leisurely life of enjoying personal interests and activities, such as painting or sculpting, building or renovating, learning or writing, travel, owning a cottage, helping their children go to school or buy a house and other personal aspirations. Others seem to strive for success and material wealth with no clear objective in mind. This reminds me of a story of a man sitting backwards on a horse while it raced by another man who yelled, "Where are you going?" The man on the horse shouted back, "I don't know, ask the horse". All joking aside, my goal is to help you achieve balance, peace of mind and contentment, by providing you with the knowledge of the investment world. Saving and sacrificing for your retirement while postponing your dreams for another day may not be the way to happiness. Although it is essential you save and invest for your future, but not to such an extreme extent you are missing the opportunity to live in the now.

From the hype or doom in the media of the great wealth or great losses made in real estate, stock and bond markets, we need to hear an honest and realistic voice of reason. Economists, analysts, journalists, authors and self-professed experts all tell us these things, yet they often get major events wrong. In fact, Wall Street Economic Analysts, Rating Agencies, the Federal Reserve, Banks and the International Monetary Fund have all failed miserably over the years to accurately predict any of the past recessions and subsequent market corrections. If not entirely wrong in their forecasts, they seem to be consistently at odds with one another. In one particular report, "...of 77 countries under consideration, 49 of them were in recession in 2009...Economists as reflected in the averages published in a report called Consensus Forecasts had not called a single one of these recessions by April 2008." Writers, analysts and commentators simply cannot do justice to the complexities of human behavior combined with the global investment world in a single article or news report. They especially cannot begin to have predictive accuracy due to the potential for "black swan events", or the unknowable's, such as mass psychology of the markets, geopolitical issues and manipulation of currency and bond markets. They can however, help us to see the trends, if not the "black swans".

* Be mindful of the hype and doom in the media *
* Listen to a voice of reason *
* A diversified portfolio is best medicine *

The media headlines often stand in the way of common sense and clarity. From the early eighties when economists, turned authors, were sounding the alarms about the "Economic time Bomb", and the late nineties when the stock markets were roaring and many experts were claiming, "it was different this time", only to watch the train wreck from 2000 to 2003. It eventually righted itself and went on its merry way for a 5 year+ bull market. Additionally, and more recently, the warning bells and sirens were ignored regarding the sub-prime mortgage circus and ultimate financial crisis of 2008-09. By mid-2016, we were at a turning point in the economy and the markets were at the peak of the cycle again. Where we go from here is always uncertain to market participants. With the recently elected President, Donald Trump the economic future is far from certain. More on this later. A long-term plan can take some of the anxiety out of investing throughout cycles. Investing in and starting a small family business should be no different from investing in publically traded stocks. You buy for the long run and do the necessary homework to ensure the investment is sound and priced right. The point being, the unsuspecting public needs to know the short and long term risks as well as the rewards to be had in the world of investing over the long run. I will share my views and ideas over the coming chapters to provide the essentials for investing for the long run.

It is a primary goal to educate non-industry investors about the various types of investments available in the "retail" investment climate, such as mutual funds, exchange traded funds, stocks, bonds, and GICs. The financial industry is highly regulated and many safe guards built into the system to protect investors from unsuitable investments or costly fees or penalties as well as providing essential client information and disclosures. That is not to say, unscrupulous Investment Advisors will not take advantage of trusting investors. Nevertheless, it deters much of the unethical behavior that occurred in previous decades. The financial markets are a challenge for professionals to navigate, so it is understandable many non-industry investors are overwhelmed by the choices and complexities of the various types of investments.

You will learn in the following pages details about financial and retirement planning as it relates to your situation. You will also learn what to look for in a Financial Planner or Investment Advisor, how to select a quality mutual fund or what the difference is between a pension and mutual fund. Alternative investment management comes from Private Wealth departments of the major banks and brokerages as well as private boutique Investment Counsel or Hedge Fund companies. They offer individual and customized investment services for high net worth and sometimes sophisticated clients. Investment Counsellors typically have advanced business degrees and designations such as the

Chartered Financial Analyst (CFA), giving them discretionary trading authorization over client accounts. I will define and explain types of insurance and a variety of investment concepts, such as mysterious hedge funds and derivatives. This will provide you with a working knowledge to ask better questions of your advisor. I cover the basics of the financial world from beginning to end and it is my wish that you will take away a better understanding of the investment landscape in Canada.

PART I

DISCOVERY

CHAPTER I

THE JOURNEY OF LIFE

"The indispensable first step to getting the things you want
out of life is this: decide what you want."
Ben Stein

"If you don't know where you are going,
you'll end up someplace else."
Yogi Berra

- ➤ The Journey
- ➤ Discovery - Knowledge - Planning - Action
- ➤ Balancing personal and financial pursuits
- ➤ Planning as a process of discovery
- ➤ Money as a necessary life component
- ➤ Accepting social responsibility
- ➤ A look at social and altruistic things

The Journey
The four parts to this book take you through the major components of *Life Planning* as it commingles with Financial Planning. Part I, Discovery will highlight all aspects of your personal, financial and physical life. Chapter I, *The Journey*, looks at how society has

come to a futuristic version of survival of the fittest. We live in a culture where it seems to be every man for himself; isolated by technological advancements (think texting or emailing), giant corporations, climbing the ladders of success, building wealth, and where material consumption are the status quo. In and of themselves, these are not terrible things, so long as your passion and desire to achieve do not meet with stress and anxiety. In fact, immersing yourself in any type of endeavor brings immense personal satisfaction.

At the time of the original writing, March 2009, capitalism and financial markets experienced its worst crash since the great depression of the 1930s. Financial markets brought to its knees. Free markets and deregulation had promoted greed, corruption and a lower standard of living for the masses. Instead of raising everyone's standard of living, it merely raised the income of the top ten percent. It was followed by commentary like, "the excesses of the past generation will be reversed as western society goes through a long period of deleveraging", (ie. paying the piper). Currently, in 2016, inequality and the gap between the top 1% and the rest of the masses have never been more apparent. Poetically, the Swiss bank Credit Suisse found that the "top 1 percent owned almost exactly 50 percent of the world's global assets, while ironically, the bottom 50 percent owned less than 1 percent." Capitalism had swung too far to the right, just as communism went too far in Cuba, leaving the masses with table scraps while being told they were the finest morsels of food available, so to speak. This reminds me of a book called, *Animal Farm,* by George Orwell. He writes a fictional tale of farm animals whereby the more intelligent species rise to power and use propaganda to deceive the rest into believing life is never been better.

The pressures are enormous for average working people simply trying to hold onto a stressful job and pay the bills, while saving for the kids' education and retirement. The executives at the top of very large corporations have difficult decisions to make during recessions must make cuts to human capital. In other words, people lose their jobs and their income. This affects thousands of people, adding stress to individual and their families. True, some people have wonderful and fulfilling jobs, with premium pension and benefits plans, but many, particularly in the United States do not have such luxuries. Despite the many day-to-day challenges we experience, regardless of income, I will maintain the importance of obtaining balance and meaning in your life through specific short, medium and long-term goals.

Chapter II, *An Investing Life* outlines the importance of investing throughout your life as well as highlighting the risks and rewards of the markets. The most recent financial crisis of 2008 will not be the last, as history shows us, economic and business cycles are quite predictable. As I write this fourth edition, we appear to be at the peak of the cycle as indicated by a number of economic indicators as well as a sideways stock market. The United States has also shocked the world with the election of Donald Trump as the 45th President. We should learn to anticipate market corrections and see them as opportunities and not a time to panic. What is less certain is the timing and duration of each cycle as it goes through its peaks and valleys.

Chapter III, *The Meaning of Life* elaborates on the premise that you cannot have meaning or purpose in your life without asking what you genuinely want and then taking responsibility for yourself and others. How will you contribute to the betterment of this world? How will you provide for yourself and loved ones? Ask yourself why you want a bigger house, a yacht, a new car, a cottage or an MBA. Ask yourself what is important to you, while keeping an eye on what is required to survive in our complex society. Quiet your mind and listen….You have the answers within you. Whether you are religious, spiritual or simply believe in the power of the mind, you will receive the answer. If not, seek advice from a trusted friend or professional. If you could slow down for a moment, discover what your true goals are, you may find that you would love to be doing something completely and totally, different with your life.

A discussion on the meaning of life would not be complete if it did not touch on life choices. Making decisions about your education, job and career should not be limited to the one you made when you were 17. I am quite certain that most of us would not let a 17 year old decide our entire life. Therefore, we can change our minds, by looking at different options from different perspectives throughout our lives. Making decisions or changing paths should be within a moral, responsible and ethical framework. Consider the consequences of your decisions when aspiring to your financial and personal goals. For instance, deciding to take a job transfer to another part of the country simply for a big pay raise, may affect family and friends. Perhaps before taking the job, a dialogue with your spouse and children and even your close friends should take place. We are free to choose, within limits. Tony Robbins said it best, *"It's in your moments of decision that your destiny is shaped."* We can indeed pilot our destiny and change course in an instant.

Chapter IV, *Goals to Motivate*, is a powerful theme that is vital to having a purposeful and meaningful life. Without goals, we merely exist, day to day. It is my contention that we must have goals to drive us to accomplishment throughout our lives. All of our basic needs are generally satisfied without much effort, in the western world. Finding food, shelter and clothing are not a burden to us. Therefore, we should have the time and energy to pursue what we love. There are other drivers of behavior that I have found to be equally if not more powerful than the instinctive drives of our ancestors. These drivers of behavior ultimately lead to the competitive pressures we feel on a daily basis. So, find your personal drivers, and set goals that feel right.

Not unlike our ancestors we are, in effect, competing to control our environment, for the biggest piece of the kill, the warmest part of the cave and the most fertile of young females or the male with superior qualities, for reproduction and passing on our genes. We know there will be a wide range of competitive spirit within the population. From very content individuals to high functioning and driven athletes, business owners and executives, professors or political leaders. Similarly, some of you are driven to pursue higher incomes, build and control your own businesses, or gather assets, such as real estate, stocks, or bonds and generally all of the comforts of living in the 21st century. While others are not as overtly driven, but derive their happiness from intellectual endeavors such as the arts, literature, history, science, philosophy or science and technology for example. Goals motivate us and are different for everyone, but will ultimately dictate what we pursue in life.

Part II, *Knowledge,* is an integral part of living for today, planning for tomorrow. This part of life planning is referring to the importance of comprehending the world around us. It is not important that you understand the details of individual topics or disciplines such as, environmental studies, biochemistry, physics, medicine or computer programing. It is important to have a general idea they exist and what each may encompass. This gives you awareness. The essence of knowledge is having a grasp or understanding of a specific subject or topic accumulated through direct experience or study; while, wisdom is an intuitive ability or capacity for sound judgment obtained *from* your knowledge. Having wisdom comes from years of accumulated experience and learning. An understanding and awareness of your societal norms results in productive members of society.

Chapter V, *Investments & The Mutual Fund Industry* and Chapter VI, Market Intelligence, emphasize that without an understanding of the fundamentals (ie. knowledge) of investing and the markets you will not have peace of mind or wisdom about investing. Due to the volatility of the stock market, it is essential that you learn about the basic types of investments and their risks and rewards. Learn what type of investment income is produced and the tax consequences of owning them. Learn how the various types of investments fit or do not fit with your objectives and risk tolerance, either on your own or with an investment advisor. This basic education will give you a sense of security and help you make better decisions. Ultimately, you will have to hire a Financial Planner whom you can trust. My aim is to take the worry out of saving and investing, by giving you a little knowledge. I will outline what to look for in a Financial Planner, in a later chapter and why I am a textbook example of who to select. All joking aside, a little bit of knowledge and wisdom will go a long way.

In the late 1990's, a few corporate executives and accountants distorted and manipulated financial statements in their efforts to achieve enormous financial incentives and payoffs. Heavily compensated investment analysts were unable to provide objective advice because of the huge financial gains for their positive spin. In the end, it all came crumbling down in 2000, when the technology and dot com bubble burst. Then over the next 3 years, the world stock markets experienced its worst bear market in 30 years, wiping out trillions of dollars of investor capital.

Following the *tech wreck* of the early 2000s, deregulation of financial institutions and loose lending practices known as NINJA (No Income No Job or Assets) loans led to the financial crisis of 2008. This crisis again wiped out trillions of dollars of market gains from the previous several years. The S&P500 fell 57% beginning in October 2007, until it bottomed out in March 2009. The worst market crash since 1929, when the S&P500 dropped 86% over 33 months. The 2007-09 events revealed that all the deregulation and propaganda of free markets did nothing to impede greed, fraud and corruption.

In my humble opinion, after the Financial Crisis of 2008, I believed it would taint the public perception of the financial industry for at least a generation. And it did, to a certain extent with mom and pop investors. Yet, by 2016, the unscrupulous behavior of the banks, primarily in the US, did not change, even with stiffer corporate governance, more government regulation and the like. It continued unabated. The Federal Reserve, bent on artificially propping up the stock market and economic growth, used massive and sustained monetary stimulus. By experimenting with the economy with a massive bond-buying program, they kept interest rates artificially low. The only result was the gap between the richest 10% and the rest of the population has never been wider due to the failure of the *trickle-down* philosophy of the corporate elite and political leaders in their back pockets. It seems more appropriate to call it the *trickle-up* effect. The middle class had their money sucked out of their wallets and into the hands of the top ten percent, if not the top one percent. Middle class indebtedness was in part their own fault, for over spending and using their homes as ATMs. This was also the fault of easy money policies of the Federal Reserve.

Part III, *Planning*, provides a backdrop about the wealth management and financial planning industry. Chapter VII,

Financial Planning, zeros in on Financial Planning as a professional service provided by accredited individuals with general knowledge in most areas of personal finance. Investing, taxes, retirement planning, insurance and budgeting are a few areas Financial Planners can help. Some planners may have several areas of expertise that are essential to you if you are to have financial independence and security throughout your life. The big banks and brokerages, mutual fund dealers and insurance companies are all capitalizing on the baby boomer demographic bulge and their desire to save for retirement. Nine million baby boomers in Canada are requiring financial, retirement, tax and estate planning advice and services. This trend will not abate for a few more decades. What credentials and expertise should you look for in a financial planner? I will highlight what to expect in the way of advice, planning and implementation. In the tradition of education, it is essential to the premise of having peace of mind and balance.

Integral to the Planning process, Chapter VIII, *Net Worth & Budgeting*, Chapter IX, *Retirement Planning*, Chapter X, *End of Life Planning*, Chapter XI, *Thoughts on Income Tax* and Chapter XII, *Funding Education*, take you through the basics of the major areas of Financial Planning your advisor can help with. Consider your Net Worth a snap shot of your current situation. It tells you where you are today and reveals your progress or lack of progress over the years. Budgeting can put you on the right track as far as defining your cash flow, paying down your debts and building your RRSPs. Retirement planning follows a process that provides a template to achieve your retirement income goals. Estate planning or end of life planning looks at how Insurance, Powers of Attorneys, Wills and Trusts will complete your life's personal and financial goals. You will see that these chapters detail many of the areas beyond the traditionally known investment component of financial planning.

Part IV, *Action*, Chapter XIII, *Live For Today*, outlines implementing all of the new discoveries about who you are and what you want. You will finally be at peace with your knowledge of investing and the markets, your wisdom to invest and begin planning for tomorrow with your newly acquired knowledge of the financial and retirement planning process. I personally have a great passion for life, love, and learning. This should come through in the final chapter Live for Today! I refer to the meaning of life in the beginning of the book, but it is not until the end that I show you the importance of using your amazing brain to achieve meaning in your life. I discuss the idea of living an active, goal oriented and creative life, not necessarily a success oriented life, as this can imply a life out of balance and too many personal sacrifices.

Continuing with the *Action* theme, maintaining physical fitness and a healthy lifestyle in general are part of the life plan. Learning all that you can about personal financial planning, finding a trusted financial planner and advisory team are essential to a life plan. Getting your finances under better control, finding balance between saving and spending then getting on with the act of living in the now are revisited. If you do not live for today you and your loved ones may live to regret missed opportunities to experience all that life has to offer. I add a caveat that becoming overextended to realize your dreams is ill advised. We cannot always have everything we want, but with proper planning and prioritizing, you can fulfill your dreams. Boredom cannot be a part of your vocabulary in my opinion. We are living in an age of infinite possibilities, infinite things to do, from sports, to games, volunteering and charity work, to taking courses at a local college. All of these infinite possibilities may compete with the infinite material temptations. Acquiring a thirst for learning is something I have a profound belief in. Living for today, planning for tomorrow is the primary message and it is my wish that some of you will also develop this passion.

Planning for Life

* A process of discovery *
* Determine what you really want *
* Develop and put your plan in writing *
* Put meaning into your life with goals *

Planning is essential to having a long, involved, enjoyable and productive life. It is a process of discovery, and finding out what you really want out of life; what you would like to accomplish, and what it is that you can give and how you will contribute. Writing or developing a plan can be as simple as scribbling a dozen ideas on a scrap of paper, but I am more interested in you developing a more comprehensive, structured and systematic approach to setting goals. I will endeavor to outline the major parts of a life plan as I see it commingling ideology with Financial Planning. I will highlight how it may serve you best on your personal journey in pursuit of happiness. After all, that is what we all hope to achieve. A life plan encompasses almost every facet of our lives, but if certain aspects are over weighted and out of balance, stress and unhappiness creeps in.

You can put meaning into your life by having goals, finding love, developing a passion for learning, becoming committed to taking responsibility for you and your friends, family and fellow man. Investing and saving are a part of the process that many North Americans will identify with and it is an essential part of the process for every household. Sadly, according to the Federal Reserve in 2014, the statistics show that the highest percentage of stock ownership resides with the top 20 percent of income earners. It is my hope that everyone be invested in the great companies of the global economy and share in the profits. I suspect the numbers would be quite similar in Canada. For a lack of a better word, *money things* are considered an essential and integral part of the life plan. Money things are a part of life, and we need to deal with them and get on with the journey of life.

Money Things

* Personal finance and investing *
* Money and meaning in your life *
* Money and relationships *

In Part III: *Planning,* several chapters outline many financial planning concepts and aspects of your life that involve money, specifically saving and spending and, investing for your retirement or children's education. Taking care of day-to-day expenses (budgeting), credit issues such as, mortgages, loans and credit cards are discussed in more detail. Understanding life and disability insurance, home and auto insurance and now for many aging baby boomers (i.e. born between 1946 and 1964) critical and long term care, estate planning issues and real estate are just a few of the money items to note.

Money things directly and indirectly tie in with many other parts of the life plan. Having money should not have an influence on having meaning in your life. Although, it should ensure that you have no excuses! Sadly, though, money is a powerful force in our lives and affects everything we do. Money directly or indirectly determines your education level, career path and job satisfaction. Many people have a great career and high paying job that will give them all of the material things our society has to offer, but if there is no internal happiness or if there is excessive stress than it is not going to last. On the other hand, some people love their jobs and are clearly passionate about what they are doing, while disregarding how much money they earn.

Money things and relationships connect in a subtle and occasionally direct ways. Wealth and social class, whether we are willing to admit it or not are often factors in who become our contacts and network of friends. Whom we mesh with on the weekends for barbeques or fine dining at a local restaurant directly relate to our money or lack of it. Sadly, this type of friendship and socializing has as much to do with money as money impacts your lifestyle. Awareness of the reality of these social norms will bring us contentment.

Social Things

* * Lifestyle and money *
* Contributing to society *
* The importance of a social network *
* How do you define yourself *

Lifestyle and money or lack of it, go hand in hand. Lifestyle can determine the place you live, the cars you drive, the restaurants you frequent, the sports events you enjoy or the places you take your holidays. Wealthy people can and do have quite different lifestyles compared with less financially privileged individuals. However, they are not necessarily happier, healthier, or more content. An interesting research study (Frank, 2010) found that as our income rises we only become happier to a point at around $75,000 per year. As of 2016, the new $75,000 is $83,000 due to inflation. It is interesting to note that once you hit the magic income level there is no gain in measures of happiness. People may have more stuff and may assess they have a *better* life, but it does nothing for the internal emotion of happiness, as defined in the study.

You need to be mindful that the ability to make and earn money today, just as our ancestors' ability to hunt and forage for food 25,000 or 50,000 years ago are critical to every aspect of our lives. Ultimately, I believe money can serve us in many ways, in addition to providing the necessities of life. It is also true that money can provide us with many of life's hedonistic pleasures. However, as mentioned above, more and more money does not imply greater and greater happiness. There are other important ways to achieve happiness. Contributing to society and helping others requires our time, energy and compassion, but pays huge happiness dividends. If time constraints are a concern, monetary donations are the primary ingredient for food, clothing, shelter and health care for the less privileged. For those with great wealth helping others can become an extremely satisfying part of life.

Personal Financial Planning as a component part of a life plan boils down to providing us with an awareness or blueprint. It provides strategies for discovering where we are today and bringing us to the point of attaining our goals and of being at peace with our lives. I would contend that almost everyone wants financial independence and financial security. I would also contend that everyone needs to have a social network and would like to have love in his or her life. I would further contend that almost everyone would love to have a lifestyle filled with every convenience if not luxury that life has to offer. However, does it not make life so much more rewarding, interesting and exciting when you work towards a goal and achieve it on your own? Many people in our society are motivated by the ultimate pleasures they derive from the rewards of their efforts.

People in western society attach or define themselves by their job title and their material wealth and success. Comparatively, the eastern cultures define themselves by their ideals, morality and responsibility to others, a collective unity with everything in the universe and a deeply felt spirituality. By keeping score relative to our neighbors, colleagues, friends or family people tend to feel superior or inferior, secure or insecure. At its worst, people feel worthless, inadequate and possibly like failures. Keeping score in its multitude of faces is not inherently good or bad. In fact, I would propose that it is an essential part of keeping us strong. However, as I believe all things to be done in moderation, keeping score often gets out of hand in sports, business and accumulation of wealth.

Before you read my following commentary, ask yourself, *"Who am I?"* Write down your answer before reading further. Ok, how did you respond to this profound question? Most people describe themselves by their job title. For example, I am a Nurse, or I am Machinist. Many others might also add what they do for a living, where they live, how big their house is and whether they are married with kids. Each of us is much more than *what we do* for a living and what we own. Although work life is important, there is so much more to life and to each individual. We are infinitely complex animals and intelligent beings capable of such wonderful love and compassion.

Philosophical Things

* Connecting with people on a deeper level *
* Looking beyond the financial world *
* Aspiring to higher moral standards *

As a Financial Planner and an individual like anybody else, I try to connect with people on a deeper level. I understand that money is very important in their lives. However, people are more than their money and it is important that I get to know the individual as well as their financial situation before I make any investment recommendations or plans. I get to know their hopes and dreams, experiences, and hear about their ideas. Most people need to accept that money is equivalent to the food and clothing, or beads required to trade for the fur coat worn by our ancestors. If you are to survive and participate in society and contribute to your fellow man, you will need to understand that money is essential. You know it can and does cause a wide range of emotions from pain and upset to pleasure and ecstasy. Of course, if you do not have enough food and clothing you will be worried and stressed. During difficult times, you can be mindful that you are much more than your material wealth, your job and title and much more than your physical body. No matter what happens in your life, circumstances should not make you feel unworthy. What you do with your life and wealth, your contribution to the world will ultimately define you.

Whether you are religious, spiritual or simply believe in the power of the mind we must all aspire to higher moral standards. I believe we were born with a built in set of values and ethical standards that guide us throughout our lives. Sometimes due to unfortunate circumstances, some people develop a short circuit in the wiring for their personal morality. I believe you are hard-wired, so to speak, with knowing right from wrong. Assuredly, we have all seen these wires defective, or crossed in terms of criminal behavior or indoctrination of one kind or another. Nevertheless, listen to the voice in your head that tells you how to make the right choices. It goes hand-in-hand that you make decisions everyday about everything from your finances to your family and friends that reflect your morals.

Financial Things

As you will read in the second chapter, *An Investing Life* is an essential part of a life plan. Developing an understanding that economic fundamentals determine employment and job growth, housing prices, interest rates and drive the stock markets higher or lower is step one. Stock market participants, you will discover are not always rational. The strength of economy is the underlying driver of corporate earnings, which dictate the direction of stock prices. When the economy is in the contraction stage of the business cycle, you should be more cautious about your stock market investments. If the economy is beginning to slow, you may coincidentally see the stock market begin to fall from its highs. The business cycle is all too predictable, in that it will take place. Pinpointing *when* a particular part of the cycle begins and what its duration is going to be, are always unknowable.

Analyzing the most recent financial crisis of 2008 is a way to learn. With naïve optimism, hoping to avoid a similar crisis in the future, many economists and market experts studied the crisis and the ensuing severe recession. Sadly, every crisis is a slight variation of anything seen in the past. I summarize some of their thoughts in the chapter, An Investing Life. I show all sides of what caused the financial crisis and how contrarian investors, market analysts and value managers believe it could have been averted.

As this is primarily a financial planning book with a component of life planning, I cover the basics of a large number of conceptual areas. By providing a conceptual basis for building your own plan, you can use this book as a stepping-stone for further study. Building a comprehensive financial plan is a lot of work, but it will give you a template to fulfill all of your goals. From a basic net worth statement, family budget, retirement plan or a complex estate plan, the concepts will benefit you throughout your life. If I can inspire, teach and open your mind to new and exciting ideas, I will have succeeded in achieving my goal.

CHAPTER II

AN INVESTING LIFE

*"One of the funny things about the stock market
is that every time one person buys, another
sells, and both think they are astute."*
William Feather

➤ An Investing Life
➤ Economic Fundamentals drive the markets
➤ The predictability of Business Cycles
➤ What really happened in 2008?
➤ What is next for the markets and Economy?
➤ An Historical Perspective on the markets

An Investing Life

* Essential to participate *
* Material luxuries vs. material necessities *
* Millionaire mind *

From the moment you begin working and can contemplate owning a car, boat or your own home you must get into the game. I refer to investing as a game not because I believe it to be of less importance than anything else, but because there are far too many unknowns, or uncertainties to worry about in the short run. In other words, it is a game compared to such matters as going to work, doing your job to the best of your ability, or perhaps dealing with a health or medical conditions in yourself or family member. I actually believe investing to be a very serious game that needs your attention. However, I do not believe that it should occupy all of your time or take away from family, friends or hobbies, unless you are a professional investor.

If you are to live and thrive in this society, I think it is essential to participate. Why should you not share in the gigantic profits of the world's largest and most innovative companies? You can easily buy and own shares in the great Canadian financial institutions and telecommunications companies, like TD Bank, RBC or Manulife Financial, Bell Canada Enterprises or the world's largest technology, pharmaceutical and Energy companies like Apple, Google or Amazon, Johnson & Johnson, Pfizer and Exxon Mobile and receive the growth and dividends generated quarter after quarter. If you are just starting to invest, for as little as fifty dollars a month you can own a basket of great companies. You can do this by planning and a little bit of sacrifice. For example, instead of going out to your favorite restaurant and a movie twice a month, go out only once. This will save you at least $100. Put $100 a month into a stock mutual fund earning 8% rate of return from growth and dividends. By investing $100 a month over 30 years, you would accumulate $150,000, over 40 years, $351,428. This sounds nice in theory, but you might ask, "Why do I need $350,000?" I will elaborate in a later chapter why you need a specific amount and how much income it will provide during retirement.

Investments are a means to an end, to provide us with the material necessities of life and to provide us with an income in our retirement. Investments can also provide us with all of the wonderful conveniences available. However, I should differentiate between *material necessities* and *material luxuries*. Material luxuries are a way to keep score and will at best, give you fleeting happiness. Whereas, material necessities provide for our food, clothing and shelter needs. So, investing can provide for both.

Throughout your life, investing plays a role, but it is the journey and the challenges you experience that give you the rewards and greatest satisfaction.

The concept of investing is limited only by your imagination. The stock and bond markets first come to mind and possibly real estate as an investment. However, this is merely the beginning of your options to build wealth. For the purpose of this book, I will focus on the passive approach to investing, such as buying mutual funds, stocks and bonds vs. the actively involved approach. The actively involved approach would be investing in yourself and then investing your saved up money to build and operate your own business. Take a quick look through your local yellow pages and see the thousands of small, medium and large business listed. It is truly inspiring when you consider all of the people that created and invested in a small business, writing their own destiny. You can do the very same with the passive approach, saving a part of your earnings from employment and investing into stocks and bonds. This will build you a secondary source of income. This approach also permits you to be an owner and free to do what you love. Whether you wish to be a truck driver, doctor, engineer or mechanic you can build a second income by saving a part of your earnings that immediately begins to pay you an income from dividends or interest.

Millionaires and billionaires around the world often invest in themselves first, then into building personal fortunes. More often than not, they fail a few times before finding the exact mix of capital, skill set, desire and filling a special niche required for wealth creation. Discipline, perseverance, genetics and perhaps a small sprinkle of luck also play a role in becoming wealthy. Thomas J. Stanley (Thomas J. Stanley, 2001, pp. 82 - 83) writes, "… most millionaires are well disciplined…." And, "The harder I work, the luckier I become." Stanley also lists the qualities or factors that determine economic success (Thomas J. Stanley, 2001, pp. 32 - 35). Integrity and high moral values and being honest ranked as being very important in a survey he conducted. Strong social skills would include leadership skills, getting along with others and the ability to communicate ideas to others ranked as very important.

Finally, investing in the stock market or one's own business and making wise investment decisions also ranked as important or very important in the survey of millionaires.

Entrepreneurial individuals build their own businesses to achieve wealth. For our purposes, I will be focusing on the more traditional means of building wealth with investment savings, for the majority of working Canadians. I will not consider real estate an investment unless it is in addition to your primary residence and it generates rental income. Investing in a diversified basket of securities such as stocks, exchange traded funds, mutual funds and bonds will be my primary focus. The ideas and strategies also apply to entrepreneurs who own businesses *and* to the employees of those businesses. I say this because creating and building a business from the ground up takes many years and before you blink, you are thinking of retirement and in need of a succession plan. At that time, all of your money and capital tied up in your business, with no easy way to obtain retirement income. This is a major risk to your retirement. Without a savings plan nor the ability to easily convert your business to an income producing investment your comfortable retirement may be in jeopardy. Therefore, it remains essential that you diversify your assets beyond your private enterprise from the first day you begin your venture.

Economic Fundamentals Drive the Markets

* Importance of Gross Domestic Product (GDP) *
* Income based and Expenditure based *
* Leading economic indicators *

You may have heard the phrase, "It's the economy stupid". This statement refers to the nature of the stock market and the economies' influence upon it. Stock market participants value companies on an individual basis by analyzing financial statements and earnings reports as well as watching the macroeconomic environment and its performance relative to its industry. Fundamental financial analysis of each company is essential to the valuation process and the efficient market theory of investing. A "clean balance sheet" means different things to different analysts, but it essentially refers to a company with little or no debt and solid shareholder equity from its' assets. Minimal debt implies less downside risk under various market conditions. A solid income statement would reveal consistent and rising earnings, quarter after quarter.

In addition to the fundamental analysis, investors look at company performance relative to its peers in the same industry. Among the various complexities of the economy, the most watched macroeconomic indicator is the Gross Domestic Product, or GDP. This is the measure of output, the revenues of an entire economy in dollar terms. Market participants often monitor GDP growth quarter over quarter and year over year as a percentage change. Statisticians measuring GDP peer into every sector of the economy including retail and wholesale trade, agriculture and manufacturing for example. Combined, this analysis encompasses a stock valuation process.

More specifically, these statistical measures look at two sides of the economy: *income based* and *expenditure based*. The GDP, *income based* measure looks at wages, salaries and supplement labor income, corporate profits before tax, interest and miscellaneous investment income, net income from non-farm unincorporated business, taxes and capital consumption allowances (Statistics Canada, 2009). Consequently, the GDP, *expenditure based* measure looks at personal expenditures on consumer goods & services, government expenditures on goods & services, business capital investment, other nominal expenditures and Exports of goods & services minus imports of goods & services. Tables showing the series data for GDP quarterly changes, year over year changes are available by Statistics Canada (Statistics Canada, 2009).

Why is GDP so important? As can be observed in the tables compiled by Statistics Canada, stock and bond market participants can make critical investment decisions using this information. For example, the Q3/08 to Q4/08 quarterly change in GDP fell -3.5%. Corporate profits fell, a substantial -20.1% and -7.3% year-over year. Market analysts and investors look for trends that will indicate the future performance of the stocks and bonds they own. This is an inexact science and numerous studies have shown that economists have failed miserably at forecasting recessions (The Economist, July 2012). Although initial GDP numbers are often a lagging data point they can reveal clear trends in the big picture of the economy.

Equally, if not more important than GDP, there are several leading or key economic indicators investors and analysts watch. According to one particular chartered bank in Canada, market participants will monitor some or all of the following indicators; the monthly US Leading Indicator, Ivey Purchasing Managers Index, Consumer Credit, Service Employment, Housing starts, manufacturing avg. workweek in hours, Exports, Exchange rate, yield curve, employment quality index and the TSX300 Composite (CIBC World Markets, 2007).

On a monthly basis, leading indicators in combination with many other analytical tools assist with economic forecasts. They are not going to give you a guarantee of the month ahead, but the analysis provides for the best estimate. On a deeper level, in-depth analysis of each sub-component can reveal contrary information. Analysts interpret the numbers within each component and relative to a broader context before forecasting. The forecasts can then provide market participants and business owners with a better idea about which direction the financial markets may go and where we are in the business cycle.

Business Cycles

* Predictability of business cycles *
* Four basic stages *
* Fundamental to stock market performance *

Business cycles are very predictable, in that they will occur, but will vary in length and strength. According to Chartered Financial Analyst, Stephen Simpson (Investopedia, 2016) a business cycle will "….go through 4 periods – expansion, peak, contraction, or recession and trough." These periods are not distinct, and will often blend and fade into the next period. Each period is highlighted by specific economic data indicating the change. The predictability of business cycles was observed from 1854 to 2001, 31 distinct business cycles of average duration of 55 months from trough to trough (National Bureau of Economic Research, 2008). However, the timing of each stage of the business cycle that is often uncertain. The Business Cycle Dating Committee of NBER also reports that since 1980 they have officially announced the peak or trough 6 to 12 months *after* they occurred. This is due to the complexities of collecting economic data.

A common business cycle will have 4 basic stages: *Contraction* (GDP *declines leading to recession*), the *trough (economy bottoms and GDP turns negative), expansion (GDP growth recovers)* ending with the *peak (top of cycle, GDP growing at full capacity).* According to the National Bureau of Economic Research, the 4 stages of the cycle start with the contractions (recessions) that start at the peak and end at the trough. For our purposes I will refer to the cycle as, Contraction (recession), Trough (bottom), Recovery (expansion) and Peak (top). Each stage will blend into the next and there are no iron clad ways to delineate when we are into the next stage with any sense of timeliness.

Firstly, a recession or contraction begins with a slowing or a reduction in economic activity/spending/earnings marked by negative GDP numbers, falling employment, falling corporate earnings and profits and perhaps falling government tax revenues to name a few. After a few quarters of negative or slowing GDP, economic growth has bottomed and all seems dire, the Trough can be said to have arrived. The trough is a time for reflection and renewal. It is often a time to restructure debt, re-capitalize, fine tune the budget, find a new job or get retraining. It is a period where corporations, individuals and governments can learn from the past and perhaps improve upon strategies that simply didn't work. During the trough between late recession and early recovery the economy stops falling on a number of measures; the stock markets tend to find a bottom for prices and valuations that may be more appropriate for the foreseeable future. Corporations tend to have their restructuring plans in place having cut costs, through layoffs, plant closures and inventory reductions. These measures lay the foundation for greater earnings and improving corporate profits as growth begins anew. Thus the stock market begins its trek upwards.

The recovery or expansion stage follows and is highlighted by improving economic data, rising commodity prices and a continuing rally, or rising of value, in the stock markets. Stock markets would have already begun to rally in anticipation of improving economic conditions and rising corporate profits. Late recession and early in the recovery stage interest rates tend to be at their lows, bond prices have peaked, as many market participants have by now shifted to safer fixed income investments driving up the prices, pushing down interest rates. This trend begins to unravel as the recovery gets underway.

Mid to late recovery, economic data shows steady improvements, corporate earnings and profits growing robustly and GDP and other key indicators show significant improvements. Stock market's rally, bond prices fall as investors shift back to stocks and interest rates begin to rise, or are supposed to under normal cycles. Bond prices and yields have an inverted relationship. That is, when bonds prices fall, yields rise. Yield is a term used in the bond market to describe the relationship between the bond price, interest coupon rate and time to maturity. I will discuss bonds in more detail in a later chapter.

The final stage in the cycle is the Peak. The Peak typically marked by an unsustainable growth rate in the economy and stock prices that are trading at very high prices relative to their intrinsic value (more on this in a later chapter). Commodity prices peak and begin to sell off ahead of stocks and prices fall at the slightest hint of slowing demand after several years of growing demand. Economic data has not proven the slowing economy at this point but the collective intelligence of the markets see it coming. The dreaded decline stage falls into place and another contraction arrives to begin another business cycle.

The business cycle is truly fundamental to the nature of the stock market. Coincidentally, corporate earnings are simply a symptom of the cycle, in many cases. Apart from the broadly defined business cycle, cyclical or defensive companies perform better or worse within the cycle. Stocks within each of these categories will be more or less in favor depending on the stage of the cycle. Cyclical stocks are often in sectors such as luxury automobiles, luxury watches and clothing, travel and hospitality or the construction and housing industries. Defensive stocks in sectors such as Consumer Staples or Utilities will outperform even as the economy slows. The products and services in the defensive industries are the necessities we need as opposed to those we want.

At the time of this writing, end of first half of 2016, we are in year 7 of a bull market. Historically it may point to a looming recession or falling stock markets. Does this mean the bull market is over or a recession is around the corner? Not necessarily, notes Lisa Mattingly of Fidelity Global Asset Allocation Group (Fidelity Investment Management, 2016). Lisa notes, "Signs of the late stage of the cycle…not necessarily a bad thing." for certain areas of the market. There are always opportunities for astute investors to achieve nice gains from stocks in the housing sector, commodity producers, large pharmaceutical companies and consumer staples companies. During the latter part of the peak and into the decline defensive stocks such as consumer staples, health care and utilities will continue to perform. While, investors shift to defensive stocks, cyclical stocks such as the industrials, materials, energy and financials begin their decline. It is important to note that this overview does not always play out in a textbook manner. With thousands of market participants, you will have some that believe the economy is in late stage recovery, while others believe it to be early stage contraction. Thus, their asset shifts and stock selections will be very different which creates a volatile market at the peak. Some investors buying and many others are selling.

Stock Markets
* Collective intelligence of markets *
* Stock market pendulum *
* Investing vs. Speculation *
* Economics the dismal science *

Collectively, the financial markets seem to be moved by an invisible hand as we only see the patterns after the fact. I prefer to refer to market moves as the collective intelligence of markets. Thousands of participants push and pull daily buying and selling. Micro moves in either direction of those participants, collectively, not individually causing market ups and downs. These market moves could effectively be equated to what Harry Markowitz referred to as the efficient market theory. He distinguishes between "the market is efficient" in the sense that market participants have accurate information (about stocks) and use it to their benefit, and the statement "the market portfolio is an efficient portfolio". The efficient market theory doesn't hold up in the real world, unless strict assumptions are applied, otherwise no investor could ever beat the market. Additionally, every individual investor, analyst and Advisor has their own set of criteria for a particular security. One investor may feel a stock is overvalued at $28, while another feels it is a buy at $28. This scenario plays out millions of times a day. If all market participants had no benefit of access to and interpretation of information, analysis and investment experience there simply would be no sense in conducting research. Of course this would introduce a paradox that I will describe later. We now know the efficient market theory to be false, misleading at best, because a small percentage of investors and portfolio managers can be predicted to consistently beat the markets (Brown W. H., 2006).

Markets are like a pendulum swinging between irrational exuberance when stocks are overpriced and panic-stricken fearful and pessimistic when stocks are underpriced. This cycle plays out repeatedly since the 1700's when even the most intelligent individuals could be caught up in the frenzy of the stock market. An interesting story retold by Benjamin Graham about The South Sea market bubble of 1720s. "In 1772, Sir Isaac Newton owned shares in the South Sea Company, the hottest stock in England. Sensing that the market was getting out of hand...Newton dumped his South Sea shares, pocketing a 100% profit totaling £7,000. But just months later, swept up in the wild enthusiasm of the market, Newton jumped back in at a much higher price – and lost £20,000 (more than $3 million in today's dollars)" (Graham, Benjamin, 1973).

Even the most intelligent individuals can get lulled into a sense of easy money with the hype and subsequently not doing the necessary due diligence and thorough analysis to determine the valuation for a specific stock. A high IQ is not a prerequisite to be a good investor. In fact, it might be a disability. There is investing and there is stock speculation. We can make a clear distinction between the two concepts. This is the primary focus of the first part of the readings ahead. Investing is having an understanding that a company is a business that has fundamental value, such as solid earnings and profit as well as a clean balance sheet. Unfortunately, and counter intuitively, a good company can be a bad stock; a good stock can be a bad company, temporarily. A company is more than a price and stock ticker symbol. Fundamental analysis of a company must be thorough and looked at relative to the context of its industry and the broader economic conditions.

Contrary to investing, speculation is the act of buying stocks or other securities based on nothing more than price movements and other technical indicators. Cherry picking of a few isolated pieces of information that motivates the speculator to believe the stock is a buy or sell. Speculating is virtually devoid of thorough research, patience or disciplined understanding of a particular company.

Stocks and bonds, mutual funds and exchange traded funds are among the most prevalent ways to save for retirement. Investment Advisers, Financial Planners and Insurance Representatives are the front line professionals selling and advising the public what to own based on suitability of the investment to the particular client. The day-to-day management of Pension Plans falls to portfolio managers and the employees generally have no say. However, in the case of Defined Contribution Pension Plans, which are similar to a Group RRSP, employees select their own mix of funds. There will be more on this in a later chapter.

The stock market had its worst 12 month period in 75 years, ending December 31, 2008, falling 50% in many if not all major markets. Not enough due diligence was taking place in the industry. Not at the regulator level, the brokerage level, nor was there enough done at the corporate level. Complacency was the word of the day from 2003 to 2008, particularly in the US. Previously and similarly, the market hit a bottom after the tech bubble burst in 2000, 9/11 terrorist attacks on New York and to finish it off. Fraud and accounting scandals broke out completing one of the worst bear markets in history...until 2008. Now, in 2016 we are eerily looking at another potential market breakdown. The US has borrowed everyone into oblivion. The US Debt Clock.org shows $19.285 trillion national debt, $161,201 per taxpayer and $59,568 per citizen. These amounts are astronomical and there is no way out. If China begins to slow, and Europe remains sluggish the US will also continue to slow into the foreseeable future. Low or negative interest rates will buy only a little time until the next financial crisis. Financial and monetary stimulus cannot help the US economy this time.

Economics, the "dismal science", is always lagging behind the curve with respects to important data indicating the state of the economy. Before the world caught wind of the declining state of the economy the global stock markets had already begun its free fall in July 2008, culminating in the ultimate collapse of every major stock market in the world, October and November 2008. Adding insult to injury these same markets surprised again a few months later hitting another all-time low March 9, 2009. This low marked the low of the crisis. A financial crisis was in full swing and the revised economic data was showing that the recession in the US had actually started 1 year earlier in December of 2007. This was an exceptionally long lead-time for the data to show a recession had already been in full force. A normal lag time is closer to 5 or 6 months for the data to prove the reality. Market and economic manipulation and ignoring clear signs were the root cause.

Market participants, investors, utilize miscellaneous indicators, anecdotal information and talk on the street to make decisions about the upcoming 6 to 12 months. They are forward thinking and continually discount, or price into the future. For example, when the markets believe the economy, an industry or individual stock is going to show negative growth, a specific stock price will move accordingly. If expected corporate earnings decline due to a particular industry dealing with weak demand, investors will sharply reduce their target prices. Consequently, many of the stocks in that particular industry will fall on the expectation that others will have declining earnings.

If the economy in general begins to shrink due to consumers reducing their spending, or housing prices begin to fall, stocks will likely fall or interest rates begin to rise sharply for example. Market participants follow the earnings and forecasts of the S&P500 index very closely. This benchmark tracks the largest publicly traded companies in the US and is a key indicator of the health of the economy. The financial markets are infinitely complex and imperfect at best. They move at the speed of light with the continuously accelerating speed of access to information. Many investors react to information minute-by-minute, day in and day out. It is the thousands of market participants and millions of buy-sell trades that influence individual stock prices. Ultimately, the market indexes widely reported in the news affect our lives, negatively or positively.

Personal Investing

* Value or Growth investment style *
* Observing historical patterns *
* Dividends, interest and capital gains *
* Stocks not always clear winners *
* Recessions and Depressions *

My primary goal is to improve your knowledge and understanding about how to invest for the long run using a disciplined, patient and common sense approach. A balanced investment strategy suits a majority of investors and savers, but it is not the only investment strategy available. Investing entirely in growth is a potentially profitable way to invest over the long run. Although, I believe this portfolio holds more risk in the short run for understandable reasons I will describe in a later chapter. A broad spectrum of investment strategies to fit your needs falls between complete safety and speculation. Finally, find an advisor that will build a portfolio of investments that will fit your risk tolerance, knowledge of investments and financial needs and goals.

When you consider investing in an individual company, you should have a basic knowledge of the life business cycle of various types of companies and its industry. Whether it is an industrial, technological or manufacturing company, they all go through four basic stages on its particular journey from its inception to decline and death. Of course there are several variations but the basic stages take place. The first stage known as a *start-up*, where an idea is born, financing is required and an individual or partners begin the first chapter of a company's history. The second stage, *growth and expansion*, finds the product or service selling very fast and more rounds of financing needed in order to continue the expansion. Growth and expansion can continue for a very long time as with the automotive or consumer staples sector. Contrarily, year over year growth can quickly slow, stagnate or shrink. At the third stage, stagnate or muted growth marks the *mature stage* of a company's life cycle. It must innovate, adapt and compete on price to remain a growth company. Otherwise, it will begin to decline, leading to its acquisition or an inability to continue as a going concern. The final stage, *decline,* is steadily decelerating growth and eventually closure.

Nokia is one notable and recent example of a telecommunications company that enjoyed a remarkable and tumultuous rise from 1998 to 2007 (CEREAL, et al... Nokia Disconnected, 2015). Apple's iPhone was introduced in 2007. Nokia then fell into rapid decline until 2013 when it announced it was selling its devices and services businesses to Microsoft. This marked the end of Nokia as a mobile phone company. It simply dominated the mobile phone market exceeding market expectations every quarter with its superior product. It then fell into a corporate culture of power struggles, management indecision, poor working conditions, off shoring of jobs to low wage countries and lack of innovation. Corporate arrogance failed to acknowledge competitive pressures building in the market place, most notably from Apple's iPhone and RIM's Blackberry and Google Android systems. Nokia stubbornly refused to change and went the way of the dinosaur.

Another interest example of business cycle at work, GM, Ford and Chrysler fell into long decline creating havoc for the US and Canadian economies leading up to the massive calls for the auto bailouts in 2008. The automotive sector itself was not in decline. The big three had new global competitors, such as Toyota, Nissan and BMW, beating them on price, quality, style and safety among a few notables. The big three eventually *got their act together* and began to innovate, build better quality and more appealing vehicles. Collectively they entered into a renewed growth and expansion period. As you can see from this single industry example, conduct ongoing research when investing in any company, big or small. Understanding which stage a particular company and industry are in factors into investing valuation models.

Benjamin Graham the father of value investing was born of painful personal losses in the stock market. He first wrote *The Intelligent Investor* in 1949 to outline his major work on securities investing. He looked at historical patterns of market indices and how stocks and bonds react under certain conditions (Graham, The Intelligent Investor, 1973). Macroeconomic variables, such as political instability and financial crisis, energy or oil supply shortages, war or trade imbalances will all cause severe reactions to the broader market. Business cycles come and go and stock and bond prices continue on their ascent upwards and to the right on the charts going back 200 years. There are periods of great bulls and other periods of terrible bears, declines in the markets. It is the periods of declining or sideways markets where prudent and intelligent investment management comes into play. For a variety of reasons, the Western world, developed nations of the US, Canada, UK, and Europe are in a long-term sideways trading market.

Historically, dividends have played a large role in the long-run return of stocks. According to Sam Ro of the Business Insider.com, dividends contributed 42% of the long-term average rate of return of the S&P500 since 1930 to 2012. Unfortunately, this statistic can be a little misleading without digging into the numbers a little deeper. In the same article, Sam Ro, showed how Morgan Stanley compiled return data for each decade from the 1930s and found that each decade looked quite different. For example, dividends contributed 64% throughout the 1940s, but only 25% in the 1950s and again 71% contribution in the 1970s. The average contribution of 42% will require some analysis, but the premise is that dividend payouts whether 3% or 5% are the constant, compared with the volatility of the market price of stocks.

Dividends from equity investments provide a steady flow of cash to your bank account while waiting for market prices to expand. From 1997 to 2016, dividend-paying stocks have been a primary recommendation to clients for their investment portfolios. Canadian's benefit from eligible dividends from Canadian corporations. Investors can only receive tax-preferred dividends outside registered plans, such as pensions, RRSP's and RRIF's. The CRA provides for a dividend tax credit, effectively reducing taxation of dividend income below the marginal tax rate for equivalent regular income from wages or interest. Capital gains yield the greatest reduction in tax on investment income. At the same time in order to achieve capital gains, the investor must accept a higher level of risk to his capital. Dividend bearing investments will generally carry less risk than growth-oriented companies' will, as they tend to be mature stage companies. Companies, which have well established brands and stable revenues, earnings and cash flow, allow for stable dividend payments. Companies will pay dividends when they no longer have the capacity to earn greater returns than the investor could on his own.

Interest from bonds, whether corporate or government issues are also a primary part of any prudent investment portfolio. Inside a registered plan, there is no tax benefit to holding stocks or dividend bearing investments. Capital gains, dividends and interest income receive equal tax treatment. Ideally, if an investor has a taxable account as well as a registered plan it is reasonable to have a heavier weighting in lower risk interest bearing investments in the registered plan. Similarly, it would make sense to hold higher risk equity type investments for capital gains (losses) and dividends in non-registered investment accounts. That said, the percentage of your portfolio in stocks even at the most ideal time should typically not be more than 75% to 90%. I say this after experiencing 3 major market crashes in the last 20 years. It takes several years to recover from a 40% decline in value. And of particular note, a 50% decline requires a 100% appreciation to get your principal back.

A typical defensive and more conservative investor will generally have a higher weighting in fixed income type investments as opposed to growth stocks. Historically, bonds have paid just a few percentage points below market indexes; however, as of June 30, 2008 the DEX Long Bond Index had yielded 10.2% annualized 20-year return vs. the S&P/TSX Composite returned only 10.0% for the same 20-year period. With the recent market crash of 2008, the S&P/TSX Composite achieved a 4.66% 10 year annualized return; while the DEX Universe Bond Index produced 6.0%. At the time of this writing, May 2016 market conditions have once again changed for the bond and stock markets. According to S&P500 calculator on DQYDJ.com, from January 2007 to May 2016 the S&P500 had an annualized 4.15% rate of return. With dividends reinvested, the return was 6.35%. Inflation adjusted, the returns were 2.31% and 4.45% respectively. Bonds yields are now at their lowest levels in decades, 10-year US t-bills at 1.44% (Canada 10-year Gov Bond 1.05%) presenting added risk to conservative investors.

Stocks are often the assumed winner where returns are concerned, but this is a fallacy. Over the really long run, starting in 1802, stocks have outperformed bonds by about 2.5%. However, early in the 19th century there was a period of 68 years where bonds outperformed stocks, another similar 20-year period corresponding with the Great Depression, and then the most recent period of 1968-2009 (Mauldin, 2009). These latter statistics refer to the S&P500 and 20 year US Treasuries (or bonds).

At the time of this writing, July 2016, it is anybody's guess, but if history is any indication, we may be in a long period of very slow growth if not recession, not unlike the Great Depression of the 1930s, or perhaps the Japanese style recession that began in 1988 and has not ever recovered. If you were to overlay the major market indices, such as S&P500 from 1927 to 1929 with a chart from 2007 to 2009 you could observe startling and uncanny similarities. The sharp rise in stock prices running up to the fall of 1929 and 2008 than abruptly falling off a cliff. As of mid-2016, we have seen one of the greatest bull markets ever. From the S&P500 lows of 667, March 15, 2009 to a high of 2130 May 2015, a 220% move. In addition, the bond market charts are also beginning to show ominous signs of collapse. So, if my thesis is to hold, the bond market may be the next shoe to drop and we may be in for a long term bond bear, not unlike the Japanese bear market still 50% below 1988 levels, 20 years after their real estate and stock market bubble burst.

Similar to the financial crisis and market crash in Japan, the US financial crisis of 2008 was of equal severity with one primary difference. The US reacted and acted swiftly to throw money at the problem. Unfortunately, bank and auto bailouts, artificially lowering rates to levels not seen for 50 years, and massive fiscal stimulus for everything from infrastructure, education and health care are short-term solutions at best. With US debt levels reaching into the stratosphere there is much concern over their ability to pay it off.

The plan was to inflate the economy and pay the debt off with cheaper dollars in the future. Unfortunately, no country that printed money for any length of time did it without dire economic consequences (Wiggin, 2006). Predictions of high inflation from massive stimulus and artificially low interest rates have to date not materialized in the general economy. However, massive bubbles developed in the stock market, high yield markets and other areas of the economy. Corporations massively enriched by low interest rates by loading up with low interest debt on their books, investing in higher returning ventures. The stock markets generally do not like high interest rates as it increases the cost of borrowing and higher interest expense reduces profits. *Wall Street* profits soared under the low rate environment after the financial crisis of 2008-09. Unfortunately, m*ain street,* or the general public, loaded up on bad debt, consumption of material goods with no return, just monthly payments. Bond markets will not react well to a rising interest rate environment as it makes existing low interest rate bonds less valuable. In other words, a great risk now lies in the bond market.

What Really Happened?

* Financial Crisis: A reasonable explanation *
* Too much debt *
* Complicated and unregulated financial products *

* Incompetence, Greed & Complacency *
* Entitlement *
* Trump and Brexit phenomenon *

Due to the complex nature of the 2008-09 financial crisis, I will share a humorous and fictional story that had been passed around the internet, anonymously explaining what happened:

> *"ECON 101 - Derivative Markets explained so all can understand it....*

Heidi is the proprietor of a bar in Detroit. In order to increase sales, she decides to allow her loyal customers - most of whom are unemployed alcoholics - to drink now but pay later. She keeps track of the drinks consumed on a ledger (thereby granting the customers loans). Word gets around about Heidi's drink-now pay-later marketing strategy and as a result, increasing numbers of customers flood into Heidi's bar and soon she has the largest sale volume for any bar in Detroit. By providing her customers' freedom from immediate payment demands, Heidi gets no resistance when she substantially increases her prices for wine and beer, the most consumed beverages. Her sales volume increases massively.

A young and dynamic vice-president at the local bank recognizes these customer debts as valuable future assets and increases Heidi's borrowing limit. He sees no reason for undue concern since he has the debts of the alcoholics as collateral. At the bank's corporate headquarters, expert traders transform these customer loans into DRINKBONDS, ALKIBONDS and PUKEBONDS. These securities are then traded on security markets worldwide. Naive investors don't really understand the securities being sold to them as AAA secured bonds are really the debts of unemployed alcoholics. Nevertheless, their prices continuously climb, and the securities become the top-selling items for some of the nation's leading brokerage houses.

One day, although the bond prices are still climbing, a risk manager at the bank (subsequently fired due to his negativity), decides that the time has come to demand payment on the debts incurred by the drinkers at Heidi's bar. Heidi demands payment from her alcoholic patrons, but being unemployed they cannot pay back their drinking debts. Therefore, Heidi cannot fulfill her loan obligations and claims bankruptcy.

DRINKBOND and ALKIBOND drop in price by 90%. PUKEBOND performs better, stabilizing in price after dropping by 80%. The decreased bond asset value destroys the banks liquidity and prevents it from issuing new loans. The suppliers of Heidi's bar, having granted her generous payment extensions and having invested in the securities are faced with writing off her debt and losing over 80% on her bonds. Her wine supplier claims bankruptcy, her beer supplier is taken over by a competitor, who immediately closes the local plant and lays off 50 workers.

The Government saved the banks and brokerages following automatic round-the-clock negotiations by leaders from both political parties. The funds required for this bailout obtained by a tax levied on employed middle-class non-drinkers. Finally an explanation I understand!"

On a more serious note: What led to the 2008 stock market collapse in the fall of 2008? Briefly, too much consumer debt accumulated to unqualified borrowers and the creation of billions of dollars of derivatives or credit default swaps (insurance on bad debts) utilized by corporations and governments. Additionally, the unregulated nature of the banking sector meant that investment bankers and lenders had the freedom to profit at will. The ensuing Global Financial Crisis caused a market selloff not seen in 70 years. This was not just about your run of the mill mortgage debt, car loans and business loans. Certain financial institutions simply ran hog wild leveraging their existing deposits up to 30 and 40 times. Banks were onto a huge money making strategy of providing mortgage financing to millions of Americans that had no means or any intention of ever paying it off. This was the Subprime mortgage fiasco and the notorious NINJA Loans (aka, No Income, No Job or Asset verification).

Mortgage brokers and the lending institutions they worked for received huge financial incentives for lending to anyone. They essentially solicited and persuaded anybody that had a pulse with the idea of the American dream. They too could have a home of their own with a white picket fence. "Just sign here and don't worry about a thing." This was the dream of the United States former President, George Bush, Jr. A policy for every American to own a home at any price was foolish and potentially catastrophic. All was good... house prices were rising for several years up to 2005/06 and it was believed that they would continue rising. Thus, if the homeowner defaulted on the mortgage the bank would take the home back and resell it to pay off the mortgage. Better still, the bank had already packaged up the mortgage and cleared it from their books. When housing prices began to fall the gig was up. One in three mortgages fell into a negative equity position. This is when the value of the mortgage is higher than the market value of the house.

Meanwhile, on Wall Street the financial sector had a panic on their hands. They had packaged and bought up hundreds of millions, billions of dollars in these subprime mortgages. They in turn repackaged them with pretty red ribbons and sold them to unsuspecting investors across the United States and the world as AAA investment quality as rated by S&P Rating Agency. Insurance companies sold contracts against these poor performing credit products, but the insurance could never cover the losses if there was ever a collapse. The interest rates were very attractive so they sold like hot cakes to investors seeking higher yielding bonds. A few years later the market realized they owned junk mortgages. Mortgages backed by residential properties that were falling in value daily and the default rate was beginning to skyrocket crashed: the bottom dropped out of the credit markets.

Investors treated the mortgage-backed securities and many other complex debt instruments like the plague. The valuations became worthless, toxic to investors at any price. Scandals, finger pointing, investigations and indictments, and government bailouts the word of the day. The situation nearly spiraled into a complete financial collapse of the credit markets, stock markets and the broader economy until the US Treasury stepped in with hundreds of billions of dollars to bail out the big bad banks. Everyone lived happily ever after...on Wall Street. The deepest economic recession in decades took its toll on *main street*, Americans. Over the next 7 years, a new President and democratic government made significant improvements.

President Obama, reduced unemployment from double digits to less than 5 percent, doubled the stock market from historic lows, reduced interest rates to stimulate the economy and brought in the affordable health care act to help 40 million Americans obtain medical insurance. As I write, President Obama is in the last few months of his 2 term Presidency and Donald Trump has won the Presidency in a shockingly surprising vote. The election campaign was as dirty as ever and Trump does not seem to play well with others, not even his own party. Meanwhile, here in Canada, Liberal, Justin Trudeau Prime Minister won with a majority government, beating out Stephen Harper and the Progressive Conservative Party. Parts of Canada are doing well, while other Provinces, such as Alberta, are suffering as a result of Oil Price wars. All these issues of the day will be resolved and most of us will carry on, going about our lives.

The Trump and Brexit Phenomenon
In hindsight, both of these shocking events should have been predicted by the pundits and experts alike. Both were a result of the majority, middle class, tired of the same old rhetoric from their governments. They voted for a shakeup of the establishment, through the democratic process. The majority sent a message loud and clear. In the Brexit case, Britain had a referendum to vote to leave the European Union and the "leave" camp won with 52%. The EU is an economic partnership between 28 countries. The EU is intended to act as a single market, allowing goods and services to flow more easily between countries. Why did UK citizens vote to leave? The people believed they had lost their sovereignty. Issues such as the environment, working hours, financial services, immigration, job security and wage compression, the mismatch between skills and available jobs, the loss of manufacturing, mining and fishing jobs all contributed to the anger of the people.

Many of these same types of issues created the Trump phenomenon. At first, Donald Trump was deemed to be in it for self-interests and provided endless hours of entertainment through news highlights. The story's about Trumps latest appalling comments on racism, immigrants, or women were incessant, yet he continued to win against entrenched Republican candidates. Trump was a complete outsider, never worked a day in government, nor had he ever served anyone but himself his entire life. But, he discovered how to win over the disenchanted voters with anti-establishment and anti-immigrant and racist rants. He discovered he could make promises and say the things his voters wanted to hear without consequence. He promised to lower taxes, to repeal Obama Care, to protect and create jobs, to secure the borders and deport illegal immigrants and to make America Great again. Well, as I write these words, Trump is President Elect, soon to be sworn in as the Republican and 45th President of the United States. A horrifying thought. It reminds me of the movie *Back to the Future II*, when Marty McFly, played by Michael J. Fox, wakes up to find the obnoxious bully, Biff Tannen has become a multi-millionaire and controls major energy company's and gambling casinos. Eerily similar to the world awakening November 8, 2016 to find Donald Trump won the election.

Trump supporters were the disenfranchised masses who lost their jobs because the manufacturing company they worked for moved operations to China or Mexico. These same individuals yearn for the old industrial age, where you could learn a semi-skilled trade and remain with the same company your whole career. Now, higher education and training in engineering, medicine and computer technologies are required to have a chance at a better life. Trump tapped into deep seated racial tensions and anger toward immigrants throughout the US. He tapped into the anger over gridlock in the White House and lack of change, poverty, health care programs set up by the Democrats and several other issues. Regardless of any of these issues were the fault of the current Democratic Party was irrelevant, they still resulted in a Trump win. He spoke their language and beat all odds. How his presidency impacts the global economy remains to be seen. Stay tuned…..

An Historical Perspective
Over the long run, stock markets have always zigzagged upwards and to the right. Thought of another way, imagine walking up a

set of stairs playing with a yo-yo. However, they are an imperfect mechanism of pricing businesses in the short-run. The pendulum will always swing to the point of overpricing then to under-pricing. Benjamin Graham, father of investment analysis, would recommend buying when the pendulum swings to under-pricing when investors are in fear mode and sell during those periods of irrational exuberance when prices are high. Market cycles never repeat in the same way for the same period of time or reasons. Thus, timing remains elusive. If we observe Peak to Trough declines in the S&P500 (Credit Suisse, 2009) we can see the wide swings in returns and the time between them.

Peak	Trough	Decline
19-Sept-29	12-Jul-32	-85.50
8-Jan-73	11-Oct-74	-40.6%
27-Mar-00	09-Oct-02	-49%
09-Oct-07	03-Mar-09	-55.5%

Source; Credit Suisse, 2009

Another descriptive way to show the extent of cycles is the table below: It shows the market highs, the market low and the extent of the decline in percentage terms as well as the duration of the bear market. It then shows the subsequent percentage increase. As you can see from the average decline of 34% compared with the average increase of 145%, the markets reward those who batten down the hatches and buckle up for the ride. In addition to the numbers below, since the lows, March 9, 2009 the S&P500 has climbed 210% from 677 to 2099, June30, 2016. Where we go from here is any ones guess. One mathematically important concept to remember is that a 50% decline implies you will require a 100% increase to get your money back. In other words, if you began with $200,000 and it fell 50% to $100,000, you know require 100% rate of return, which doubles your money. As we all can comprehend this does not happen in 1 year, 3 years on most likely not even in 5 years. So, patience will be tested. Diversify your investment portfolio and you will not likely suffer such great losses as the broader market.

Bull-Bear Cycles in the U.S. Since 1946

Market Top	Market Bottom	S&P 500 High	S&P 500 Low	% Decline	Subsequent % Increase	Bear Mkt Months
May-46	Jun-49	19.25	13.55	30%	267%	38
Aug-56	Oct-57	49.74	38.98	22%	86%	14
Dec-61	Jun-62	72.64	52.32	28%	80%	6
Feb-66	Oct-66	94.06	73.2	22%	48%	8
Nov-68	May-70	108.37	69.29	36%	73%	18
Jan-73	Oct-74	119.87	62.28	48%	126%	21
Nov-80	Aug-82	140.52	102.42	27%	229%	21
Aug-87	Dec-87	336.77	223.92	34%	65%	4
Jul-90	Oct-90	368.95	295.46	20%	417%	3
Mar-00	Oct-02	1527.46	776.76	49%	90%	32
Oct-07	Mar-09	1565.15	676.53	57%	178%	17
			Averages	34%	145%	17

Source: CI Investments

As I wrote in the Third Edition, March 3, 2009, the S&P500 fell to a low of 667 and has since risen to a high of 2130, May 21, 2015. A monster move of 220%, from its lows, but still not even close to a past increase of 417% from the lows in October 1990 until hitting a peak in March 2000.

Articles relating the financial crisis of 2008-09 and stock market crash to 1929 were coming out daily in the early days of the crash. Similarities for the causes of the current crisis and the 1929 crash are eerily coincidental. The stock market crash of 1929 took place in October. The financial crisis and ensuing stock market collapse began in October 2008, nearly 80 years later! Both markets crashed due to the reckless use of leveraged investments and consumer borrowing, and complete negligence on the part of the banks and financial institutions. Did we learn from this? Not likely, market participants will find ways around the new regulations put in place to reduce the possibility of *those* events happening again.

Nevertheless, new and even more creative and sophisticated strategies will be employed to make money that could not have been predicted.

A well-known theory about stock market trends over the long term describes and predicts this phenomenon. Ralph Nelson Elliott developed the Elliott Wave theory in 1920 by observing that the stock market moves in small to increasing sized waves, culminating in the Grand Super-cycle (Investopedia, 2009). His theory is based on crowd or investor psychology as the herd moves from periods of excessive optimism to fatalistic pessimism. Interestingly, the theory predicts the largest wave is 40 to 70 years from beginning to end. From 1929 to the crash of the Technology bubble in 1999 and following 3-year bear market is exactly 70 years! I could argue that the bull market from 2003 to 2008 was merely an economic illusion created by greed, speculation and the mass creation of money by the easy money policies of the US government. However, it is now 2016 and the U.S. Federal Reserve essentially printed trillions more, implementing a massive monetary stimulus package known as Quantitative Easing. It was intended to stimulate economic activity and growth, through trickle-down economics. Unfortunately, it failed to sufficiently enrich the middle class or lift the poor out of poverty. Low and slow growth seems to be the phrase of the day. Consumers are paying off their debts, saving more and banks have tightened their lending practices to remain compliant with new regulations. I would hazard to say the next Elliott Wave began 2009.

The rationale for the economics and business 101 lessons above is to offer some insight into the complexities and uncertainties overhanging our economic and financial systems. From this point forward, I shall endeavor to transition to a completely different perspective on the traditional Financial Planning model. Understanding the economy, stock markets and personal investing are all meaningless without looking to the bigger picture of our financial lives.

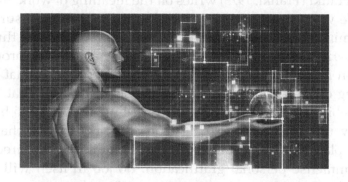

CHAPTER III

THE MEANING OF LIFE

"Happiness is...
Something to love,
something to hope for
and something to do."
Anonymous

➢ Discover the importance of finding meaning in your life
➢ Making choices and controlling your future
➢ Choosing the ideal job and career for happiness
➢ Personal life expectancy and retirement planning
➢ Solving problems through power of mind
➢ Finding contentment in it all
➢ Differentiating between success and winning

The Meaning of Life

* Developing a sense of purpose *
* Responsibility and contribution to society *
* Live with passion *

Viktor Frankl (Frankl, 1973) writes on the meaning of work, life and love. He was an Austrian Psychiatrist and a Holocaust survivor. His seminal work, *Man's Search for Meaning* takes you through his experiences in captivity. His writings have had a profound effect on my outlook on these topics. We often ask, "What is the meaning of life?" He proposes that we should ask, "What is our responsibility to life"? How do we contribute to society to build a better world? How can we change and adapt rather than changing people, places or things around us. Although a job or career can bring immense personal gratification, no job in itself will bring ultimate satisfaction and contentment. Therefore, it is essential that we have outside interests and a deeper perspective that can sustain us. Many people hold to the neurotic thought that if I only had a better job or made more money I would be happier. If I was a doctor, engineer or baker – If only I was fatter, thinner, richer, smarter or more beautiful, then my life would be different and I would be happier. This is the ultimate delusion of our society.

> *"Everything can be taken from a man but one thing:*
> *the last of the human freedoms - to choose one's attitude*
> *in any given set of circumstances, to choose one's own way."*
> *Viktor Frankl*

Without meaning in our lives, we have mere existence. We all need to have a sense of purpose, become hungry for life. Imagine prisoners of war or entire societies of enslaved peoples over the centuries. They became prisoners or slaves, held captive by enemies of the political systems of other men. Tortured and inhumanely treated for no other reason than being of another nationality, religion or from another country. History has shown that people can adapt and survive when held captive, if the human spirit becomes determined to transcend the physical body. We cannot imagine being held captive in the traditional sense, in our modern society, but we can on some level, identify with feeling at least a little trapped in our jobs, a horrible marriage or family situation or the like. We have a powerful ability to decide to ignore or minimize the human emotions of fear, hopelessness, anguish, and loneliness.

We can choose to have hope and acceptance. The human mind or spirit can overcome the most horrific of conditions and survive physically by finding meaning in it all.

Life Choices

* An end to complaining *
* Infinite options available *
* Power to change *
* Happiness*

I have learned firsthand that life is precious and life is too short to be whining and complaining about the state of the weather, politics, crime, and war in the Middle East. I am on occasion, guilty on all counts. We stress about our jobs, our finances, and the broken fence, the car that is in need of repair and the in-laws that keep dropping by unannounced. Many of us are robots going through life on autopilot doing a job that we may dread, but getting up every morning to arrive early for another round of repetitive and tortuous job duties. Our world provides us with infinite options if we choose to seek them out.

There are millions of subjects to learn, hundreds of places to go and things to experience. Many of the people, places and things that we see on television are also available to see firsthand for all those who are adventurous enough. No excuses; Make a decision, for example, that you will visit Egypt, Hong Kong or Africa and find a way to do it. Your life may be changed forever. Your perspective certainly will be. If you have dreamed of owning your own pastry shop, or a limited edition Ford Mustang, or meet your sports hero, make a decision and find a way to accomplish the dream. Sacrifices will be required, but I can assure you worthwhile.

Elaine St. James (James, 1994) wrote a wonderful little book entitled, Simplify Your Life. She reminds us that we have choices. We can move to a smaller house, change jobs, bow out of the holidays, get out of debt, pay off the mortgage and stop being a slave to your calendar. She is very clear on rethinking how we live our lives and how to get a handle on what we want to do with our lives. One particularly important suggestion she has is to figure out what kind of job you want. This may require some soul searching, researching your options and possibly retraining or returning to school. She contends that it is vitally important to enjoy what you are doing 8 to 10 hours a day. There are options available. If you are unhappy where you are, you need to be somewhat selfish and make some changes.

Happiness is not something everyone is born with. It may not be an innate or inherited trait. "A student once asked the Dali Lama, "What is the true meaning of life?" His answer was very simple: "Happiness" (Howell, Kelly, 2016). Kelly Howell is the founder of BrainSync.com and specializes and reshaping our thinking, attitudes and consequently our daily lives. She utilizes meditation techniques with music to alter the four different brain waves. She goes on briefly commenting on recent work by neuropsychologist Rick Hanson, Ph.D. and author of *Hardwiring Happiness*. He has found that our brains "...have a bias toward negativity", fixating on bad news and ignoring or dismissing offsetting positive information. For some bizarre reason, people seem glued to stories about personal tragedy, bad economic times, famine, drought, hurricanes, and apocalyptic climate forecasts... Researchers believe this bias is a trait leftover from our primitive brains. For hundreds of thousands of years, our ancestors lived every waking moment in fear of predators, lack of food and water, injury and illness and the elements. Most do not have these worries in the western developed countries like Canada, US and Europe, yet many remain in a constant state of worry. The research shows that we can re-wire our brains to react more positively to the world around us and choose to live happier, more inspired lives.

Pilot Your Destiny

* Developing a sense of self-worth *
* Looking inward for direction *
* Permission to say "no" without guilt *

Dr. Wayne Dyer (Dyer, Pulling Your Own Strings, 1978) has spent his whole career writing about how we can be the pilot of our own destiny. He writes extensively about the social milieu that imprisons us within its social structure, family constraints, corporate and government bureaucracies that strive to regulate, bully us and dictate how we are to behave, what to say, what job we should be in and create doubt and guilt if we fail to conform and perform. Dyer has made it his life mission to educate the masses about developing a sense of self-worth, looking inward for direction, rather than following the status quo. I would further add that we have free will and the power to make a decision to be happy or sad with single thought or action. Just try skipping down the street without a big smile on your face! We can choose to be an artist, musician or photographer knowing we would be unlikely to have the financial security of becoming a doctor, lawyer or accountant or obtaining a government or bank job. The only thing stopping you is fear of what others might think. Find a job that you can be passionate about and will allow you to pilot your own destiny while paying the bills.

Dr. Dyer tells us to be selfish in a positive way, by giving us permission to say no without guilt. That is, he tells us we do not have to allow any manipulation into behaving a certain way for the family name and reputation. Nor being made to feel guilty by family, friends or co-workers with phrases like; "we have always done it this way..." or "why can't you be more like your brother Bobby" or worse, manipulation and tyranny from your employer with phrases like "it's company policy and that's the way it has always been". Dyer understands very well the pressure we feel in our society to conform to the norms of the day. He wants us to be aware that we have options and we can turn off the guilt and make decisions based on what we want and not what everyone else wants, often for their own self-serving reasons.

Dr. Dyer offers insightful and powerful advice, yet undoubtedly very difficult for most of us to execute and act on. Imagine telling your boss and colleagues you were not going to the annual summer barbeque because you do not want to go! That you wanted to attend your regular weekly yoga session, you had baseball or you wanted to finish reading a good book you had started last night or god forbid you might want to spend a moment with your children or spouse. These excuses might not go over very well with the boss, company, friends, or colleagues. However, if you feel in your heart that you do not want to attend another one of the company events and are going to be made to feel guilty or worse, be coerced by the manipulative tactics of company managers and colleagues. Get creative! Make up a believable story, white lie if you will, and do not feel guilty. It is for your *own* self-preservation.

Simplify Your Financial Situation

Each day I meet with clients and assist them with their investments and personal finances. Whether I am helping them save enough to buy that dream house they unfortunately will pay for 2 ½ times over the next 25 years, or building a million dollar investment portfolio for retirement income, I build into the meeting a discussion about keeping their financial situation simple. I offer suggestions to keep annual bills, receipts, statements, taxes and the like in a single annual file box that costs $9.99 at a local office supplies store. I have personally done this for 30 years and have every box saved and stored. I keep them, not only to ensure I can find receipts or tax returns quickly and without stress. I also keep them to have as annual time capsules. That said, if you have substantially more complicated personal financial situation, such as owning and operating a small or medium size business, you will require accountants to prepare financial statements and income and expense statements to keep track. My wife and I keep memorabilia from vacations, pictures of family, friends, and homes we have lived in, as well as receipts and statements. We have always maintained this organization knowing it will reduce the stress of finding something in the future.

Furthermore, I also suggest to my clients to consolidate their banking and credit facilities with one major institution and consolidate their investments with 1 or maybe 2 investment advisers, using self-directed plans. This will minimize the number of statements they receive on a quarterly or annual basis and make for easier tracking. At first, many people will feel uncomfortable with this idea, as they believe, especially anyone born pre 1940, that they should not put all of their eggs in one basket. This might be true of Americans as they have smaller less solvent banks and financial institutions that can and do indeed go bankrupt, but the probability of a Chartered Bank, Insurance Company or any of the major Financial Institutions going bankrupt in Canada are slim. Having all of your savings and investments at one institution does not imply risking everything in one investment unless of course you have not diversified. By diversification, I mean that your investment adviser or portfolio manager has invested your money into each of the major asset classes such as stocks, bonds, and cash, not just investing in a single stock or bank term deposits.

In fact, I would contend that depositing your savings at the bank vs. stock and bond mutual funds may be riskier. This is due to the risk of being in only one company, and the possible erosion of purchasing power from historically low returns, inflation and taxation. At least if you own shares in stocks you are participating in the ownership and dividends of multiple companies rather than simply earning interest from a single company. Moreover, the Canadian Deposit Insurance Corporation or CDIC insurance will only cover your cash deposits and term deposits up to $100,000 per person, plus one joint account per institution if the member institution fails. I recommend that you pick up a CDIC brochure from your local bank or the DICO brochure from the local credit union and read the details on what you can expect from this insurance coverage.

For many small investors, mutual funds are a way to diversify your assets while at one institution, but there is no consistent rate of return or principle guarantee in the short run. Excellent, objective investment advice must be found if you are to consolidate your assets with a single institution. An upcoming chapter on what to look for in a Financial Planner will help you in your search. If the institution provides advice on all of the mutual funds and investment options available in Canada and can provide objective advice without funneling you into their proprietary products. Then you can have the highest level of comfort in holding all of your investments in this one institution. The reason you can do this is by virtue of having outside investment companies managing your money you have eliminated the concern of having all of your eggs in one basket.

#1 Stress: Money

* Learn about money and reduce stress *
* Money and happiness are not necessarily related *
* Reduce your debt and your stress *
* Savers and Spenders *

Dale Carnegie (Carnegie, 1948), one of the first self-help guru's wrote a book in 1948 called How to Stop Worrying and Start Living. He wrote that 70% of all of our worries are financial. I would prefer to say that the number one stress in modern society is money or anything-related to money. However, that is just semantics. A social and cultural phenomenon of the endless pursuit for material wealth and success causes great stress in our lives. In particular, many people are not merely obsessed with money but many are ironically and functionally illiterate about it. Additionally, most people are unfamiliar with strategies to manage it. Many are also unaware of what it can and cannot do for us. We get bombarded with powerful messages on television, in newspapers and flyers, from the mega malls and big box retail stores that subliminally tell us we must have more stuff...If we are to feel and look successful we need more money and more stuff.

I suspect that people have the false belief that if they only made more money they would have no more worries. The unfortunate fact is that the more money people make the more they spend. Anecdotal evidence would suggest that happiness and wealth have a weak correlation. Additionally, the scientific literature has shown higher rates of suicide observed in professionals, such as Physicians and Dentists, as well as the impoverished (Stephen Soreff, 2006). There is no apparent relationship between happiness and prosperity at least not in any meaningful or permanent way. However, researchers found that measures of happiness do climb with higher annual income to about a $75,000 benchmark (Huffington Post, July 2014). Interestingly, the study found a wide discrepancy between the happiness-income relationships, depending on which state you lived in. That is not to say that people can be happy living in third world countries or subject to stark poverty. Impoverished and starving people generally have little energy to be happy, hopeful, or enthusiastic. Happiness is not widely experienced in western society despite our vast wealth. Happiness replaces anxiety, worry, guilt and frustration when money is not the focus of your life. Ultimately, it is your thoughts and not your money that can create or destroy happiness.

People, corporations and government are all deficit spending, spending more than they earn. According to Statistics Canada, the average Canadian has a debt to disposable income ratio of 167% in 2016 Q1 (Statistics Canada, 2016). That means that Canadian households on average held $1.67 in debt for every dollar of disposable income. Twenty-one years ago, 1995, that ratio was well below 90% and prior to 1985 it was 55%! A Stats Canada survey (Statistics Canada, 2007) of 13.3 million households over a 6 year period from 1999 to 2005 found a 47% increase in family total debt load; a 41% increase in auto loans; 58% increase in credit card and installment debt and line of credit debt more than doubled. The survey further added that 75% of the increase in total debt was due to the increase in home prices and numbers requiring mortgages. One in three homeowners in Canada has a mortgage.

I meet *Savers and Spenders* in my office every day. I can make the determination which camp they fit into within 10 minutes. By looking at their age, income, savings and investments, size of credit card debt plus loans and mortgage I can determine their general spending habits. It is that simple. Savers often have virtually no debt other than maybe a small mortgage and a single credit card with any balance. Relative to their same income peers, spenders often have large mortgage debt, 3 or more credit cards, 1 or more car leases or loans, small retirement savings and a very small net worth.

In contrast, wealthy or high net worth clients, by definition, have no mortgage or other debt, a modest home, large amounts in RRSPs and other investments. Many of these individuals are typically over the age of 55, but managed to live within their means throughout their lives. True, they may have had different circumstances that brought them to their great wealth but generally, but their secret is moderate spending habits. All of this debt causes unnecessary stress for families and marriages that often fail because of the heavy financial burden. Make a choice to eliminate debt and the endless pursuit of having more stuff. Live for Today, Plan for Tomorrow!

Don't Postpone Today For What Might Never Be

* Act on wishes you have today *
* Look at your individual longevity *

As a Financial Planner, I have met with seniors who accumulated significant amounts of wealth over their lifetimes. Unfortunately, I am also witness to a very sad and tragic phenomenon. Couples married for 40, 50 or 60 years, lived, saved and sacrificed together so that they might have a comfortable retirement of travel, leisure and relaxation, die without ever enjoying the fruits of their labor. Couples who on the surface had it all, only to have one of the spouses fall ill, become immobile, or pass away. At this point, many but not all of the surviving spouses often lose their motivation and enthusiasm for dreams of travel and life of pleasure with nobody to share them. Such is the main reason for this book. We must live in the here and now. I say with strong conviction that you need to act today on wishes that you have and not to delay, keeping in mind not to cause harm to yourself or others, nor become indebted.

It is a statistical fact that tomorrow may not come for many people who are looking forward to a comfortable retirement. Life Insurance actuaries have all the numbers you can imagine and they tell us repeatedly that many of us with heart disease, stroke, cancer and other age related tendencies will not reach retirement in comfort, or at all. So, look at your own health, family history and longevity and you may get a hint about your personal longevity and life span. I will elaborate on individual life expectancy and how you can determine how long you may life, based on family history and the new health adjusted life expectancy statistics. Plan and live accordingly.

Education, Job & Career

* Finding the right job and career *
* Refuse to accept being unhappy in your job *
* Knowledge and strategies for job hunting *
* Using your transferable skills *
* Find you dream job and go after it with passion! *

An important part of a life plan is education, training, and finding the right career path. These parts of life are paramount if we are to enhance and bring our lives to a new level. We spend on average 8 to 10 hours per day working. We might as well enjoy what we do. It all starts with a good postsecondary education or training. Regardless of whether you attend a community college for the hands on approach to learning or attending a big city University to obtain an undergraduate degree in Science, Business or Engineering take the time to discover what you love doing. There is a published directory of thousands of job titles, each title categorized into two or three dozen major job areas. Find the job or career that you can wake up to each morning with excitement and enthusiasm. Otherwise, as I will reiterate throughout these pages, make a change and find another job. Refuse to accept being unhappy in your work. There are alternatives and solutions. Job and career are huge topics and beyond the scope of this book, so I will provide a basic outline and suggest you then seek professional career counseling advice and guidance. If you are not satisfied with the advice, seek out another counselor.

You need to get more out of your job than a paycheck. Finding the right occupation requires some soul searching, experimenting, personal discipline, and skills assessment. I personally experimented from the age of 16 to the age of 21, with various career paths, before finding something I could sink my teeth into and become passionate. When that was completed, I discovered it was not what I wanted. Therefore, I continued my search for the ideal occupation. I am thrilled to have found a stimulating and gratifying occupation as a financial planner. Things change and you may have to dig deep to find the courage to change direction. As Tony Robbins quoted so eloquently, "It is in your moments of decision that your destiny is shaped".

I could not possibly discuss job and career without referring to a book written by Richard Nelson Bolles (Bolles, 1995), *What Color is Your Parachute*. Since his first printing in 1970, Bolles has given job hunters and career changers unmatched knowledge and strategies to determine their unique career path, specific job, and skills to obtain that perfect job. The basic premise of the book is helping the job seeker take a personal inventory. The strategy has you looking at your experiences and recognizing what you are good at and what you enjoy doing most. The process helps you determine whether you are good with people and social interactions, working with data and information, or with physical things such as designing, building or manipulating objects. A little preparation will go a long way to ensure you are in a job that will yield years of gratification rather than years of unhappiness.

What Color is Your Parachute is the most popular resource for job search strategies that I have known. It is an invaluable tool to help you find the right vocation or career. If it does not help you, visit a career counselor and another and another if you do not find what you are looking for. Corporations are losing productivity from an unfulfilled workforce. Stress and possibly career boredom are a major cause of absenteeism and stress related illness. When we enjoy our jobs and are at peace with our career choice, we eliminate stress. We are at peace in our jobs when it is a good match with our capabilities, personality, and natural characteristics. Find a job that your academic credentials, personality, interests and skill set are a good fit. Do not worry about how much the job pays. True, cash is important, but is down on the list of why you want the job. Whether you are a graduate or you are changing jobs you will hear a lot about specific jobs that have barriers to entry and in high demand with applicants. If it is truly your dream job, go after it with passion! If it is your dream job, tell the employer or recruiter it is your dream job and why you are the best candidate for the job. If it is your dream job, you will have spent a great deal of time researching & speaking to individuals doing the job or retired from the job ensuring both pros & cons of it. Be prepared and win that dream job.

You are qualified for more than one job. You may not realize it but you have many transferable skills. You have skills other employers can utilize in another capacity. Take the time to discover what they are. There are literally hundreds if not thousands of job titles and classifications to choose from, listed in the National Occupational Classification (NOC) (Statistics Canada, 2011). In this 899-page directory of occupational classifications, there are 10 broad occupational categories, 40 major groups, 140 minor groups, 500 unit groups and over 40,000 specific job titles. The NOC provides for skill level criteria, such as education, training and experience for each category or group of occupations. If you are unfamiliar with the many specialized areas of your discipline, go to the website www.sdc.gc.ca/ and local college or university career center. You will find a wealth of information on job qualifications, company data, and compensation.

Starting Your Own Business

* Financially and emotionally gratifying *
* Requires personal skills assessment *
* Pros and Cons *
* Requires expertise of lawyers and accountants *
* Doing your homework *

Self-employment can be infinitely gratifying financially and emotionally. However, it requires an immense amount of planning, preparation, and knowledge of your personal skills, aptitudes, and experiences. Starting your own business requires a very concentrated focus, but most importantly passion! This focus and passion must be for the service or product you propose to provide to the consuming public. Regardless of the business, you will need to do an in depth and comprehensive market analysis, financial analysis and personal skills assessment and inventory. A market analysis will require you to understand what the market demand is for your product or service. You will have to determine whom your competitors are, what price to charge, how to make a profit, what are the pros and cons to working in this business and industry.

A financial analysis will help you determine if you have the financial resources to start and run a business. A personal inventory will ensure that you indeed have what it takes to run your own business and deal with the long hours and difficulties of being self-employed. Unless you are independently wealthy, or have a source of capital from family or friends, there will be a great deal of risk in beginning most businesses. Despite all of the challenges for sole proprietors, thousands of individuals begin and carry on successful business ventures every day.

A quick review of the Business Directory of Yellowpages.ca of any major city and will show the vast extent of human creativity, ingenuity, and perseverance. Yet, many ventures will not succeed. The business was either ill-conceived or there was a lack of drive to do what it takes to make the venture work. Nevertheless, understanding your skill set and knowing you have a marketable service or product will clearly be the starting point. After doing your market research, seeking expert advice from accountants, small business bankers, and lawyers is part of the due diligence process. Having a written business plan is the key. There are dozens of books and computer software programs on the market to assist if you are on a shoestring budget and cannot afford a marketing firm, accounting firm, or lawyer to do all of the initial legwork.

Ultimately, you will require the services of an accountant to provide bookkeeping and tax advice. A lawyer will be required for formal legal advice. The lawyer will set up the articles of incorporation or at least advise whether to incorporate. A Certified Financial Planner can be your quarterback directing you at each step of the process. Finally, having the support of your family and friends is important, but not critical. If this is your dream they should not stand in your way, nor should you permit it. Listen to their opinions if they are knowledgeable and objective. If they are simply negative opinions based on their own fears, such as, "nobody has ever done that before, or it's already been done, you'll never make any money..." My recommendation is to thank them for their vote of confidence and leave them in the dust. Good luck to you!

Life Expectancy

* Saving for retirement and your longevity *
* Life expectancy statistics *
* Health-Adjusted Life Expectancy *

The title of this book, *Live for Today, Plan for Tomorrow* speaks volumes in terms of our limited time on this Earth. The financial industry tells us to save for our retirement and that we must have hundreds of thousands or millions of dollars saved by the time we retire to support our life style. Common sense reminds us that material wealth will not extend your life nor will it provide peace of mind or happiness. I am somewhat biased as a financial planner that we need to save and plan for tomorrow, but I also believe strongly in living for today. Due to the high rates of cancer, heart disease, diabetes and other medical conditions, life can potentially be very short. However, we need to plan in case we live to a ripe old age and do not want to work beyond a certain age.

Financial and retirement planning software programs used by industry professionals assume we will live to 90 years old. Thus, exaggerating how much we need to save or deposit with a financial institution or investment fund. Yet, statistics tell us another story about longevity, or life expectancy. Statistics Canada (2012) reports that life expectancy for males at birth 79 and females 83, more or less. This is less than 15 years of retirement for men and less than 20 years for the average woman! Think about this alternatively, these statistics highlight that half of all males will die by the age of 79 and half of all women by 83.

Drill a little deeper and we discover that males may only have a *health-adjusted* life expectancy of 69 and females 71. An interesting new statistic reported by Statistics Canada (Statistics Canada, 2012) that, *"Health-adjusted life expectancy is a more comprehensive indicator than that of life expectancy because it introduces the concept of quality of life. Health-adjusted life expectancy is the number of years in full health that an individual can expect to live given the current morbidity and mortality conditions. Health-adjusted life expectancy uses the Health Utility Index (HUI) to weigh years lived in good health higher than years lived in poor health. Thus, health-adjusted life expectancy is not only a measure of quantity of life but also a measure of quality of life."* Investigate your own longevity and come up with your individual life expectancy. It may be very different from the average. The odds are stacked against most of us for the longevity of a George Burns or Bob Hope and living to a ripe old age of 90 and beyond. So we need to Live for Today!

Life Expectancy Tests

* Discover what *your* life expectancy is today *

Life expectancy tests can give you an idea about your own longevity. Online tests completed through various web sites on the internet will give you a sneak peek. The tests ask questions about your parents and grandparents medical history, such as heart disease, diabetes, or cancer. In addition, high blood pressure, high cholesterol, alcoholism, and addiction to smoking all affect your life span. The questionnaires even ask questions about your driving record. Whom you drive with and whether the driver is male or female also affects your score.

A scoring system assigns specific number of points to weight critical aspects of your behavioral and medical profile, but the output is an actuarially calculated age of death. The program instantly gives you a personalized life expectancy. This basic questionnaire is an eye opening exercise as it gives you the opportunity to change a few of your bad habits or seek medical help to minimize the risk of certain killer diseases with proper treatment and medication. I would recommend that you do the tests on two or three different web sites and use the average score to help you plan your life.

Three Months to Live

* More life expectancy and mortality statistics *
* Leading causes of death and preventable deaths *
* Overcome genetic predispositions with knowledge *

This idea will encompass the thought that goes through everyone's mind from time to time, "What would I do if I had only 3 months to live". This is often the case with a cancer diagnosis. What if a life altering disorder or illness strikes, such as Parkinson's, Heart Disease, Diabetes, or Alzheimer's? I promised myself that I would not write a technical book with a lot of statistics or numbers. However, I will give you a few highlights of the leading causes of death as reported by Centers for Disease Control and Prevention (CDC, 2015), and a few other organizations, to get you motivated to *Live for Today*.

Statistics present a few problems in terms of the way researchers use or design the variables of a study. For example, various research groups define major categories differently. In other words, one group may include all cancers in once category while another may just include top 3 types of cancers separately and the remaining as "other cancers". This will skew the results. As reported by the CDC, the leading cause of death, of all persons in the US, 2015 was Heart Disease(23.3%), a close second in rank, Malignant neoplasms (or cancer)(22.5%), third in the ranking is death from chronic lower respiratory diseases (5.6%), unintentional injuries (5.2%) and cerebrovascular diseases (5%) in fourth and fifth spot respectively. I have referred to the US statistics as it has a population 10 times the size of Canada and amplifies the serious nature of the types of diseases we might be susceptible to in Canada. The study breaks down deaths by sex, age, race, Hispanic origin and further provides death rates of a variety of specific types of disease. It is possible, that many of the annual deaths are a result self-destructive behavior, such as smoking, poor nutrition and a sedentary lifestyle. However, genetics assuredly plays a vital role as well.

Statistics Canada has found somewhat different causes of death results in Canada. For example, 2012 research shows that the leading cause of premature death are from malignant neoplasms or cancer (30%) and ranked heart disease second (19.7%) then cerebrovascular diseases or stroke (5.3%). Whereas the US leading cause of death ranked heart disease first. WorldLifeExpectancy.com provides us with World Rankings of causes of death. Coronary heart disease ranks first world-wide, followed by stroke, lung disease, influenza and pneumonia, lung cancers, HIV/AIDS, diarrhoeal diseases, diabetes, traffic accidents, hypertension and continues to list 75 more causes of death. Clearly, some of these causes do not affect us in developed countries, but many do. The World Health Organization (WHO) provides the most reliable source for International data and comparison of death rates since they standardize the data by separating different forms of heart disease and cancer. The WHO data reports that coronary heart disease ranked first in both countries and Alzheimers/Dementia ranked second in both countries, as was Lung Cancers both ranked third leading causes (WHO, 2014). Thus, there are variations in the data reported but the message is clear about what is killing people.

TABLE 3.1
Top 15 Leading Causes of Death in Canada (WHO, 2014)
1. Coronary Heart Disease
2. Alzheimers/Dementia
3. Lung Cancer
4. Stroke
5. Lung Disease
6. Colon/Rectum Cancer
7. Diabetes
8. Influenza and Pneumonia
9. Breast Cancers
10. Falls
11. Lymphomas
12. Pancrease Cancers
13. Prostate Cancers
14. Kidney Disease

15. Suicide
Data Source: Published by WHO May 2014

A little less than a quarter of annual deaths in the US and nearly a third in Canada are cancer related. Cancer is an insidious disease because it tricks your body into believing everything is fine, until it has taken over an organ or destroyed some other vital bodily function. There are often no symptoms until it is too late. Some cancers are preventable through exercise, proper nutrition, cessation of smoking and early detection and routine checkups for higher risk individuals. Cancer is still a major challenge for the medical community. Research is an ongoing necessity, to find new treatments or discover cures. A close sister to heart disease is cerebrovascular disease or stroke. It is also a major cause of death on an annual basis and is tied to poor nutrition, lack of exercise, smoking and of course a genetic component plays a role. Dozens of other minor causes of death are from alcohol, violence, poisoning and drowning to name a few. The point being, you need to be aware of what your personal risks are. Look at your family history and your personal lifestyle regarding smoking, drinking, eating and exercising.

Further commentary on life expectancy refers to statistics about how many years you can expect to live beyond a particular age. There are significant differences in men and women, but if you are male and you live to 50 you can expect to live another 32 years. If you are a female, you can expect to live another 35 years. So, how is this information useful in retirement planning? If you use this information in conjunction with your personal life expectancy, you can make a better determination of how much money you will need during your retirement. There were 2,239 deaths from road traffic accidents in Canada in 2014. In the US, there were 33,838 deaths from road traffic accidents. Statistics Canada reports that the probability of developing any type of cancer throughout your life is 41% for men and 37% for women. The probability of dying from any type of cancer is 27% and 23% respectively. Therefore, if heart disease or a cancer does not take us, we have to be aware of other risks in life.

It is not my intention to scare you with the numbers above or send you off screaming hysterically to your family physician for a full physical, blood tests and MRI or CAT scan to determine your fate. Basic information gives you some ammunition to get up and get moving. With knowledge and awareness, you can seek preventative treatments, reduce your risk factors and overcome genetic predispositions. With access to information through the internet, there is truly a world of knowledge at your fingertips. With technological advances in medicine, nutrition, engineering, telecommunications, computers, construction, transportation, finance and access to information there is quite simply no rational excuse for us to sit around waiting to die. Go and live everyday with passion! Develop an insatiable hunger for knowledge. Yes, go out into to the world and experience all that life has to offer. We are living in the greatest era in the entire history of humanity.

Solving Problems

*Understanding the difficulties of solving life's problems *
* Accepting certain grand problems won't be solved
by any of your individual interventions *
* Sometimes our perception is the problem *

We often think we can solve our personal problems, financial or otherwise, on our own, using a pragmatic or logical strategy. However, without having an infinite amount of data stored in our brains we probably fall short of having the correct information to make the most accurate decision or solve the problem. The most complex problems are the psychosocial problems we run into. Problems coping with difficult people at home, work, school, or in the community will always be a challenge to solve logically. Similar to mathematics, without an understanding of the fundamentals, math problems will be difficult to solve. You may find it difficult to come to terms with world hunger, human rights, homicide, geopolitical problems, or terrorism. To illustrate, the 6 o'clock news shows us terrible and unthinkable crime occurring every day, in addition to wars, starvation and suffering around the world. Are these problems the ones we can fix or solve by worrying about them or getting upset? No. These world issues come into our lives through a visual medium that provides us with only bit pieces of information and awareness of their existence. Unfortunately, news often sensationalized for ratings, not to provide understanding.

Our logical and reactive brain tells us to get depressed or angry over the sad state of the world. We feel helpless and tortured at the thought of the starving and sick children. These are realities and problems that no single human can solve on their own. This reality will not go away because you are worrying about it. Therefore, you have a choice. You can become actively involved in finding a solution to these problems or you can completely ignore these things out of your control. They do not directly affect you in your daily life and you can choose to let the powers to be deal with them. They are not *your* problems they simply are *a* reality.

To give you an analogy think about being a gazelle on the grasslands of Africa. You know that every day a predator will stalk and kill one gazelle from your herd. It could be a young, old or sickly member, but one more is taken. Lions are not inherently evil or malicious for their act of killing and eating one of the herd members. It must hunt and eat and it simply is a reality of the jungle to be accepted. If you are genuinely interested the watch and learn. Otherwise, gather the guilt, grief, anger, and feelings of helplessness, bag it and toss it away. You are not being cold, indifferent, or evil. You are simply accepting life as it is and living your life, as you need to in order to survive.

Another example of learning acceptance – your adult children never want to visit you. They say they are too busy or it is too far to drive. You gave them life. They give you grief. This is a problem right? No. Your perception of this situation is a problem. It again is simply a reality. The Buddhist philosophy speaks about attachments and desires. Once you eliminate your unhealthy attachments to people, ideas and material things, you will become enlightened and free. In other words, you will be free from your guilt about the past, your worry about the future. Your attachments cause your pain and despair. If your children are not able, or do not want to visit, it must be respected and accepted. Otherwise, you will be carrying emotional baggage that will impede your moving forward. Meanwhile, you are to continue with your life as an independent and loving person with no guilt or anger. Carrying around anger, guilt, frustration, jealousy, and envy are not healthy, physically or emotionally. Be at peace with these realities of life.

We Have All The Answers

* The awesome power of your mind *
* Using the power of mind to find answers *

It is my contention that we have the capacity to find all the answers to our deepest questions within us. Our mind figures things out for us continually and constantly providing direction. We have all heard the phrase that we only use 10% of our brains. This may be partially true, but the other 90% is actually thinking and working for the 10% that we consciously control! Much of our brainpower is involved in managing the business of breathing, pumping blood through your circulatory system utilizing micronutrients from our most recent meal and rebuilding millions of cells throughout our body. Sadly, and somewhat facetiously I contend many people consciously use only 5%, not even the 10% widely talked about. Have you ever been working on a problem such as how to arrange the furniture in your house, how to put a new gizmo together, or how to solve the crossword puzzle but could not come up with the answer until you walked away for an hour or even slept on it? You proceed to go back to the problem and presto, you figure it out just like that! It was the 90% of your brain doing the thinking for you while you slept. Therefore, it seems like perhaps we do use 90% of our brain, albeit not to its optimal ability.

Yes. This is the amazing power of the mind, the unconscious part of the brain. If you are religious, maybe you prayed for the answer to come to you. If you practice meditation, you would utilize the deep relaxation of the meditative state to receive the answer. Whatever you attribute it to, if we can slow ourselves down for a few moments, listen and ask ourselves in quiet meditation we will find the answer. It will come to us in time. Sometimes the answers come to us immediately and sometimes the question is more complex and requires a little more attention, but it too will come to us if we listen. It is important to note that some questions simply demand more information. Ideally and intuitively, you will know this.

Lost Contentment

*The reward is in the journey, not the destination *
* Develop a passion for learning and sharing

We can live our lives today like the proverbial dog chasing its tail, never quite succeeding. Alternatively, we can accept the fact that it is not important whether we grab the tail or obtain that big promotion, bonus or luxury automobile. What is important is the pleasure that chase brings us. If it is bringing us stress and misery, it probably is not a suitable place to be in our life. In Thomas J. Sanley's book, *The Millionaire Mind,* he writes of highly intelligent people as being "more challenged, more excited about doing heart surgery or solving high order math problems than counting every dime."(Stanley, 2001) Living life, challenging ourselves to be better people by sharing and being compassionate toward others is the road to follow. Thoughtfulness, empathizing and being mindful of our words and actions towards each other are the moral teachings of religious leaders and philosophers throughout the ages.

Live for Today! Plan for Tomorrow is not a how to book. It is an educational approach to learning about some of the most important aspects of our lives. My hope is to share with you an alternative way of thinking outside the very restrictive range of social and behavioral constraints our society imposes on us. Learning a trade, getting an education, getting married, buying a house, and having kids are all pretty much the status quo. If you want to get beyond these ingrained and cultural rules, it is imperative that you learn to think in different ways. Philosophy offers us this grand path to knowledge. History's greatest thinkers from Aristotle to Bertrand Russell and Nietzsche have brought us the basis of modern law, medicine, psychology, and ethics. Every year, creative, thoughtful individuals write and publish hundreds of thousands of books, academic journals and articles. You cannot imagine how the world will open up to you, if you read a few of these great works. You will wonder why you never had such a passion for reading and learning before.

Learning the Hard Way
* A story of the futility of striving for more without knowing why *

After completing a few thousand financial and investment planning interviews with clients over the past 20 years, I discovered that most people want the same things. They want to be able to retire in comfort, to protect their families in case of death or disability, to pay off the mortgage and other debts and have financial independence over time. Here is a fitting story that highlights the premise of this book.

A Mexican fisherman, we'll call Yuan Valdez, living and working in a sleepy village came into dock after a few hours of early morning fishing to find a fast talking and sharply dressed boat salesman, named Jose Perez, standing waiting while he tied his small boat to the dock. Jose said, "If I could help you to catch more fish, make more money so you can provide for your family, all of the best things life has to offer. As well as help you to retire with financial independence, so that you could spend more time with your lovely wife and children, would you be interested in what I have to offer?" Yuan said in a very slow and relaxed manner, "Ok senor, I will listen." They talked for hours. The salesperson ended up selling him five fully operational, fishing boats, financing the purchase with long-term bank loans and assisting him to hire 15 extra fishermen to help him catch more fish, and make more money.

Ten years had gone by and Jose Perez came back to the small fishing village to see how Yuan Valdez was doing. It was getting dark that evening but heard that Yuan would be in soon from his long day at sea. When Yuan arrived, they began to talk and Jose asked how he was doing. Yuan was exhausted and perturbed, he said, "Since I met you I have worked 6 days a week from 5 am to sunset. I rarely get to see my wife or my children. I am tired when I do see them. All of my money is tied up in the aging fleet of boats you sold me, or going to wages, or bank interest on the loans. I do not think this was a good idea for me. Prior to meeting you, I worked but a few hours each day, played with my children, made love to my wife every afternoon during siesta and sometimes all night if I was successful in catching a few extra fish! I had no stress in my life. If I had simply continued to work with one fishing boat and saved part of the profits from the sale of the fish that I caught I would have had much less stress and could have retired in a few years. If I had not been greedy, I could have spent more time with my children and my wife would not be running off with my friend, Julio, who works at the local bakery down the street. Jose, I am selling everything and will fish with 1 boat, get to know my children again and enjoy a peaceful life once again."

This story illustrates the futility of solely focusing on success and planning for your future without living in the now. If Yuan had truly been passionate about fishing and building a quality business, he would not have been so unhappy. Had he been aware that he had options to get out before any further harm came to him and his family the end may not have been so tragic. Live for today as there may not be a tomorrow.

To be fair, Yuan entered into the venture to make a lot of money, to provide for his family. This alone is not enough. He was not passionate about fishing. I think he was passionate about relaxing. The other side of the coin would reveal that a small percentage of the population actually finds the job or career they are completely passionate about and the money comes rolling in. These fortunate individuals discovered what they truly loved doing and the financial rewards were always secondary to their commitment. I do not believe Bill Gates founder of Microsoft, Stephen Jobs founder of Apple or Mark Zuckerburg founder of Facebook set out to become multi-billionaires. They were so focused and passionate about their quest for the best software, personal computer technology or connecting everyone on the planet, becoming wealthy simply was not in the equation. The bottom line, find a job, career or any endeavor you can be passionate about and the money will come. If money is the sole focus of your journey, you will be unhappy.

Success vs. Contentment

* Defining success *
* Success is the act of challenging yourself
in any endeavor regardless of the outcome *
* The opposite of success is not failure *

There are as many definitions of success as there are people willing to attempt a definition. Most people have a desire to be successful. Not everyone has the "burning desire" Napoleon Hill speaks about in his famous book called, *Think and Grow Rich*. In the traditional sense, success will often mean winning as well as achieving some higher level of recognition, having a good job, good income to support the family and owning a nice home. For many, success consists of "material success". Material success is possibly a way of keeping score. Healthy competition is essential for the human spirit and for the ultimate survival of man. Competition keeps us physically strong, intellectually and mentally sharp and compels us to be the best we can be. That said competition at the expense of our health and happiness is probably not worth it.

Success in any endeavor is about making the effort and challenging yourself to be your best regardless of the outcome. Winning is not synonymous with success. I do not accept that it is a failure if you have challenged yourself in education, a sport, game, job, or other activity simply because the outcome was not first place, an 'A' or the Presidency. I believe that, *it is better to have tried and failed then never to have tried at all*. Unfortunately, too many people have the mistaken belief, consciously or unconsciously, that if they try but fail, everyone will think and *know* they are a failure. Therefore, they do not take risks. I say, jump in with both feet, challenge yourself, and never mind what anybody thinks!

It is my contention that we need to all work towards a balance in our lives. Putting in a 60-hour workweek, to succeed, at the expense of our physical and emotional health, leisure time for self with our spouse and children is probably not a reasonable direction to take. *If you love what you do and you are not harming yourself, your family or other relationships then I say, do it!* If we truly ask ourselves what it is we want and deeper yet, why we want it. An answer will come from within. The answer may astonish you and turn your life upside down. You will not know until you listen. The power of mind is there for you.

In a later chapter I talk at length about the many ways we can experience and live life to its fullest. I realize it is much easier to delude ourselves into believing we are content with our present life. Nevertheless, I would highlight again the premise of this book is to motivate you to new challenges and experience all that life has to offer. Do not allow life to pass over you. It is much too short and too easy to sit back as a spectator instead of a participant.

Success vs. Winning

* The cost of being a "winner" *
* Ultimately successful through the experience *
* Success is not synonymous with winning *

Little league baseball and minor league hockey have become brutally competitive on and off the playing fields. The parents the coaches and spectators want to win at any cost. The kids just want to play a sport that makes them feel good. When I played minor league hockey in London, Ontario and other Southern Western Ontario hockey towns, I was in my glory. Being on the ice, skating, passing, shooting was a euphoric, fully focused state of mind, no different from any other animal in the wild doing what comes natural. I was in this glorious state until, at age ten, I was bumped up to a "travel" or "all-star" team, whereby the players were fierce competitors and the parents and coaches were downright militant. The young players, myself included were made to feel like stars if we scored or made to feel badly after every shift and game if we had missed a pass or worse a goal was scored on your shift. I decided to play in a less competitive "house-league" and was ultimately successful by having a more enjoyable experience from then on.

We all have our own set of questions about a successful life and various aspects of our own lives. It remains vital that we continue to seek answers through quiet meditation, by slowing the pace, reflecting, and listening to the inner dialogue, which is quite miraculous in its ability to solve problems for us if we listen. Some may call this prayer; others may call it meditation or simply the power of mind. We have the answers we simply need to learn to listen quietly. Dr. Wayne Dyer (Dyer, There's a Spiritual Solution to Every Problem., 2001) writes about the constant inner battle between ego and spirit or conscience. The ego is determined to keep you focused on physical pleasures of the flesh, success and winning at any cost. Meanwhile the spirit is moving you to transcend the impulses of the ego driven body. One essential part of the meaning of life is that we grow to understand that we are more than our material wealth and success, winning and achieving. We are capable of transcending the imperfections of the physical body through power of mind and move to a more mindful or thoughtful life. Lastly, with knowledge and awareness we can overcome the emotional upsets associated with the fear of failure or not succeeding in the traditional sense.

Saving The World One Child At A Time

* Acting on our responsibility to others *
* Eliminate your paralysis and acknowledge it *

I mentioned earlier of our responsibility to others and the importance of contributing. My wife and I became foster parents for a little girl living in Africa. Initially when I signed up, I was watching Foster Parents Plan on television and for once, I committed to sitting through the program to begin to understand. As I watched in shock as the narrator described the horrific living conditions, lack of food and drinking water, inadequate clothing & shelter. Nor were there any means of attaining these necessities let alone material wealth we take for granted on a daily basis. My heart was wrenched, partly out of guilt, but mostly from a very deep sadness for their plight. I realized I had to do something to help these souls. I picked up the phone, dialed the 800 number and made a monthly pledge to assist a sponsored child. It is still not enough but it was something. We received pictures of our sponsored child and her parents and received correspondence telling us all about the way of life in their village in Sub-Saharan, West Africa. It is a life far removed from ours. It is a way of life that is rich in social life but impoverished materially. Necessities of life, such as food & water and medicine are luxury items, as are pencils and paper for school. Our foster child grew up and we have lost track of her, but the experience forever changed us.

A billion people are starving around the world and the developed world does very little to minimize their suffering. Maybe we feel helpless, yet we are insensitive and desensitized when we see the starving children living in the filth and famine on television. They are unaware of their desolation and isolation. They are unaware of what is possible and can only hope to live to see tomorrow and have a small bowl of rice, corn mash or some other miserable excuse for food. The blankness in their eyes and the sadness that we see in them is a tragedy of the human spirit. What can we do? We can firstly acknowledge this horror then we must begin individually to take responsibility which can then develop into solutions that work on a massive scale to build the foundations of what amounts to providing the resources and teaching these poor nations to fish and farm. Education is the key to economic growth if not prosperity. Perhaps we can also assist financially in bringing enough resources to the people to allow them to have food, clean drinking water, clothing, and shelter to all. This I believe is possible if there is a will by the people of the wealthy nations of the world.

CHAPTER IV

GOALS TO MOTIVATE

"Your Goals, minus your doubts, equal your reality."
Ralph Marston

➢ The importance of personal and financial goals *
➢ Awareness of the drivers of human behavior *
➢ Primal motivators of pain and pleasure *
➢ Discover what people really want *
➢ Understanding the concept of self-reliance *

Goals

I speak at length about goals throughout the book. Financial and personal goals intersect and are undifferentiated in terms of their importance to your life. Without something to work toward for 1 day, 1 year or 25 years forward, we tend to feel a sense of emptiness. Even more than feeling empty, we may feel a sense of futility or hopelessness, of being on a treadmill. Not all the time because we are busy working, doing yard work or spending time with friends or family. Nevertheless, we will feel like there is something missing in our life. Occasionally, we may need a rest from goal oriented behavior so we go on a vacation, but the goal, if there is one, is still in the back of our minds driving us on. We are passionate, motivated, and driven by our goals to achieve or obtain something of significance in our lives. For those seeking recognition, living your life consumed or obsessed by your passion is unhealthy.

You may have a goal to achieve a first or second place finish in a marathon or golf tournament. You may have a goal to make more money and buy a new car in 2 years. Alternatively, you may have a more altruistic goal of volunteering your time, at the local hospital to help terminally ill cancer patients in their final days.

* Find a balance between materialistic
achievements and social responsibility *

All are worthy goals; however a balance between materialistic achievements is needed, such as a promotion at work that pays more, or buying a new car and goals of personal knowledge, health and social responsibility to your fellow man. Do your planning, and then get on with the business of living in the now.

Goals: Planning for Tomorrow

* Discovering why you have a specific goal *
* Prioritizing your daily, weekly, monthly, yearly goals *
* A fictional story of putting your goals in writing *
* Using the power of mind to achieve your goals *

Goals such as having a cottage, traveling, charitable giving, wealth preservation, tuition for the kids, mortgage free at retirement and having enough money to retire in comfort are all noteworthy. Taking courses at a local college or University, achieving a diploma or degree in something that interests you are also highly rewarding goals to have. Dig a little deeper and ask yourself why you would like a cottage? How would this make you happy and what is the price you must pay, financially and emotionally. Why do you want to travel? Is it to learn about the culture, the history, for the food, the weather, or some other reason? Moreover, what will the price be, financially and emotionally? Why is wealth preservation important to you? Is it out of fear of running out of money? Is it from your parents or grandparents telling you stories of the great depression of the 30's or some other experience that you may have had? Is it simply to be financially independent or to leave an estate for your children or grandchildren? There are many reasons why we have goals, but they are often just fleeting thoughts or subliminal images we have seen on the television or magazine. Give your goals some serious thought and write them down. It will give them the power to be realized in your life.

Personal, professional or job related, and financial goals can all be developed for daily, weekly, monthly and yearly planning. Priorities those goals and have the most important items as your primary focus. Stephen R. Covey writes extensively about work life and personal productivity strategies in *The 7 Habits of Highly Effective People* (Covey, 1989). By creating and prioritizing your short, medium and long-term goals, you will begin to feel the control come into your life. You will begin to see the world in terms of possibilities. You will accomplish a great deal more with much less stress because you will know with clarity and focus what must be done and what can wait.

Here is a story about a graduating class at a large Educational institution to illustrate the value of goals and planning. A survey conducted on the class found that only 3% had written goals of what they wanted to achieve throughout their lives. A number of years later, the same individuals were surveyed again. They found that the 3% that had written goals for financial success had a net worth higher than the entire 97% of other students combined. Regardless of whether this story is fact or fiction, the power of a written plan cannot be understated.

I know from personal experience that writing a list of things to do around the house on a Saturday increases the likelihood of getting it completed. My wife will attest to this! Similarly, having a written goal plan for 1, 3, 5 and even 10 years works in mysterious an miraculous ways. Our subconscious mind grabs hold of this plan and sets things in motion for you to achieve them. This again is the 90% of your brain working for you below the surface of awareness. The more specific you are in your vision the more powerful it will be in directing you over time. The power of the mind will help you Live for Today! Plan for Tomorrow.

Financial Planning - Short-term Goals

Short-term goals would include money that may be required within 1 yr. A cash emergency fund would generally have 3 to 6 months of income available in the event of a layoff or job loss. Through dealings with clients, I have found that many people will utilize a Line of Credit in combination with savings as a source of emergency money. Unfortunately, credit cards are used more often a cash cushion for car maintenance, home repairs, purchase of a new lawn mower or other unexpected expenses. In times of low interest rates, a line of credit can clearly be a feasible solution. Your cash cushion or savings would not be yielding a very high rate of return and the interest income is taxable, while a line of credit is available immediately at a low rate. If a line of credit is not a solution for you, set up a high interest savings account, separately from your regular checking account. Moreover, a Money Market mutual fund, with your local bank or financial planner will yield a slightly higher rate as well. Money Market funds are liquid and very safe, although not completely guaranteed like a GIC or term deposit with the bank. CDIC insurance covers up to $100,000 for each individual, held by a financial institution and member of CDIC. In contrast, your principle in a money market fund are protected not guaranteed to the degree the investments held in the fund are backed by the good credit history of the issuer.

Financial Planning - Medium Term Goals

These goals would include money that may be required within 1 to 3 or even 4 years. Saving for a new car, traveling costs, or saving for a teenage child's education would be examples of medium term funding. How can you go about saving for this timeframe? Investing on a regular basis into a low to moderately risky bond or income mutual fund will give you the best result. There is no need to risk your capital in this relatively short period. For example, money market and bond funds often allow as little as $500 initial investment and $50/mth. You may need to negotiate a low front-end commission to buy a money market or bond fund. Do not buy a mutual fund with a back end or deferred sales charge basis, for a short-term holding period, as you would be subject to a penalty to withdraw within the 4 to 7 year schedule. This makes the investment liquid unlike most GICs, locked-in for specified term. However, many institutions offer cashable GICs, often redeemable on the anniversary date with a reduced rate for early redemption.

Financial Planning - Long Term Goals

Longer-term aspirations, defined as goals that are set for 5 to 10 or more years and often between 20 to 40 years. Paying off the mortgage, saving for retirement or buying a summer cottage are a few examples of long term goals. These goals are achieved over long periods through a disciplined and planned approach. A financial adviser or planner can help determine what the monthly payment should be if your goal is to pay off the mortgage in 10, 20 or 25 years. The math is a little complex, so using amortization schedules or software available on the internet will work. You can create numerous scenarios making assumptions about the term, interest rates, and payment amount. Using time value of money (TVM) calculations or software programs, your financial planner can assist you in calculating what is required to accumulate $500,000 by age 65. Short of going through the mathematical equations, using widely available software or calculators, inputting an assumed rate of return, the future value of $500,000, time-period and number of payments into the formula, the monthly or annual payment amount is calculated. See illustration below:

Illustration of Time Value of Money
  (*using TI BAII Plus calculator)
  FV=$500,000; PV=$0; N=25 yrs; I/Y=6%; P/Y=12; CALC; PMT
  Where:
  FV = Future Value
  PV = Present Value
  N = Number of Years
  I/Y = Annual interest rate

P/Y = Payments per year
CALC = Calculate
PMT = Payment amount.

In this case, to save $500,000 in 25 years, assuming a 6% average rate of return the investor would have to deposit $717.50 each month for 25 years. Over 50 years, the saver would only have to deposit $132.00 each month to achieve $500,000! This shows the power of compounding and starting early. Start a regular investment plan for your retirement, for that dream car or vacation or set up a trust for a child or grandchild today. Plan for Tomorrow!

Drivers of Human Behavior

* Power *
* Wealth *
* Recognition *
* Love & Companionship *

Humans are no different from other animals in the wild in that we are primarily driven by our instincts for survival. However, we no longer have to hunt and forage for food other than driving to a nearby grocery store or mega mall to buy everything we need to satisfy our thirst, hunger or craving for chocolate. We do not have to worry about the saber tooth tiger ripping us apart or gored by a charging mammoth. Law and Police enforcement protect us from the criminal and predatory elements in our lives. Dangerous animals remain in secure cages in zoos or wildlife preserves, with the exception of stray dogs or pit bulls without a muzzle. We also do not worry about dying of exposure to the elements, since the advent of affordable housing for the masses and the development of gas heating and electricity. Therefore, we have essentially transcended the primary drivers of behavior, or instincts, in modern western cities.

What drives us towards becoming the best we can be? What are the motivators of our achievement-oriented behavior now, given that all of our instinct driven motivators are eliminated? There are many reasons for driving us to achieve and get to the top. *Power, Wealth, and Recognition* will be the result of climbing to the top of the corporate ladder, building a successful business or obtaining a high level executive or management position. Along with *power* comes control over your environment, your employees. Whether there are 5 or 50,000 employees, as with a large corporation they are ultimately your subordinates and generally must submit. This is no different from the alpha male in a pack of wolves or a large clan of chimpanzees. And to be fair, the larger, more ferocious female Hyena of Africa is leader of the pack. Being in a position of power is usually better than the converse.

Wealth is also a driver of behavior no different from hunting and foraging for food and mates to pass on your genetic offspring. With greater wealth comes greater power and control over your life and environment. Great wealth will also bring you recognition as a successful and top performing person in your field of endeavor. Wealth provides the ability to obtain the highest quality food, shelter and mate or mates! It has been said that men will marry a female 6 years his junior in second marriages. Moreover, higher wealth may bring even younger females. I refer to Donald Trump, soon to be President of the United States and his younger wives. After Ivana Trump came Marla Maples, after Marla came First Lady to be, Melania Trump, 46 years old to Donald Trump's 70. I refer to Harrison Ford and Calista Flockhart; Michael Douglas & Katherine Zeta Jones; and Tom Cruise and Katie Holmes. Need I say more? Of course, these are high profile examples, but I have personally seen enough similarities to confirm the anecdotal evidence.

Recognition is another driver that is a result of achieving top status as an executive, premier athlete, artist, or doctor. Even a local politician, surgeon or professor will achieve esteemed recognition from the public from their prestigious positions. Recognition can also be a driver for altruistic reasons. There are many wonderful, loving, and generous individuals helping the poor, the sick, and the desolate. They give tirelessly to others. They truly want to help and ease the pain and despair of the less fortunate. However, I also believe there is a seed of desire for recognition for their good deeds. They embark on writing books about their good deeds to bring awareness to the population. But, is it possible they would like just a hint of appreciation if not recognition?

Canadian, Stephen Lewis has been writing, speaking, and playing an active political role for decades. He is United Nations special envoy for HIV/AIDS in Africa, a humanitarian, diplomat and advocate for children's and human rights. He is the all-time greatest good deed doer. He continues the fight to eliminate poverty and fight for human rights in third world countries. He should know that mere awareness and the lack of resources, $50 billion needed ($5 for each starving person in the world) to feed and medicate the millions of sick and hungry versus $1 trillion for the US war effort in the middle east will not change quickly nor easily. The reality of suffering around the world is far too horrific and overwhelming for politicians and average people alike to deal with. So the paralysis and desensitization continues. Ultimately, Stephen Lewis wants to help the needy and change the world for the better, but he wants and needs recognition, not necessarily for himself but for the plight of the poor and starving.

* True greatness comes only with love and companionship *

Finally, I think the most important driver of behavior is *love and companionship*. The human feelings derived from love and companionship gives us meaning in our lives. Humans came hardwired with a need to be part of a social group. I truly have a hard time believing that anyone can achieve greatness without the support and love of a husband, wife or life partner or even the love and support of a few good friends or family members. Statistics show that married people are healthier and live longer than if single. Many animals will die if isolated from their social group. We share intimate physical and emotional moments with each other. Unconditional love and support gives us the strength and confidence to try new and risky things with a safety net to fall into if needed. The common cliché that we rarely hear, in this politically correct world, is "behind every great man is a woman" has more truth than we realize. Although, I would modify it to read:

> *Behind every great man is a woman,*
> *Behind every great woman are her kids and then her man,*
> *And, behind every great person is the love and support of*
> *loved ones.*

Drivers of behavior are all very personal, but many can identify with some or all of the above-mentioned drivers. If the primary drivers for food, clothing, and shelter are not satisfied, there will be a challenge to transcend them and move toward greatness in terms of a recognizable human achievement. It has happened in our history, with the likes of Mother Theresa giving her life to help the starving and impoverished people of India. She transcended the basics of food, clothing, and shelter barely obtaining these things except at a subsistence level, but she overcame them by the love and adoration of thousands of people she had helped.

I am of the belief that drivers of behavior do not come naturally to us all. If they come at all, they come in a wide range of strengths. If someone falls at the weaker end of the spectrum, they may need to begin with baby steps, learning, and building a little bit at a time. Having meaning in your life is a choice that you make alone. Having a purpose or goals will give you the strength and confidence needed to achieve them. How are you contributing and being responsible to your fellow man and your world while striving to achieve personal goals? As JFK so eloquently put it (Reeves, 1992), "And so, my fellow Americans, ask not what your country can do for you; ask what you can do for your country."

* Taking responsibility will put meaning into your life *

Will the world be a better place because you have lived? At the early part of the twentieth century, Gandhi made an extraordinary difference in India with his philosophy of non-violence. A small, meek, and fragile man took on the ruthless dictatorship of the British Monarchy and was victorious. He had a vision, a goal and consequently through his special purpose put meaning into his life. By taking responsibility, he inspired thousands of his fellow citizens to do the same.

* Surround yourself with positive, enthusiastic people *
* Live every day in awe and without fear,
doubts, regrets or anxiety *

Find and surround yourself with positive and enthusiastic people. If you need to join a YMCA, take a cooking course at a local college or take karate lessons then sign up first chance you have. You will not regret it. You will begin to feel the life sustaining energy that is there for us all. Pick up a self-help book on self-confidence, building self-esteem or positive thinking. I have listed a number of books that have inspired me to live for today, plan for tomorrow at the back of this book. Learn all you can about successful positive people. Not just the rich and famous, but also the courageous, enthusiastic, creative and self-reliant individuals that live every day in awe. Live without fear, doubts, regrets or anxiety. Go through the local yellow pages and look in wonderment at the thousands of individuals that have struck out as independent business owners. Imagine for one moment at what courage it took to begin a business with no certainty of income or success. Sustaining enthusiasm and passion takes a great deal of energy and courage, and possibly fear, as it is too easy to sit back and be a spectator. Keep active and live life to its fullest!

Pain & Pleasure

I previously discussed issues around human motivation and the drivers of behavior. Master motivational speaker and author Tony Robbins writes about the concept of "pain and pleasure" (Robbins, Unlimited Power, 1986). He contends that each of us is motivated to maximize or optimize the pleasurable experiences and minimize the painful or the most uncomfortable sensations, emotional or physical, that we might experience in our lives. In contrast to Robbins, Freudian psychology refers to the "id", raw instincts and the "ego", the mediator between instinctive drives and demands of reality, as the driving force of behavior. In addition, the "superego" steps in and takes the role of our conscience. I would agree that these forces are real, but I would extend the idea that we can control all of the instinctive drives and ultimately attain a finer balance between id and ego and pain and pleasure driven behavior. You might be asking yourself why he is referring to Sigmund Freud and Tony Robbins. If we understand some of the reasons why we are motivated to pursue or not to pursue our goals and dreams we can begin to write our own future.

Procrastination can illustrate how pain and pleasure are at work in our lives. It is a common approach to avoiding uncomfortable or painful emotions. You know you have a major report due on your supervisor or professor's desk by Monday morning, but you delay and delay, coming up with excuse upon excuse that other things are more pressing. Finally, Sunday afternoon panic sets in and you begin putting the report together, working into the night to finish. Postponing the inevitable is not a rational way to go, but it does succeed in the delay of pain if not in some way avoiding it altogether. Unfortunately with every moment of delay comes anxiety and worry about completing a routine project. It makes more sense to chip away at it from the moment of assignment. You will feel less stress, a degree of control and accomplishment. In the end, there is no panic or concern about not completing the assignment.

It makes reasonable sense that some of our actions initially begin with the desire for pleasure and the elimination of pain. Our bodies' physiology instinctively acts to moderate our body temperature, so we are not too cold or too hot. We consciously and actively seek a good job that will provide us with the money to buy food, clothing, and shelter. Moreover, we instinctively seek a mate that can bring us feelings of love, companionship, and intimacy. Generally, we instinctively act to avoid pain in every situation. Given two alternatives that are equally uncomfortable, we choose the less painful of the two. For example, you stay in a job either that you dislike or accept that you will have a lower standard of living by switching jobs. If having a lower standard of living is going to be socially embarrassing and limit your ability to provide for your family or drive a nice car. You will choose to stay in the job you dislike because the alternative is even more painful emotionally than the job. This is a powerful concept to be aware of in terms of what might be motivating your behavior in your day-to-day decision-making.

The Magic Wand

* Financial independence *
* Travel and leisure *
* Freedom to pursue our dreams *

What would people want if they could wave a magic wand and have or do anything they imagined? Many of the people that I have had the honor of advising over the past 20 years have expressed the importance of financial independence and wealth preservation. Although many people enjoy their jobs, it may not provide complete fulfillment and freedom to pursue their dreams. Sufficient financial resources may only help self-starters and independent personalities. For most people having a job to go to each day gives them a sense of purpose, but may not satisfy life goals, desire to spend more time with loved ones, learn and understand the world, travel, play more chess or paint. Working 40 or more hours per week, managing a household of kids, pets and other obligations does not always allow us the time or flexibility to do everything we wish. However, working and saving a part of your earnings can provide for a comfortable lifestyle when time becomes available.

Another wish is to travel and experience the world. You can realize such a desire today or in the near term with a few simple financial strategies. Forced savings on a monthly or bi-weekly basis over a one, 2 or 3 year, period, depending on your level of income can result in a dream vacation. Why do we then delay what we desire the most? I have seen heart-breaking situations when loving spouses finally retire with more wealth than is imaginable to an average person, but one of them falls ill, or becomes immobile or passes on. The surviving spouse lives with many of their personal dreams unfulfilled and nobody to share them. Travel now if it is truly, what you wish. Save a part of what you earn not just for your retirement, but also for your dream trip. One caveat is that I need to emphasize moderation. Instant gratification can become a way of life and may squash plans for the future.

Self-Reliance

* Self-confidence and independence without
approval seeking behavior *
* Following your heart, unmoved by criticism *

When we decide to have children, our primary wish is that our children will be safe, happy, and healthy individuals. Our hope is that our children have a better life than we have had. Of course, we do not think too deeply about what that might look like. Nevertheless, we always wish them the very best of everything. A parent's hope is that their child is self-confident, independent, and capable of making her own informed decisions without seeking the approval of others. According to Dr. Wayne Dyer, self-reliance is a concept that describes an individual that has confidence in themselves and the world in which they live. It is a parent's dream that their children develop the skills to think independently, to take absolute responsibility for their lives, and not find fault or blame (Dyer, What Do You Really Want For Your Children?, 1985). Watching over time as our children develop independence and self-confidence gives us peace of mind. Far too many adult children in our society are financially and emotionally dependent on a spouse, a parent or on a government social program. This is a sad commentary on parenting skills in this country, if not an observation of more fundamental problems in our society as a whole.

Teaching our children to be responsible for their own life and destiny by giving them the opportunity to build the skills required to survive in a very competitive world. Self-reliant and confident children and adult children are willing to take risks and follow their hearts knowing it may not work out, but not letting that thought get in the way of their personal dreams. Individuals who have the courage to move forward and get back on the horse after falling off for a second or third time succeed in a number of ways. Unmoved by criticism, negativity or doubt they forge onward putting meaning into their lives. I can only imagine the mental strength of a mountain climber as she is half way up the cliff and must overcome any doubt in her mind she will reach the top. Nobody to help, you must be self-reliant!

Common Financial Goals

* Differentiate between Financial and Personal goals *

I have found that most people cannot articulate their goals when asked. We may know intuitively what we want, but until the goals are solidified in writing, they will not have energy. Writing and prioritizing your goals will give them life and you will begin to see them materialize. Make this a list of short, medium, and long-term goals. Ask yourself what you are doing to achieve your goals now. What is your timeframe to begin and how much time, money or effort will you require? I have provided a list of common financial goals people may have at any single point in their lives. Some goals may not apply to you depending on your life stage, but check off the ones that are most important to you. Then, prioritize in terms of importance and ask yourself what you are doing right now to achieve them. Finally, begin your search to find the information and the action required to achieve these goals.

- ✓ Reduce Income Tax
- ✓ Retire Early
- ✓ Own my own home or cottage
- ✓ Own a trailer/boat/plane
- ✓ Preserve my wealth for my beneficiaries
- ✓ Save for Annual Travel
- ✓ Save for my children's education
- ✓ Save for my retirement
- ✓ Learn how to invest
- ✓ Keep ahead of inflation
- ✓ Protect my assets from over taxation
- ✓ Insure myself in case of death or disability

✓ Write or Update Wills or POAs
✓ Pay-off debts or mortgage
✓ Own my own business
✓ Own a dream home

This is not a comprehensive list, but gives you a glimpse at some of the financial and retirement goals you may have. Do not confuse these financial goals with personal goals that might include running in a marathon, losing 10 lbs., learning a new language, inventing a new way to iron clothes or to improve your relationship with your children. A list of personal goals could be infinitely long, only limited by your imagination.

Goals and Goal Setting

In the inspirational words of Tony Robbins, "determine what you really want then take massive action towards achieving it". I am a big believer in identifying and clarifying your goals in life and your financial goals. Is it fear of success, fear of rejection or fear of some other unknown that is stopping you from moving forward? Realizing what is holding you back from achieving all that you desire is the critical first step. Tony Robbins and other motivational, educational masters teach us that focus and clarity are the keys to your ultimate success. Focus and attending to what you truly want in your life is the key to happiness and elimination of conflict.

Many people believe they would be happier if only they were rich. This simply is not the case, as studies have shown that happiness measures reach a peak at about $80,000 annual income. Beyond that, more income or wealth merely gives you the perception of happiness as you bathe in your solid gold tub filled with gold coins. I agree, owning a 95-foot yacht, Ferrari F12Berlinetta and a magnificent 15,000 square foot mansion, with 48 bedrooms, 15 bathrooms, indoor pool would be nice. Nevertheless, how happy would you be sitting in this fine home alone because your friends and family were working? Wealth is merely a state of mind, a conceptual idea. How you identify with wealth and what it can do for you are the questions you must answer. Most of us have more financial resources than the majority of the world's population.

Comparatively, North Americans are very wealthy by world standards, so it is how we define wealth. In many other countries around the world, wealth could mean owning 5 goats and 6 chickens. In Grenada for example, the poverty is so prevalent that kids would be elated with new shoes shipped in from the US (Catherine Alford, 2013). They would wear them every day until another shipment came in next year. Wealth in Grenada means having the opportunity to eat at KFC, fast food restaurant. Considered a status symbol eating at the only fast food restaurant on the island, people actually walk around with KFC cups and bags for few days. True, financial independence is having enough financial resources to live your life without work. You would then have the freedom to do what you want, when you want with whomever you want. In the end, perhaps you would still work because it is what you love doing, not because you have bills to pay.

PART II

KNOWLEDGE

Stock Markets · Bond Markets · Commodity Markets · Money Markets · Derivatives Markets · Futures Markets · Insurance Markets · Foreign Exchange Markets

Financial Markets

CHAPTER V

INVESTMENTS & THE MUTUAL FUND INDUSTRY

"Rule number 1 of investing is never lose money.
Rule number 2 is never forget rule number 1."
Warren Buffet

➢ Learn about the basic types of investments
➢ Learn about different types of mutual funds
➢ Commissions and Fees
➢ Stocks, bonds and foreign currency
➢ Real Estate investing
➢ Derivatives explained at last

Three Types of Investments

* Safety = GICs, T-Bills, Money Market Funds *
* Income = Bonds, Dividends, Income Funds *
* Growth = Stocks, Stock Mutual Funds *

If you remember nothing else, I will instill in you that there are three basic types of investments, yet hundreds of intricate branches for each of them that you may not need to understand. The first group of aptly named investments is *Safety*. Safety type investments will generally provide a principle guarantee or virtual guarantee and a prescribed interest rate or return for a specified period. A Government of Canada T-Bill, Guaranteed Investment Certificate (GIC), Term Deposits, and Money Market Mutual Funds to name a few are what I would describe as Safety Investments.

The second group, *Income investments,* includes Government and Corporate Bonds, Preferred Shares and Utilities stocks for dividend income, carry no principle protection. These types of investments trade on the open market and fluctuate in value daily. Although they are relatively safe over the long run or term to maturity, they offer no principal guarantee. Income investments provide a steady stream of either interest from bonds or dividends from common or preferred stocks. Income trusts have been spinning off tax preferred income to unit holders. Although, the recent announcement of a change to the way Income trusts can spin off tax-preferred income to unit holders is no longer allowed effective 2011. The Canada Customs Revenue (CRA) office taxes Income Trusts like any other Canadian corporation. Government of Canada bonds, Provincial and Municipal bonds, low to high quality corporate bonds and dividend bearing preferred stock are all examples of income investments.

Finally, *Growth Investments* provide no principle guarantee, experience wide fluctuations in value daily and will often appreciate and yield little or no dividend income. Many common stocks are widely considered as growth investments. Risk can be relatively high in common stocks but the rewards can also be equally great. There is a great deal of variation in the risk level between the thousands of publicly traded stocks. However, a significant portion of the large capitalization or blue chip stocks rate as moderate risk over the long-term. However, note that large losses can be felt in the short-term and even in the long-term if the investor has purchased a single individual stock or is improperly diversified. Familiar to most investors are Mutual funds, which are diversified baskets of bonds and or stocks and can fall into anyone of the three types of investments.

Mutual funds still have a credibility problem with the public and may be lacking transparency and full disclosure at the sales level. If the truth be known, a simplified prospectus for each mutual fund, if read, provides the transparency. In 1932, the first mutual fund in Canada, The Canadian Investment Fund Ltd was established. There may not have been clear investor transparency, but there would have been audited financial statements and an Investment Policy Statement for the managers to follow. The amended *Simplified Prospectus* came out in the early 2000s, due to poor transparency, to provide, in plain language primary aspects of the fund. Again, investors and advisors ignored the document. It was simply too time consuming to go through 200 pages to find information about the single fund they purchased. Effective May 30, 2016, advisors are to provide the 4-page Fund Facts document to the client prior to the sale of any mutual fund in Canada.

Mutual Funds

* $1.27 Trillion Invested in Mutual Funds *
* 5 major asset classes *
* 53 categories of funds in Canada *
* 36,516 mutual funds available to investors *

As of May 31, 2016, IFIC (Investment Funds Institute of Canada-www.IFIC.ca) reported that Canadians hold $1.27 trillion in mutual funds. Seven years ago, July 31, 2009, IFIC reported total mutual fund assets of $556.7 billion. The industry supported 192,000 jobs, generated a $17 billion economic footprint and contributed $7 trillion in tax revenue. The FundLibrary.com reports 437 fund companies in Canada, 36,516 mutual funds including their clones, as of July 19, 2016. One in three Canadians holds or invests in mutual funds. This is largely due to many Canadians' participating in company sponsored pension plans.

The CIFSC (Canadian Investment Funds Standards Committee, July, 2016) recently announced the new mutual fund categories and classification definitions as well as detailed review of their screening process. The Committee classifies security types into five broad asset classes: Cash, Fixed Income, Equity, Commodity or Other. The Committee also defines Regional and Sector Classifications of specific funds. Common groups, such as Money Market, Fixed Income, Balanced, Target Date, Domestic or International Equity, or Commodity Funds will be familiar to many investors. Without defining each of the 53 categories of funds, I have given you several of the basic types of funds below.

Types of Mutual Funds

As I have mentioned previously, mutual funds and indeed all investments, are simply the tools to help you achieve your financial goals. Although essential, financial planning incorporates dozens of other strategies alongside of mutual funds. You should have a basic understanding of what funds are and what they can and cannot do. Each mutual fund has a written investment policy or mandate to follow. The Committee screens the mandate along with the actual holdings on a security-by-security basis and places the fund into a specific category. I have briefly outlined a few of the more common categories (CIFSC, 2016) with the hope of providing you with a level of comfort in selecting any specific fund.

1. *Money Market Funds*: Often Canadian or U.S. versions are offered. The manager must invest 95% of assets in cash or cash equivalent securities, such as short-term government of Canada T-bills, short term Bankers Acceptances, investment grade short-term corporate notes. Your principal protection goes only as far as the investment credit worthiness of the issuer.

2. *Canadian Short Term Fixed Income Funds*: The fund must be 90% Canadian dollar denominated holdings. They typically have less than 3.5-year duration and investment grade, BBB or better. The manager will also invest primarily in government issued bonds, either Federal or Provincial Bonds or Corporate bonds with a high credit rating.

3. *Canadian Fixed Income Funds*: The fund must invest 90% in Canadian dollar denominated fixed income with duration between 3.5 years but less than 9 years. They must also be investment grade (ie. BBB or better).

4. *Canadian Long Term Fixed Income Funds:* The fund must invest 90% in Canadian dollar fixed income securities with a duration of 9.0 or greater. The fund cannot hold more than 25% in high yield fixed income. The fund must primarily invest in investment grade securities (ie. BBB or better).

5. *High Yield Fixed Income Funds*: Similar in nature to a "regular" bond fund but the manager must invest primarily in non-investment grade credit quality (equivalent or below BBB). In other words, the average credit quality must be below investment grade. The general strategy is to achieve a higher return by investing in higher yielding fixed income instruments, while managing risk within the mandate.

6. *Preferred Share Fixed Income Funds:* The fund manager must invest 90% of the holdings in Preferred Shares. Preferred shares are a hybrid of a stock and a bond. They generally will not receive growth as a common stock, but will receive a reliable dividend payment quarterly, depending on the issuer.

7. *Balanced Funds*: This group of funds must invest between 5% and 90% into equity securities and between 10% and 90% in fixed income securities. They can be Canadian, Global, Neutral or Tactical Balanced funds, each category having specific mandates to follow.

8. *Canadian Dividend and Income Equity Funds:* The mandate for these funds is to invest 70% into Canadian equity securities and further, they must invest at least 50% in income generating securities. They must also invest in securities

exceeding the Small and Mid-Cap threshold. Therefore, the securities must be of a large-cap nature.

9. *Canadian Equity Funds:* This category states that the manager must invest at least 90% in Canadian domiciled securities of a large cap nature.

10. U.S. Equity funds: Similar to Canadian equity funds, the US equity mandate states the manager must invest at least 90% in US domiciled securities.

11. *International Equity Funds*: This category has a geographically diverse mandate and must invest at least 90% outside Canada and the US and at least 70% in developed countries, such as Europe, UK, Australia, Japan, etc...

12. *Global Equity Funds*: This fund mandate has even more flexibility, it can invest anywhere around the world with a few stipulations. First, the fund must invest more than 10% but less than 90% in Canada or the US and must be of a large-cap nature.

13. I have listed 12 categories, but the Committee has 53 special categories in total. Each fund must follow the mandate set out by the definitions. The fund categories highlighted above are some of the more common, largely diversified funds often recommended as core holdings. For a full list of categories, visit www.CIFSC.org/mutual-fund-categories.

The Mutual Fund Simplified Prospectus; A must read...
The Simplified Prospectus highlights some of the important disclosures related to your mutual fund investment. I have listed some of them below:

* What is a mutual and what are the risks *
* Organization and management of the funds *

* How to purchase, switch or redeem you funds *
* A discussion of the Management Fees and Expenses *
* Dealer and broker or adviser compensation *
* Income Tax considerations when owning a fund *
* Your legal rights *
" Additional information: financial statements, performance, and management commentary *

The document provides investors with enough useful information to help them make an informed investment decision. The simplified prospectus follows strict guidelines to provide information in plain language for Canadian unit holders of all levels of knowledge. It sets out how the fund is managed and how the manager must invest the money deposited by the mutual fund unit holders according to the level of risk mandated by the funds' stated objective. This document discloses management fees, dealer compensation, commissions, and penalties for early redemption. It discloses and provides disclaimers on investment risk and returns. The Simplified Prospectus sets out the parameters of the fund and the industry and its managers. It is necessary read if you are to be a fully informed investor. It is not mandatory that a mutual fund investor receive a copy of the Simplified Prospectus. Effective May 30, 2016, investors must receive a copy of the Fund Facts document.

Fund Facts Document

Fund companies and investment advisers need to educate their clients about the different types of risks inherent in all the various types of mutual funds. New regulation, effective May 30, 2016, requires delivery of the Fund Facts document pre-sale or prior to buying a Mutual Fund. Advisors can no longer recommend a mutual fund over the phone without this minimum disclosure, pre-sale. Fund Facts provide several critical pieces of information so the investor can make an informed decision. The document highlights key points for the lay investor, without the industry jargon. A typical Fund Facts document for a stock fund will include several key sections on four manageable pages, as follows:

1. Quick Facts - provides fund codes, date of inception, total value of fund assets, management expense ratio, name of fund manager, distributions and minimum investment.
2. What Does the Fund Invest In? The top 10 holdings in the fund are listed according to their percentage weight. Total holdings is disclosed as well as investment mix by sectors, such as Financials, Energy, utilities and country weights, such as Canada, US and Europe.
3. How Risky Is It? A brief paragraph or two presents the fund in an understandable language, such as, "You can lose money." Additionally, an industry wide Risk Rating of: Low, Low-to-medium, Medium, Medium-to-High and High.
4. How has the fund performed? This section highlights year-by-year returns, and best and worst 3-month returns. This information can truly give the investor a feel for what might happen if the markets drop.
5. Who is the fund for? In plain language, four concise statements, it states what type of investor this fund is suitable. For example, it might state, "can handle the volatility of returns of equity investments…" or "plan to hold their investments for the long-term."
6. A word about tax. A few brief paragraphs explain the investor will have to pay tax on any distributions or capital gains earned, unless held in a tax- sheltered plan, such as an RRSP or TFSA.
7. How much does it cost? This section highlights sales charges. Deferred Sales Charges and the subsequent 6 or 7 year schedule of penalties for early withdrawal; Low Load Sales Charges and subsequent 2 or 3 year schedule of penalties; Fund Expenses are disclosed and explained as well as trailing commission which is an ongoing commission paid to your advisors firm for as long as you hold the fund.
8. What if I change my mind? Explains that your rights allow you to withdraw from an agreement to buy mutual funds within 2 business days of receiving a simplified prospectus

or Fund Facts; and cancel your purchase within 48 hours after you receive confirmation of purchase.

9. For more information. Name, address, website and telephone numbers for the fund company are found in the last section.

With all the disclosures in the Fund Facts, for an individual to lose all of his money invested in a diversified Canadian or US Equity fund for example, every company held in the fund would have to go bankrupt simultaneously. It is possible, but not likely. If it were the case that all of the stocks in the fund went to zero, including the major banks, insurance companies, food manufactures, oil and gas and utility companies there would clearly be many other terrible things happening in the economy to worry about. What can and does happen is that the prices of the stocks in the fund fluctuate and fall significantly every so often. A *Market Correction* occurs when a broad selloff across all stocks takes place. Therefore, mutual funds, whether they are bond or equity type funds can never guarantee your principle remains intact in the short term, but as history has shown, will generally grow over the long term of 10 years or more.

Specific Mutual Fund Selection Criteria

Now you have some ammunition to go out and select a portfolio of funds for your savings. I would again recommend that you seek out an accredited financial planner, holding the Certified Financial Planner (CFP) or Canadian Investment Manager (CIM) designation, to assist you with the individual fund selections. The Planner or Broker should have a set of 5 to 10 criteria for his "picks". If he cannot describe to you how he picked the funds other than it did 32% last year he has not done his due diligence and you may not want to deal with him. *It is not just about the returns.* As outlined below in more detail, some of the selection criteria I use are:

1. 5-year average annual compound rate of return relative to peers, i.e. Quartile ranking.
2. Manager tenure: long or short.

3. Management fee relative to peers is it high or low.
4. Standard Deviation: a risk measure for 3 and 5 years, relative to peers and benchmark index.
5. Beta: a measure that compares the movement of your fund with the benchmark index. It is a measure of how sensitive the returns of the fund are relative to the returns of the index.
6. Sharpe measures the risk adjusted return. It may well be the single best indicator of a top performing fund.
7. Tax efficiency of a non-rrsp portfolio.
8. Calendar year vs. compounded returns relative to benchmark and peers.
9. Value or Growth Style/Large or Small Capitalization
10. Size of the fund; it's assets under administration.

There are several dozen more criteria to analyze, but let this be a starting point when questioning your planner or broker. *It is essential that you and or your adviser know that the fund you are investing in is of a superior quality. It can mean short-term disaster or long-term success. Of course there are never iron clad strategies that will avoid every possible land mine, but this will minimize risk.*

Wrap Accounts

* A basket of several mutual funds managed like one *
* Packaged to match a specific risk tolerance *
* A "hands-off" approach to investing *

This is just another way to market and package mutual funds combining several mutual funds into a single basket: Sometimes known as a *fund of funds*. Purchasing a wrap account typically involves an interview process. An investor answers several questions in a questionnaire and then receives a risk tolerance score. One of the six or seven wrap or portfolios of funds will then be selected as a match to the investors risk tolerance. Typical asset allocations are weighted according to a quantitative computer models, basing its assumptions on historical past performance of various risk measures. For example, a balanced growth portfolio may have 15 percent short term bonds, 20% medium term bonds (Canadian and Global), 10% preferred shares, 25% Canadian stocks, 15% US stocks, 15% international stocks. The packaged product appeals to the general-public, comfortable with the idea of a managed solution, lower costs and a hands-off approach. Ultimately, the wrap account is a creatively packaged product of 8 to 12 pools or mutual funds that will broadly diversify your assets. The benefit to the wrap account investor is very little or no involvement in the management of the fund and typically lower volatility because of the diversification. Sometimes I refer to this broad diversification as *de-worsification*. In other words, you can over diversify and water down the returns by having everything lumped into one investment. An underweight position in your best investments, or an overweight in your worst can also detract from performance. For example, the downside here is that if preferred shares are significantly underperforming the market, the manager must retain the asset weighting, according to the investment policy, and mandate.

The Case for Active Management

* Passive Investing vs. Active Investing *
* Selecting a superior manager to beat the index *
* Selecting a manager with expertise in specialty markets *
* Selecting a manager for higher risk adjusted returns *

First, it is true that mutual fund sales people and brokers can make more sales commissions if they sell a back-end loaded mutual fund than if they sell a stock or an ETF (Exchange Traded Fund). It takes similar level of knowledge to select an ETF as a managed fund, but the adviser is required to be more hands on if building a portfolio of ETFs. Research and portfolio management duties are required. Whereas, owning a Balanced Mutual Fund, for example, is virtually a hands-off solution. The fund manager makes all the investment decisions about what securities to buy, what weighting of bonds or stocks to hold, etc. The advisor has little to do, freeing up his time to do the Retirement Planning, Tax and Estate Planning for his clients. Furthermore, managing a portfolio of ETFs adds a more sophisticated level of investment management by the advisor, as he must make the asset allocation decisions. Managing ETF or stock portfolios takes time away from the planning aspect of an Advisor's role. Second, by selecting a managed fund you hope the manager can beat the index, increase your returns, and manage the risk of being in the market during a crash or correction. Unfortunately, the manager cannot be expected to beat the market consistently and simultaneously manage the *market risk*. He can only manage the risk of the individual securities he owns in the portfolio. The only way to beat the index is by investing outside the index. That said, there are some superb fund managers that will beat the markets for long stretches. There is also growing evidence to support there are indeed superior stock pickers (Brown W. H., 2006). Determining who they are is the challenge for advisors and investors.

There are two additional reasons to buy an actively managed stock fund. First, you want the expertise of a fund manager to invest in a specialty market that is not available through indexed investing. For example, if you want an expert in precious metals and mining stocks. You can search for a top performing portfolio manager in that sector. The second reason is to own a stock fund that will give you reasonable risk adjusted returns or lower volatility in general, than the index. In the end, most investors are risk averse, but want the highest possible return with the least amount of risk. I would contend that owning a stock fund managed with a fundamental bottom-up, value approach is the best long-term option. A growth fund or index fund will not protect your capital in a bear market. A value fund will shine as the herd shifts out of growth to protect capital. The higher management fee is fair if you are not simply matching the performance of the index but earning consistent and low volatility returns during every part of the economic cycle. Many experts in the industry will say that if it is a long-term investment you should not worry about volatility. I disagree. *It is exactly the fluctuation in the value of principle driving people out of the equity markets.*

In the end, like anything, there will be a ranking of performance within each of the mutual fund categories. Picking mutual funds and designing a portfolio that is appropriate for an individual's personal risk tolerance, time horizon, financial resources and personal goals is an essential and critical process to follow. It is a combination of art and financial analysis. I will admittedly tell you there is no guarantee of outperformance with any particular investment strategy. Assuming it is high returns that you are looking for. There are, however, some sure fire ways of avoiding big losses, while obtaining relatively good returns in the short, medium and long term. I will discuss these strategies of diversification and tactical asset allocation in upcoming chapters.

Beating the Index

* Thousands of Investors = Efficient markets *
* Few Investors = Less efficient markets *
* Statistics are conclusive: Indices beat active managers *
* Large efficient markets are difficult to beat *
* Managers can outperform in smaller specialty markets *
* Management fees are part of the performance problem *

Information is so readily available to the thousands of players in the market it is near impossible to develop a strategy that will "outsmart" the majority of the players consistently. Information clearly plays a role in financial decision-making. However, when it comes to beating the market index, the majority of the money managers fall short. I am referring to mutual fund and portfolio managers doing worse than the performance of an index or index fund, passive management. Ted Cadsby provides a thorough analysis of index funds vs. actively managed funds. His conclusion, "It's a simple historical fact that most fund managers have great difficulty beating the index."(Cadsby, 1999). Cadsby goes to great length to show statistically, in large, efficient developed markets, such as the Canadian or US markets the majority of active managers underperform the index by a wide margin. In less efficient, such as the emerging markets or specific sectors, fund managers will outperform the index as they can take advantage of inefficiencies in the pricing of individual securities. Cadsby suggests that indexing is a solid strategy to maximize long term returns and should be part of every investment portfolio.

Since Cadsby conducted his research in 1999, the debate continues to reflect the merits of both, but passive investing outperforms. Active managers use a variety of strategies to try to beat their benchmarks and perhaps achieve higher risk adjusted returns than their respective benchmarks 1 or 2 years in a row, but not long term. By conducting fundamental analysis and using complicated valuation methods to find mispriced securities they believe they can outperform. Active managers charge significantly higher fees than passive indexed investing and most experts agree that active managers simply will not consistently outperform after fees and taxes. In a recent 10-year period, Wharton, University of Pennsylvania found that, "On an after-tax basis, managers of stock funds for large and mid-sized companies produced lower returns than their index-style competitors 97% of the time, while managers of small-cap stocks trailed 77% of the time."

Why Buy Mutual Funds?

* The pros and cons *
* Instant portfolio of stocks or bonds *
* Can appear to be expensive vs. index funds *
* Own mutual funds that meet investment
objectives and risk tolerance *
* Historically, equity managers will protect the downside *
* Fund manager expertise, reporting and hands off approach *

There are hundreds of reasons, for the average investor, why mutual funds are the best way to invest. Yet, interestingly enough there are an equal number of reasons why they are an inappropriate and expensive way of investing. Generally, if you want high returns they cost too much for the value and risk. They often underperform less expensive passively managed index funds and individual growth stocks are the route to the highest potential returns. Selecting a mutual fund that outperforms the benchmark consistently is like picking the winning hockey team for the Stanley Cup each year. In Canada, management expenses are often way out of line at 2 to 3%. It simply does not make sense to me that the fund continues to charge high fees, as the fund gets larger and larger. Research costs do not go up because you are simply buying a bigger block of 1,000,000 shares vs. 100,000 shares of the same company. At a minimum, there should be economies of scale and the management expense should fall. Coincidentally, the marketing expenses of the firm often rise as the fund grows. This in turn brings in more investment dollars and the fund or funds will continue to grow. Nevertheless, the 2 or 3% management fee continues. At the same time, there is a low probability the active fund manager will even perform as well as the benchmark.

To be fair, for many small investors, mutual funds are clearly a wonderful way to invest into a diversified portfolio of securities for a reasonable cost and great convenience. For larger investors of $250,000 or more, the alternate way to invest is into ETF's, exchange-traded funds, individual stocks and bonds. Buy and hold is not something that I would recommend for all mutual funds, as the managers do not have your personal interests in mind. Growth managers are managing the fund to outperform on 1, 3 and 5-year periods. The managers do not consider when individual investors get into the fund and will not tell you when to get out. It could be at the top of the market, which is a poor time for new investors but not a bad thing for existing unit holders. They often take on a great deal of risk to squeeze out every point of return, even if it means remaining in the market at outrageous levels. It would then be up to the individual mutual fund investor to pull some money out of the fund and go to cash or other asset if they believed the market was set to fall. *It cannot be overemphasized; it is up to the mutual fund investor and his adviser to pull money out of the fund if the markets become expensive. Mutual fund managers are paid to manage and hold equities, not to hold cash.*

Timing is of course very difficult to do with any degree of success, but there are strategies such as tactical asset allocation (think pie chart and big and small pieces signifies different asset classes or sectors of the economy). This will allow for a shifting of money from top performing asset classes to poor performing or better-priced asset classes, essentially buying low and selling high. Tactical asset allocation shifts money between sectors such as financial, oil & gas, telecommunications or health care as well as between countries' equity and bond weightings. As one market becomes more overvalued on a relative basis good managers will begin to reduce the weighting of that asset class while increasing the weighting in another. This is not so much timing as it is prudent portfolio management.

Holding value funds for the long run has its risks. Historically, value funds do not succumb to the wild fluctuations of the markets, as would a growth or momentum fund. Although midway through 2007, growth stocks soared while value fell terribly out of favor around the globe. Value managers buy stocks at discounts and hold for a relatively longer period, until the company turns around, or the market takes notice. As the price begins to rise as more market participants begin to buy the value stocks, the value manager will begin to sell into the demand for the stock. Value managers take a bottom up analytical approach and do not factor in what might be taking place in the broader market.

Of course, there are pros and cons to the argument of trying to buy and sell stocks and bonds on your own or buying growth funds then trying to time the markets. Firstly, many people do not have the time, money, or expertise to invest in individual securities. When buying and owning individual securities there would not be a management fee if executed on a discount brokerage account, but there would be commissions to buy and sell. If a full service broker is providing advice and executing the trades, the broker will likely charge 1% to 2% commission or an annual fee, depending on the size of your account. This is not necessarily a less expensive way to invest than mutual funds and I would question whether an individual broker with less educational credentials is going to outperform the likes of major mutual fund companies or provide the diversification of even a single mutual fund.

As far as the sophisticated investment knowledge that is required and ongoing monitoring of the individual stocks, it becomes apparent that it is not for everyone. Mutual funds provide small and large investors alike with a "hands free" approach to investing and saving. Finally, I would argue that an average management expense of 2.25% annually is a relatively small price to pay the opportunity to improve returns and build your wealth.

How to Select a Money Manager

Let me rephrase that question: If you choose to use actively managed mutual funds, how do you select a particular Mutual Fund? First, not all mutual funds are created equal as we learned in the previous chapter. Although many of the hundreds of mutual funds available are mere copies of each other, within a specified category of fund. With a few different stocks sprinkled in to add the management team's own flavor of the month. Some fund managers clearly have a stock picking gift even though the largest funds often have the same top holdings. They may not have remotely similar stocks on balance.

I will outline specific selection criteria below, but one essential criterion for selecting a qualifying a fund for your portfolio is a minimum of a 3 to 5 year track record. The fund should have a three, four, or five star rating from Morningstar rating system. Review the Manager tenure (3+ years at the helm); Compare the 3 and 5-year standard deviation statistics against peers. Standard Deviation is a critical statistic showing how much the price of the fund goes up or down on average over 36 or 60 monthly measurements. Therefore, a high standard deviation vs. similar funds in the same category may be a fund you would stay clear. Consider the Beta of a fund. It will tell you if its performance is sensitive to movements in the tracking benchmark index, such as the TSX/S&P60. For example, a Beta of 1.0 would imply that the fund's performance exactly tracks the index. A Beta of .5 indicates that if the index drops 3% in 1 month the fund will fall only 1.5%, on average. Similarly, a beta of 1.5 indicates the fund will likely see a 4.5% return for the month, if the index did 3%. Additional ways to weed out fund managers is the management expense ratio compared to peers. Three, five and ten year calendar year returns should be reviewed and compared with peers, with careful consideration of larger than average fluctuations in returns. I also review several other very important statistics that assist me in selecting funds that have a proven record of managing the fund within the stated level of risk. The Sharpe statistic, or risk adjusted return, gives us a measure of the return the fund has yielded for a given level of risk. For instance, you may be looking at a fund that yielded a very high return of 32% in 1 year, but the fund had huge volatility within its stock portfolio on a monthly basis. Losing big on some stocks but winning big on a select few; Rather than having steady returns from the whole portfolio. In other words, the manager was taking big risks to achieve the return. All said, selecting a mutual fund on the return in isolation, is ill advised.

Qualifications to Look For in a Mutual Fund or Pension Fund Manager
Mutual fund managers, Pension fund managers, and Private Investment Counselors should ideally have the CFA designation. The Chartered Financial Analyst designation is awarded to those individuals passing a series of three 6-hour examinations over a minimum of 3 years. The examinations run once a year only, with the exception of Level I, which is now available two times each year internationally. Over 100,000 candidates in 140 countries sat for the three examinations in 2006, for example. The examinations cover comprehensive and complex material from such diversified fields as corporate finance, international investments, economics, statistical analysis for investments, portfolio management, financial statement analysis, derivatives and ethical and professional standards. At each level of the examination process, approximately half of all candidates will pass allowing them to write the next level and become eligible for the CFA designation, upon meeting other work related experience criteria. Each level contains a new additional mountain of information and body of knowledge requiring a minimum of 250 hours and often up to 350 hours of concentrated self-study. Finally, a little more than two-thirds of Level III candidates will succeed. The CFA is quickly becoming the gold standard in the industry for all portfolio managers, equity,

and fixed income analysts hired by mutual fund companies and pension funds.

Commissions, Management Expense and Fees

* DSC = back end loaded commission *
* FE = front end or upfront commission *
* MER = Management Expense Ratio *
* Fee Based Account = Annual fee, no commission *

Bank employees and Insurance representatives often sell proprietary mutual funds, their own branded mutual fund line up. Bank employees, mutual fund representatives are quite often on salary and sell funds with an initial sales charge (ISC), zero commission. The commonly used term for the initial sales charge is front-end load. While mutual fund, investment and bank dealers, typically sell third-party mutual funds, either front-end commission (ISC) or on a back end or deferred sale charge (DSC). Front end loaded mutual funds are sold with a 1% or 2% commission charged up front. The benefit of buying with a front-end load is that there is no penalty to redeem early. However, if the fund is sold back end loaded (DSC), or low load (LL) it may have cost nothing to buy, but if it is redeemed within the first 6 or 7 years, or 3 years for LL, there can be a 1% to 5.5% penalty. For example, based on the DSC schedule, if you purchase a fund on a DSC basis and sell it for cash in the first year there could be a 5.5% penalty. Additionally, if the fund has gone down in value, the penalty is on the book value, not the market value.

Often in the second year there could also be a 5.0% penalty and so on based on a DSC schedule disclosed in the fund company simplified prospectus. The fund companies allow for a 10% free units redemption each anniversary of deposit date, for any reason. Moreover, this option works nicely for retirees withdrawing funds for retirement income. Fund companies permit switching funds within the fund family, no charge. However, the fund company may charge a switch fee for early switches. Deferred sales charges act as a deterrent for short term investing. Banks and mutual fund companies have a line-up of no load funds. While mutual funds additionally have DSC and LL fund versions, banks have NL for in-house representatives and "Advisor series", similar to DSC, for external investment advisors.

Management Fee

Every mutual fund, pension fund and insurance segregated fund has a specified management fee. Canadian equity funds, for example have a management fee of approximately 2.5% specified in the simplified prospectus. However, at the end of the year when the mutual fund managers add up all of the expenses to run the fund, as a ratio to the net asset value of the fund, the management expense ratio may be even higher than 2.5%. That is, if the fund had higher *actual* expenses than the stated fee or the value of the underlying investments fell over the course of the 12 months. The management fee takes care of the portfolio managers' salaries, analyst salaries, administrative expenses, technology & research, and sales & marketing expenses. Additionally, if the fund sold on a DSC basis, the investment dealer/advisor receives a .5% annual trailer. On a front-load commission basis, a 1% annual trailer or service fee is paid to the dealer/broker as part of the 2.5% management expense.

Service Fee

The trailer or service fee is an on-going compensation paid to brokers and planners to provide service to the investor. In reality, the investor gets no guarantee of service for this .5% or 1%. New regulations, beginning in January 2017, requiring a fee page on statements will show the amount of service fees paid to the investment dealer in dollars. It is important that you have your adviser provide you with an outline services you could reasonably expect. If you, the investor and your advisor agree, sign a written letter of engagement to ensure no broken promises. Again, in practice, financial planners rarely use letters of agreement, in any formal manner. Even if the broker meets with the client 1 or 8 times per year on a $100,000 account, the mutual fund company pays the investment dealer from $500 to $1,000 depending on the investment mix and the broker receives a percentage from 40% to 90%. In other words, if the broker sold the fund on a back end loaded basis, the Investment Dealer is paid 5% commission up front, but receives only .5% per year as a service fee. In fairness, the 5% upfront commission is appropriate due to the challenge and costs of acquiring a new client, costs of overhead for research, expertise and administration that goes into the initial investment plan and recommendations. The industry is looking at ways to minimize any possibility of conflict through very strict disclosures, compliance and auditing procedures. A recent option of selling low load funds where only 3% is paid up-front, but a higher trailer or service fee is paid every year thereafter is becoming more popular as an incentive for better after service. In fairness to the vast majority of financial planners and investment brokers working on commission there is a significant amount of accreditation and professional advice provided to clients on a long-term basis, to earn a living.

Stocks: Common Shares vs. Preferred Shares

* Common Shares = minimal dividends, potential growth *
* Preferred Shares = safe regular dividend, no growth *

The media are generally referring to common stock when they talk about the markets. The United States S&P 500 and the Dow Jones Industrial Average or the Canadian TSX/S&P60 are a few of the most common North American stock market indices. They are the indices that observers will comment on in the business news and papers. Common stocks pay dividends but if they pay at all they are very low yields. Common stockholders can be voting or non-voting and will share in the growth of the company and have no guarantee of dividends or principle. Although rare, common shareholders can lose their entire investment. In contrast, in a bankruptcy situation, preferred shareholders will recover their capital before common shareholders, but only after bond and other senior debt-holders are paid. Nevertheless, preferred shareholders will not necessarily share in the growth or appreciation of the company, as they provide safety of capital and a regular stream of dividends.

Full service or discount brokers execute trades for a commission or charge a flat fee annually to buy and sell stocks in an investment account. There is no management fee on stocks held in a discount brokerage account since there is no management. A full service broker or Investment Advisor can either charge a commission for each transaction or charge a flat annual account fee. Nominee or self-directed accounts hold common and preferred stocks as well as mutual funds, GICs, Bonds and ETFs. Investment Advisors and Financial Planners administer, manage and monitor these accounts.

Preferred Shares

"Ladies & Gentlemen Prefer Dividends"
* Capital Preservation*
* Preferential tax treatment of dividends *
* Steady flow of income *

In the aftermath of the 2008 financial crisis and stock market meltdown, investors once again became risk averse, demanding safety. Many investors threw in the towel at the end of 2008 and market lows of March 9, 2009 sitting in cash or money market funds earning virtually no returns, missing the ensuing sharp market recovery. Understandable that investors dumped stocks, but they also sold their holdings in Preferred Shares, running for the safety of Bonds and Government T-Bills. This was all, very temporary as the markets took a sharp V-turn March 10, 2009 after hitting the multi-year lows. Anecdotal evidence suggests that investors sell at the exact wrong time, and then become paralyzed with fear about when to jump back in. Investors finally realized that in a low interest rate environment there was no place to go except the stock market. They began the search for income yielding investments. There was a solution for all those investors unable to make a decision about how to invest their savings. However, I know of no guaranteed strategy to earn big money (or losing big money) in the stock market without making speculative bets. There are however, straightforward strategies to earn decent returns without taking on too much risk. It is simply a matter of buying quality dividend paying investments and patience. Of course, the catch 22 is to know which securities are the "quality investments".

A little known way of achieving steady investment returns comes from owning preferred shares of Canadian and US corporations. Quality common stocks pay dividends, but preferred shares often pay higher dividends with less volatility and risk. That fact fell apart at the beginning of 2015 when the Canadian interest rates fell below the existing preferred share dividend payouts. Fixed Rate Reset preferred shares essentially began a 25% descent for the next 15 months. The problem was the existing Fixed Rate Reset issues have a contract that states that at the end of the 5th year the issue will adjust the dividend to a certain fixed percent, such as 1.25% above the Federal Governments 5 year Bond rate at 2.0% for example. If the existing issue has a 5.25% dividend and will reset at only 3.25%, the price falls. Therefore, as of July 2016, the Canadian preferred share market requires 35% to 40% to recover losses.

Referring to the S&P/TSX, the June 2009 issue of The CFA Analyst, it stated that, "between 1929 and 2004, 65% of the return on equities has come from reinvestment of dividends." This fact shouts at the importance of receiving a regular stream of income from your investments. Preferred shares are closer to a bond in terms of yield to the investor and relative safety of capital. With exceptions as mentioned above. They are unlike common shares of publicly traded companies other than they are ownership stakes.

Why would you want preferred shares after reading the above? Here are a few important things to keep in mind when considering preferred shares. First, in terms of capital preservation, preferred shareholders rank ahead of common stock holders, but after bondholders, if the company was to file bankruptcy. Second, preferred shareholders will not participate in the growth of a company as would common stock holders; nor will they participate in major market crash, as would the common stock holders. Generally, the price of preferred shares will fluctuate only nominally compared with common stock. Third, preferred shareholders typically receive a set quarterly dividend, for an unknown term. The prospectus will state whether it is cumulative or non-cumulative. This refers to the possibility of a dividend cut or suspension, if the company is in trouble. Non-cumulative preferred shares would not receive the missed dividends when reinitiated. Cumulative issues will receive lost dividends if missed for any number of quarters.

Fourth, in the case of straight (or "perpetual") preferred shares there is no maturity. This type of preferred share, considered the riskiest and carries with it higher interest rate risk than other types. Although this was the theory until Fixed Rate Resets were created in 2009. If you purchase a straight preferred with a 6.25% dividend and 2 years later the long term interest rates go up, the value of your preferred shares will go down. The reverse is true. If rates go down, the value of your preferred shares will go up. I would add that the dividend continues regardless of the price of the preferred, so long as the company financials remain solid.

Fixed rate reset preferred shares issued by the major Canadian banks and insurance companies over the past several years. Another way to look at this type of preferred share issuance eliminates the long-term risk of higher interest rates as it provides for a dividend rate reset after 5 years to adjust for prevailing rates every 5 years. Fifth point on why you should still consider preferred shares, dividends from Canadian corporations receive the dividend tax credit if held in taxable accounts. For example, if you are in average marginal tax bracket, $75,000 annual income, an Ontario taxpayer pays 31.48% tax on his next dollar of interest on a bond or GIC. By comparison, with the dividend tax credit the same Ontario taxpayer will pay only 8.92% tax on eligible dividends.

To put this in perspective, a current dividend of 5.25% pays $46.92 in income tax on $525 of dividends and if it were interest, the investor would pay $165.27 of income tax. In other words, a GIC has to earn a significantly higher interest rate to equal the same after tax dollars. So there it is, *ladies & gentlemen,* and not speculators that prefer dividends for their serious money. Investors and Advisers alike are advised to read the prospectus. Each issue of common or preferred stock set out different provisions in the prospectus, found on the website www.SEDAR.com, the System for Electronic Document Analysis and Retrieval.

Preferred share ratings in Canada

DBRS ratings for preferred shares in the Canadian securities market give investors an indication of the credit worthiness of the issuer. DBRS provides a scale based on qualitative and quantitative analysis. How reliable is the dividend payment based on the earnings strength of the issuer and how solid are the financial statements and balance sheet? These are just a few of the criteria analysts and investors will look at. The table below will also highlight the major ratings of preferred shares issued in Canada.

Superior Credit Quality	Pfd-1
Satisfactory Credit Quality	Pfd-2
Adequate Credit Quality	Pfd-3
Speculative	Pfd-4
Highly Speculative	Pfd-5
Default	D

Personally, I would give an issuer an 'F' for Default, but all joking aside, Pfd1, 2 and 3 are generally of investment grade quality. Capital preservation and dividends are acceptable, but Pfd-3 becomes less reliable in adverse conditions. According to DBRS, a rating of Pfd-3 or better corresponds to BBB category for senior bond issues. Each category has specific quantitative criteria that each issuer must meet or exceed to receive the rating given. Again, earnings and balance sheet strength will be the key to ratings. Analysts then dig deeper to determine how well the dividend payments will stand up during adverse market and economic conditions. Similarly, DBRS rate bond issuers according to their balance sheet and strength of their ability to make interest and principle payments.

Bonds: Government and Corporate Bonds

* Governments and Corporations borrow by issuing bonds *
* Investors lend the money for interest *
* Government Bonds: Federal, Provincial, Municipal *
* Corporate Bonds issued by business' requiring money *

Bonds are defined firstly as fixed income investments. Fixed income implies a stated coupon or interest rate, for a specified term. Corporations and governments of all levels issue bonds to fund various operations or projects. When the government or a corporation issues a bond, it is asking for investor money to fund a capital project or some other business venture. In return, the issuer will promise a specific interest rate be paid to the investor on a semi-annual basis and return of principle at the end of the term. Government, Corporate, or other types of bonds have no principle guarantee, although investors buy bonds of investment grade on this premise. Furthermore, many high quality bonds, as rated by the Dominion Bond Rating Service (DBRS), rarely default. However, if you purchase a 5 year bond for $1,000 with a coupon of 4% and interest rates rise to 5% in 1 year your bond is now only worth approximately $956.30 on the secondary bond market. The market will not pay $1000 for a 4% coupon when they can buy a new issue with a 5% coupon. Therefore, if you wanted to cash out you would have to settle for a capital loss of 4.37%. This is interest rate risk. Ultimately, the investor receives his principle if held to maturity in addition to receiving the semi-annual interest payments.

Bonds can be low risk or high risk depending on credit worthiness of the company or government issuing the bond. The DBRS, bond-rating agency goes through a rigorous analysis of the government or corporation issuing the bond and its ability to repay the bond. For example, the Federal Government issues bonds that are of the highest quality and would be considered low risk while receiving a single to triple AAA rating. Lower risk bonds will often have the lowest yield or interest rate vs. a B or C rated corporate bond, or *junk bond* that must pay a higher rate to investors for the added risk. Triple BBB, for example is still considered a relatively high investment grade bond but investors will want slightly higher return for the higher level of risk.

Bond Ratings

Canadian and U.S. market participants use rating services of 3 major agencies: DBRS, originally known as Dominion Bond Rating Service, Moody's Investor Services and Standard & Poor's each have their own methodology and rating terms. See chart below for overview of each rating agencies as detailed in the TDSecurities. com web site, Capital Markets tab.

Credit Quality	DBRS	Moody's	S&P
Superior	AA(low) to AAA	Aa3 to Aaa	AA- to AAA
Good	A(low) to A(high)	A3 to A1	A- to A+
Adequate	BBB(low) to BBB(high)	Baaa3 to Baa1	BBB- to BBB+
Speculative	BB(low) to BB(high)	Ba3 to Ba1	BB- to BB+
Highly Speculative	CCC to B(high)	Caa to B1	CCC to B+

This is a very general overview of ratings used by market participants. The methodology and credit analysis for hundreds of issuers is beyond the scope of this book. Mutual Fund and Pension managers conduct their own individual bond research and credit analysis, although they will utilize the credit ratings of the major agencies as a starting point.

GICs and Canada Savings Bonds (CSB)

All of the major financial institutions issue Guaranteed Investment Certificates (GIC) across Canada. They typically sell in terms of 1 to 5 years and will guarantee the rate and principle for the term. The Banks and insurance companies offer various forms GICs, such as fixed term, cashable terms and escalating or stepped rates over various terms. The federal government issues Canada Savings Bonds (CSB) and Canada Premium Bonds (CPB) (CSB.gc.ca., 2016). Both issued and "fully guaranteed by the Canadian government to help Canadians meet their savings needs". CSBs are only available through employee payroll savings plans, for 3-year terms, rates announced each year for 1 year, by the Minister of Finance. The annual interest rate based on prevailing market rates. "Certificated Canada Savings Bonds can no longer be purchased through financial institutions, dealers or by phone." CPBs are available at most if not all financial institutions, including banks, credit unions and investment dealers, and by phone. Each year the government issues a new series with new regular and compound interest rates offered. For more detailed information on how to buy, redeem CSBs and CPBs go to www.csb.gc.ca.

Exchange Traded Funds (ETFs)

ETF manufactures package their product like an index fund and they come-in numerous types, but are bought and sold like a stock on the open market. Black Rock's iShares are a popular brand name for a basket of ETFs packaged to provide access to the major indices. For the most part, the price will reflect the underlying stocks in the index, but at times, the ETF will sell at a discount or premium depending on supply and demand. They have very low management fees compared to mutual funds, often lower than competitive index funds and are as liquid as most stocks. ETFs meet the needs of every type of investor in the market place. Suppliers created ETFs to track widely held indexes like the S&P500 as well as specialty ETFs that reflect various sectors such as the health care industry, financial services sector and technology. Researchers avoid a great deal of research by simply buying the entire market sector.

* Baskets of stocks or bonds *
* Low management fees *
* Leveraged and inverse bull and bear ETFs *

Over the past several years, the ETF category continued to expand with creative and innovative investment offerings. In addition to the basic ETF, that tracks major indices or specific sectors, Jovian Capital Corporation (now Horizon ETFs) created leveraged, inverse, and actively managed funds for stocks, fixed income, currencies and commodities. According to Howard Atkinson, of Horizons BetaPro ETFs, an associate of Jovian, they are the result of barriers to entry into the broader ETF market, erected by the major indexes, such as the S&P500, TSX/ S&P and the DOW Jones. These indices provided exclusive rights to a variety of companies such as iShares for several years. As long as iShares' trading volume met certain benchmarks each year, they would retain the rights to use the index exclusively. Therefore, the Jovian group of companies developed a new family of ETFs that have filled a much-needed niche, primarily for institutional money managers, and sophisticated retail investors. I will discuss each type in turn, but for now, it would be wise to note there is generally a higher level of knowledge required for their use.

These alternative ETFs (Horizions BetaPro ETFs, 2009) are bought and sold on the Toronto Stock exchange not unlike stocks, and other familiar ETF brands and are "...used by investors to profit when the markets are rising or falling, or to reduce the risk by hedging an existing market exposure. The Inverse ETFs are designed to offer daily performance opposite (inverse) that of the underlying index or benchmark. The Leveraged ETFs are designed to offer double the daily performance (inverse daily performance) of their underlying index or benchmark." The leveraged Bull & Bear ETFs allow investors to double their investment profits if the market goes up(Bull ETF), and double their profits if the market goes down, using the Bear ETF. Of course the reverse is also true. If they have purchased the Bull ETF and the market goes down they will have magnified the loss. Similarly, if they had bought the Bear ETF and the market goes up they will have magnified the loss.

The technical mechanisms involved in the structure and design are beyond the scope of this book. However, leveraged ETFs use derivatives such as futures and forward contracts extensively to execute the delivery. It is highly recommended that investors read the prospectus as it will provide details of the holdings, investment strategy and the risk and reward disclosures approved by the regulators.

International Equity vs. Domestic Equity

When you read the word equity, it commonly refers to ownership in common stocks individually or in mutual funds. Domestic equity refers to Canadian common stocks, such as Canadian banks or oil and gas or industrial stocks. Many publicly traded Canadian stocks derive their revenue and income from business in Canadian dollars from Canadian consumers. However, Canadian companies can also have dozens of subsidiaries in other countries, thereby deriving a part of, or even a majority of the income from foreign consumers in foreign currencies. This adds another layer of complexity to the analysis and valuations of these companies.

International equity refers to non-North American common stocks in countries such as the UK, Germany and Japan for example. Canadians investing in International Stock funds are adding currency risk to the market risk of the investment. However, by investing in International stocks you are diversifying your holdings and minimizing your long-term risk and in an ideal world increasing potential returns. Investing in Canada alone eliminates any currency risk but exposes your capital to domestic market risk, interest rate risk and political risk for example. The Canadian market is less than 4% of the world market capitalization and has limited investment opportunities. By contrast, the US market is 40 to 45%, Europe is 25% and Japan is 20% of world market capitalization. By investing in Europe, South America, Japan, and Asia, you can share in the profits of the largest and most successful companies in the UK, Switzerland, Germany, Hong Kong and Tokyo. Small and large investors alike can share in the profits and growth of the largest banks of Europe, steel manufactures of Japan or the largest electronics and auto manufactures of Japan such as

Sony and Toyota. Generally, most experts would agree that global or international diversification is and will be the way to minimize risk and maximize returns going forward. This claim is despite the huge returns from the Canadian market of late.

Real Estate Investing: Risks and Rewards
Investing directly in residential real estate can be a moderate risk strategy assuming you have done your homework. Investing in a rental property with a 25% down payment and mortgage on balance can yield long-term rewards. Investors benefit from tax-deductible mortgage interest, capital appreciation, ongoing rental income and an asset to provide for your retirement income needs. The downside is the risk of vacancy or renters that refuse to pay rent and property management and maintenance costs. This will leave you making the mortgage payment, property tax and utilities payments and costs to maintain the property. Interest rate risk is also a concern as mortgage interest rates go up the cost of holding the asset goes up and you may not be able to raise rents. On the flip side, if interest rates go up, inflation is also rising and therefore you may have rising appreciation in the value of the property. On the other hand, if you have tied up all of your savings in real estate and prices collapse in the housing market as we experienced in early 1990s, you would be missing other investment opportunities such as high yielding bonds or stocks. As a part of a diversified portfolio of investments, real estate can comprise up to 1/3rd of the total, stocks being 1/3rd and Bonds another 1/3rd, as a general rule.

Options, Futures and Forward Contracts
Derivatives require a sophisticated level of knowledge to utilize in a portfolio of investments. Derivatives are investment instruments, which derive their value from the underlying security. For example, investors calculate the market price of a *Call Option* using the market price and the strike price of the stock, the time to maturity and the expected volatility and liquidity. Registered Investment Advisors who trade Options for their clients require specialized courses and a comprehensive application to the regulators. Options, such as puts and calls limit the risk on an underlying investment

such as a stock or bond. To generate income, the owner of a stock writes or sells calls options. A call option allows the buyer or holder of the call option the right to buy the stock or bond at a specific price within a specified period. If the price of the stock goes up, above the strike price the option holder will exercise the option for a quick profit. If the price of the stock goes down, the holder of the call option will let the option expire and will be merely out the price of the option. Therefore, an investor who believes the stock price will rise significantly and make a profit can purchase call options. Moreover, the option buyer will only risk the price of the option and not the entire downside of the stock if it crashes.

A *Put Option* is the mirror image of a call and provides the holder the right to sell a stock or bond at a specific price during a specified period. It is like buying insurance on the stock or stocks an investor owns. To protect the downside of a stock, an investor can buy a put option. It allows the investor to exercise the put, gives him the right to sell the stock currently trading at $15, for $10 even if it happens to fall to $5, for example. In other words, the investor can "put it" to the put seller. Options are complex and used by sophisticated investors and their advisors and institutional investors for a number of reasons, which are beyond the scope of this book.

Briefly, *Futures and Forward* contracts are very similar to each other, with one main difference. Futures trade on specialized *futures markets* using standard contracts and a clearing center to protect the parties from default by a counter party. Forward contracts by contrast are custom contracts between two parties that have offsetting financial objectives. For example, a mutual fund manager would like to buy a $10 million bond in 90 days at a specified price. This locks in the future price for the manager. However, if the price of the bond drops below the agreed on price he must still pay the agreed on price, essentially taking a loss. In contrast, the counter party essentially realizes a gain as the price had dropped and he could immediately buy the bond back at a lower price for an arbitrage profit.

To illustrate a futures contract think of when you buy a house. You put an offer to buy a house for $250,000 with a 90-day closing.

In 90 days, you pay the $250,000 and take possession of the house. If by some strange reason, the market price of the house appreciates to $300,000 before you take possession and a buyer wants the house, you could sell the house and have an immediate capital gain of $50,000 less selling commissions. If you had not taken possession, it is called a flip. Investment and Real Estate speculators will use this strategy in rapidly rising real estate markets.

What Kind Of An Investor Are You?

* Investment Knowledge = Poor, Limited, Good, Sophisticated *
* Low risk tolerance = GICs, Money Markets, CSBs *
* Moderate risk tolerance = Bonds, Preferred Shares, diversified common stock mutual funds...*
* High risk tolerance = Specialty stock mutual funds, individual stocks, high yielding corporate bonds *
* Speculative risk tolerance = Smaller startup companies, leveraged investing and derivatives investing *

Before ever investing a single dime, it is imperative that you determine an initial investor profile for yourself, as would an Investment Advisor. This will involve a minimum of taking a questionnaire to determine your investment knowledge, risk tolerance and investment preferences. Investment knowledge is more a subjective measure. In an initial client interview, the client is asked about their profession and knowledge of and experience with stock markets. Does the client watch business programs that discuss the daily market movements of major indices, economic data about GDP, unemployment rate, productivity and the like? Can the client understand financial statements, or understand the various types of investment vehicles, such as mutual funds, stocks, bonds and exchange traded funds? Have they ever taken an investment course? Depending on their responses, they are rated poor, limited, good or sophisticated. Risk tolerance is a measure of how you will likely accept the swings in your investment capital. It is more of an emotional measure than scientific. A moderate risk investor can accept some fluctuation in the value of his principle, perhaps up to 25% in a short or long period; while a high-risk investor can accept wild fluctuations in his principle in the short run of between 25% and 50% of his capital. An aggressive or speculative investor is willing to accept a total loss of his principle in order to achieve maximum returns.

If you are a novice investor, or low risk investor, you will need to stick with safer type investments such as guaranteed investment certificates, T-Bills and investment grade corporate bonds or Government bonds. This strategy will immediately begin to grow your money without worrying that you have made the wrong decision. If you rush into individual stocks or equity mutual funds without fully understanding what they can and cannot do for you there may be disappointment. The industry talks about the long term, but this cliché serves the investment industry and not always the investor. It is true that in the long-run stocks will yield the greatest returns. However, if you do not diversify you may also lose a part of your capital if you are in the wrong market at the wrong time. Or, at the least it may take many years to recover your loss. Your peace of mind is essential if you are to Live for Today!

CHAPTER VI

MARKET INTELLIGENCE

"I will tell you how to become rich....
Be fearful when others are greedy.
Be greedy when others are fearful."
Warren Buffett

- ➤ An argument against the status quo and buy and hold
- ➤ Diversification and Indexing
- ➤ Timing the markets and beating the Index
- ➤ Stop worrying about the markets
- ➤ Beware the Expert's and Guru's
- ➤ Financial Shenanigans

Market Wisdom
The thesis of this book, in part, will argue the status quo, evangelical preaching of the financial and investment community. The mutual fund industry in particular continues to chant buy and hold for the long run. Admittedly, timing the markets is indeed very difficult and I will discuss this in more detail later, but over the past 100 years, there have been prolonged bull and bear markets where buy and hold could mean great wealth or great loss. I would argue that when you have had an abnormally high return

in a specific security or investment during any specific period, sometimes it makes sense to take a profit. At least, trim or reduce your weighting in that particular investment. I am not advocating that you try to time the timers, ie. Trade the Mutual fund managers if you have a broadly diversified fund. Rather, I am suggesting you review the valuations and trade a specialty fund or stock that has gone up very rapidly. Try adhering to the old adage buy low and sell high. It will pay dividends. Unfortunately, most investors buy high and sell low.

Many investors in fact, have not had the high average returns the major funds report because they buy the fund when it is doing well and sell it when it is down, only to watch the returns soar thereafter. Would it not make sense to be cautious about investing new money in a market that had gone straight up for several years? For example, toward the end of the nineties the markets were rising at a staggering rate, completely and totally, unsustainable by historical standards. The market gurus and experts were claiming that it was "different this time" and that the markets and the technology index in particular were going to continue to rise in value and that technology was here to stay. Yes, technology was here to stay, but the rise in stock prices by all fundamental analysis was absurd. Some analysts, the loudest with the most celebrity, were using new valuation metrics, such as Price-to-Clicks for web-based and dot com companies, instead of Price-to-Earnings, Price-to-Book or Price-to-Sales. Price-to-Earnings multiples and tech stocks soared....until they did not.

During the late 90s, towards the end of the tech bubble, a small handful of economists and analysts were beating a contrarian's drum. They claimed that the markets would inevitably return to the historical average. A "reversion to the mean", was inevitable according to Bill Sterling of CI Mutual Funds. In other words, the markets were primed to fall. Nevertheless, history tends to repeat itself and the herd mentality kicked into high gear, in the late 90s. Memories are short lived. Investors and savers who had never invested in the stock market were moving out of GICs and buying highly speculative technology stocks and specialty equity mutual funds with their sacred retirement savings. In the end, small and large investors alike "lost their shirts" due to irrational exuberance and had fallen prey to greed. The NASDAQ index of technology stocks fell over 70% from its highs. The S&P500 fell over 40% during the ensuing bear market from 2000 to 2002 and climbed back to near record highs in 2007 then crashed again over 40% in 2008-2009. The S&P500 finally reached its record highs in 2015. Fifteen years to recover had you invested at the top of the market. Caution is the word of the day in any hyped market. Invest in a diversified basket of mutual funds for your core holdings and try not to get caught up in the hype.

Further to the lesson of the technology bubble of the late 1990s: What kind of an investor would invest in a company with no assets, no earnings, and no reasonable prospects for revenue growth let alone profits and dividends? Sadly, investors purchased billions of dollars of stocks on a whim and a prayer. Along with a lot of hype from some of the most well respected analysts and Financial Institutions in North America, small and large investors alike lost their shirts. These analysts and "experts" knew better and chose not to disclose the absurdity of the prices, perhaps out of fear of a negative market reaction and the perception they were pessimistic. A more likely reason was a compensation program that was simply too tempting to turn down. Honest and objective reporting would not have been pessimistic; it would have been and should have been a moral and fiduciary duty to disclose the reality of the situation. There were of course a number of great stocks of the old economy that were undervalued at the time, but were completely overlooked as the big money shifted to *new world stocks* that drove up the prices. *Old economy stocks,* such as the banks, manufacturing and oil and gas and mining companies with real hard assets sold off and prices fell. Things have since turned around but the losses on the new world dot coms and tech stocks are permanent to those investors who chose to file one by one off the cliff.

Many experts will agree that if you hold on to stocks long-term you will outperform other asset classes, including bonds. For instance, Aswath Damodaran, a Professor at Stern School of Business, NY., compared long term performance of the S&P500 stock index with 10 year Treasury Bonds. He found from 1928 to

2015 the S&P500 had a geometric average return of 11.41% vs. 4.96% for Bonds; from 1966 to 2015 S&P500 9.61% vs. 6.71% for bonds; and, 2006 to 2015 S&P500 returned 7.25% vs. 4.71% for Bonds. To be conservative, the arithmetic averages were significantly higher for both asset classes. According to the June 30, 2006 ANDEX Chart, the US Large Stock Total Return Index(CAD) has produce a 12% average annual return since January 1, 1950; the Canadian S&P/TSX Composite Index a 10.7% average return and the Canadian Scotia Capital Long Term Bond Index a 7.5% average return. Fast-forward to June 30, 2014 the Andex Chart shows us the following rates of return in percent:

	1 year	5 year	20 year	30 year	since 1950
U.S Large Stk Tot Ret(CAD)	26.4	16.8	8.4	10.8	11.4
S&P/TSX Comp Tot Ret	28.7	11.0	9.3	9.4	10.1
FTSE Long Bond Index	7.6	8.1	9.3	10.8	7.5
GIC 5 year Rate	1.8	1.8	3.7	3.7	3.7

As you can see from the short and long-term average annual returns, they are all positive, near double-digit equity returns, single digit, interest rates of return. Average annual returns can be deceiving because they do not show the extreme volatility in specific calendar years or periods. Long-term asset class and sector performance charts show us the volatility the markets are capable of producing. Beware of industry experts and authors expounding the virtue of buy and hold for the long run. What long run is good for one investor may be completely unsuitable for another, depending on their stage in life. In addition, an article by Professor Siegel, of "Stocks for the Long Run" notoriety, is again professing the merits of buy and hold for the long run (Siegel, 2009). He cites statistics going back to 1871 showing that equity investors do better than fixed income investors do. He states, "...for the 13-10 year periods of negative returns stocks have suffered since 1871, the next 10 years gave real returns that averaged more than 10 percent per year. This return has far exceeded the average 6.66 per cent real return in all 10-year periods, and is twice the return offered by long term government bonds."

Therefore, it would appear that equities generally outperform bonds over long periods. Again, not so fast....A few noteworthy exceptions, to make a point. According to 2004 AndexChart, the period from July 1, 1974 to June 30, 2004, the Canadian Scotia Capital Long Bond index outperformed the Canadian S&P/TSX Composite Total Return Index. Long bonds actually outperformed over multiple periods of 3, 5, 10, 20 and 30-year time periods. That was a long time to be sitting in stocks waiting for equity out performance. This anomaly was in large part due to the high interest rates of the 70s, 80s and 90s. The stock markets do not do well in high interest rate environments. Subsequently, over the past 25 years, bond yields and interest rates in general have fallen while the stock markets have enjoyed high double-digit returns. That was until the financial crisis and another market crash in late 2008 knocked the markets down as Muhammad Ali knocked out his opponents, Joe Fraser, George Foreman and Sonny Liston. Nevertheless, like Rocky Balboa, the markets keep picking themselves up to move higher. Nevertheless, over long periods, due to the risk premium on stocks they must theoretically, yield a higher return. Otherwise, there would be no financial incentive to invest in a riskier asset class.

The equity indices may beat the bond index over extend long periods, but the incredible statistic that is not being disclosed is that a majority of equity fund managers have lower returns than the major market indices. Not only do the indices not have to deduct a management fee of 2 to 3%, but they also outperform the active managers despite the lower fees. So why are you being sold a managed fund? There are several reasons that I know of.

The Indexing Paradox

* No Portfolio Managers or Analysts = chaos! *
* Too many Indexers = opportunity for stock pickers *
* How to beat the Index *

The paradox of indexing and the efficiency of the markets is that if there were no portfolio managers or analysts doing their due diligence and research, the markets would no longer be theoretically efficient! That is, if all the investors, mutual fund managers, pensions and brokerages decided to use indexing instead of researching and actively picking stocks we can imagine the chaos. As a consequence the markets would be completely unpredictable, individual stock prices would have no rational basis and ultimately investors would not have faith in investing in this platform. Therefore, it is clearly essential that investors do their due diligence and analysis. The rewards are there for the investors that do their homework better than the pack.

If too many investors decide to index, the pendulum swings too far, pricing inefficiencies creep in and stock pickers would be there to take advantage. The collective intelligence of the markets is often difficult to beat. In other words, most individual investors and mutual fund managers alike cannot outperform the index. That said, the collective intelligence quotient (CIQ) ebbs and flows over time. The CIQ tends to be at its lowest when markets are at their peaks and valleys. At those points, the arbitrageurs step in and buy the mispriced securities at discounts until the prices return to fair value. The more players there are the more difficult it becomes to outperform the market, which is a culmination of all of the wisdom of all of the players at once. The S&P500, a US market index comprised of the largest stocks in the US market is generally difficult to beat since it has thousands of investors, buying and selling on the open auction market. When a stock is selling off because they believe the price is too high or there is a problem with fundamentals, a buyer is usually ready to buy for other reasons. In contrast to the larger companies of the S&P500, the prices of small and midsize US companies will have wider discrepancies to take advantage of by astute investors. Similarly, the emerging markets are less efficient due to fewer investors doing proper analysis and therefore can take advantage of pricing inefficiencies for profit.

However, if the markets are efficient according to theoretical models, how does a portfolio manager beat the markets year after year? You cannot beat the market by imitating the index of stocks in a particular benchmark index or following the herd, says Bill Miller. The book entitled, *The Man Who Beats the S&P*, Bill Miller

(Lowe, 2002) talks about how he did it. Janet Lowe describes how Bill Miller, portfolio manager of Legg Mason's Value Trust, beats the S&P 500 for 11 years and running. He was eventually beat after 15 years in a row. His run lasted from 1991 to 2005. Bill Miller's investment strategies are complex and beyond the scope of this book. I can tell you that his strategies and investment philosophies are born of in depth security analysis and a value investment approach similar to Benjamin Graham, the father of value investing and billionaire Warren Buffett, of Berkshire Hathaway Inc. A value investment style, as I have alluded to in previous pages, looks for companies' with the following characteristics. The company has the ability to generate substantial cash flows and earnings, sell at discounts to its intrinsic value, sustainable dividend growth rate, trusted and competent management and have low debt/equity to name a few basics. A portfolio manager cannot hope to beat the index if he invests in the same stocks of that index in the same weights. Bill Miller invested in companies outside the box. Therefore, the index can be beat but not by investing in all of the same stocks making up the index. The conflict of interest arises when the portfolio managers are under pressure to match the performance of the index so they are less likely to invest in companies outside the index for fear of underperforming the benchmark index. So the vicious cycle of under performance by the majority of mutual funds continues.

Market Timing

* Expertise of Mutual Fund and Pension Managers *
* "Timing" is a loaded term *
* Stock and Technical Analysis is the source of timing *
* Getting in and out at precisely the right time *

"Timing the markets" is a term loosely used to describe someone that has no foundation for buying and selling other than the stock went up-or-down. With up to 70% of all trades executed on a daily basis by computer-generated algorithms, developed by thousands of analysts, it seems nearly impossible to beat "them", or to outguess them in any short-term period. For an active manager to beat the market index he must know something that none of the other players in the market know. The only way to do that is to acquire and act on illegal insider information. The investor has to outsmart the consensus, legally, using an eclectic approach. This implies putting together all of the available information and formulating your investment selections. The "markets" are comprised of thousands, if not millions of participants, consisting of the brightest and most talented money managers in the world. It is often amazing to see how many small investors buy and sell stocks in their self-directed investment accounts on a part time basis, believing that they can do better than the mutual fund and pension fund managers who live and breathe the markets. It is remotely possible that small investors will do better for a year or two. Nevertheless, real acumen comes into play when the markets are falling in a bear market. A bear market can last from 4 months to 3 years to decades as Japan recently and is currently experiencing as recorded throughout the history of the markets.

As much as fund managers delude their unit holders and themselves they are *not* market timers, they are in a sense timing the markets. Although, they do not time in the sense that amateurs will time. Based on their very sophisticated forecasting models they will make the determination that it is the "time" to buy or time to sell. That is, according to their personal or collective opinion that a particular stock price is undervalued or overvalued. Investment managers look at the macro-economic or top down picture and make the determination that "the stock has further to run". This is code for timing.

Technical analysis or charting is an art as much as it is a sophisticated strategy for valuing and trading stocks. It looks at trends in a stock price, volume of trades, industry groups and sectors and up days vs. down days, advancers vs. gainers, price momentum up or down among many pieces of data and then the determination to buy or sell if the charts tell them their criteria is being met. Even good managers using excellent research analysts are timing the markets in a sense when they make subjective decisions about the financial ratios such as P/E, P/S, P/B or what part of the market cycle they are in.

When small investors or even institutional investors alike make a decision to buy or sell based on scant information or emotional reasons, the true challenge begins. Not only does the investor have to be right in timing to get out, but also must now be right a second time when he decides to get back in. *If he gets out too early he will miss the upside and higher returns. If he gets out too late, he risks losing capital when the stock price falls.* Anecdotal evidence would suggest that nobody has consistently been able to do this. This rings true since nobody knows for certain when the market is going to change direction. It they did, they would be fantastically wealthy. Some very astute players may occasionally have a hunch the markets are due to go up or fall and get it right. However, doing it consistently is not going to happen.

Foreign Currency: $€£¥

Foreign Currency and exchange rates deeply affects a Canadian's portfolio of foreign investments. The US greenback (ie.US dollar) is still the currency of choice for world trade, although the Euro was becoming a powerful currency in itself until Brexit. With the "Brexit" vote, for the UK to leave the European Union, mid 2016, I suspect the Euro will no longer be a contender. For Canadian investors, holding US stocks introduces an additional level of risk. Not only is there market risk but also currency risk as Canadian's have learned the hard way in the recent past. Between 2002 and 2008, the USD/CND exchange rate fluctuated wildly and consequently the USD fell from a high of $1.60 USD/CAD to $.90 USD/CAD (par) against the loonie (ie. Canadian dollar). Put another way $1.60 USD/CAD reads as follows: $1.00 USD equals, or buys $1.60 CAD. Or the inverse, $1.00 CAD equals, or buys USD $.625. USD denominated stocks held by Canadians fell over 35% due to currency alone. Even as the S&P500 index gained over 50% during the same period, in Canadian dollar terms, Canadian investors realized virtually no gains on US stocks. Contrast that period with 2013 to 2016 when the USD gained 30%. Canadian investor returns on US stocks appreciated significantly by similar amounts. Investing in US stocks without adequate currency protection increases the risk of owning stocks that may not be as risky to American investors. Similarly, currency fluctuations affect European and United Kingdom stocks without protection.

Hedging

Canadian fund managers could not have known for certain, the USD was going to depreciate so much against the loonie and other major currencies. As of December 31, 2007, the loonie was trading at 1.0196 to the USD (United States Dollar). During the 1970's the strength in the Canadian dollar was due to price of oil and commodities (aka Petro-Dollar). The Canadian economy was a resource based economy and thrived during the global economic boom. Despite a few blips to 1.30 USD, the loonie maintained par or near par from January 2008 to December 2013, again due to the strength in price of oil and a few other natural resources. Many portfolio managers had the misunderstanding that hedging currencies cost too much and made no difference to portfolio returns over the long run. This may be true, but it could take 15 or 20 years to right itself after a big move one way or the other. Not everyone is on the same investment time horizon. As we have just experienced, some Canadian investors suffered losses of 10% to 30% on their foreign investments in the recent past.

Importantly, mutual fund managers have permitted allowances so they can hedge the currency exposure in their portfolio of stocks and bonds. This does not imply it is a *Hedge Fund* per se. A Hedge Fund can utilize any number of alternative or derivative investments, such as call and put options on stocks, futures or forward contracts, buying long or using short selling strategies. Hedge funds have very little regulation versus mutual funds because they have qualified to use the accredited investor exemption to raise funds from qualified accredited investors. The law assumes accredited investors do not need protections offered by prospectus because they can analyze the financial information and accept the loss of the entire investment. The Ontario Securities Commission (OSC), the regulatory body in Ontario sets out the criteria to qualify as an accredited investor (AI). To qualify as an accredited investor, an individual or combined with a spouse owns financial assets of $1 million before taxes and net of liabilities. Secondly, an individual requires income of $200,000 or combined with a spouse $300,000. Thirdly, to qualify as an AI, the OSC requires an individual who currently is, or once was, a registered advisor or dealer. Fourthly, financial institutions, governments, insurance companies, pension funds, registered charities and certain mutual funds also qualify as accredited investors, as recognized by the OSC.

A currency hedge is an insurance against wide moves of a specified countries currency by putting a contract in place that will guarantee the value of the underlying assets in domestic currency. It is not a *bet* on the currency. It simply eliminates or neutralizes the currency risk. The portfolio manager enters into a forward contract. No money exchanges hands to lock in the price of the Canadian dollar, 90, 180 or 360 days in the future, for example. If the Canadian dollar strengthens against the USD the buyer of the contract will receive a profit on the forward contract large enough to offset the loss on the USD exposed stocks in the portfolio. In retrospect, it would have paid off, over the past few years, but over the long run, it remains to be seen if the costs outweigh the reward. So again, many managers have a policy of calculated hedging rather than full 100% hedged positions. In other words, if a fund holds 60% US stocks the manager may only hedge half of it back to Canadian dollars if the risks are not obvious.

Short Selling
Shorting the market implies a bearish forecast for a stock or stocks in a particular market index. In contrast, buying long is the traditional purchasing of stock, bond, ETF or mutual fund. Investors sell short by borrowing the stock (from the broker firm), immediately selling it, and putting the cash into a brokerage account. The investor is now "short the stock". If the stock price then falls, the investor buys the stock at the lower price and replaces the short stock with the brokerage. The investor pockets the difference after transaction costs for a profit. Shorting the entire market index is done in a similar fashion through ETFs. Shorting

allows investors the potential to make money in good and bad markets.

Stop Worrying About the Markets

* Ignore the headlines *
* History of rising stock markets *
* Zigzagging upwards and to the right *

The headlines will always sensationalize the negative events and skim over positive events occurring in the world. At the very heart of the sensationalism is profit. A more tragic story will sell more copy. A more tragic story on the six o'clock news will grab more viewers and the television station can demand more advertising dollars. "Markets Crash on news of lower than expected Corporate Earnings" Next week... "Markets recover from previous sell off with better than expected employment numbers"....And on and on it goes. Weekly headlines can and do affect our collective psyche. Consumer confidence is driven by what the public are hearing on the news. Many investors lose all reason as they obsess about the headlines. Newspapers and Television news broadcasters report their observations in the most captivating way they can to make money. They do not necessarily report so you are more informed. If they did report to inform us fully they would tell you the other side of the story as well. Professional money managers are not reading the headlines; they are reading financial, economic and analyst reports from reputable sources to make their decisions. The headlines are what drives most investors buy and sell at the exact wrong time. The majority of amateur investors buy at the top when they feel good about the economy; the markets have moved substantially upwards and subsequently watch their investments fall. The same group will hold all the way down, selling at or near bottom into the hands of the professionals.

History speaks for itself in terms of the rising stock markets. Stocks generally outperform bonds and bonds outperform cash. In any specific period throughout centuries of market history, bonds may have done better or even cash under the mattress would have been a better investment. You can review any chart of long-term performance of stocks and it will invariably show a zigzag line on a 45-degree angle upward and to the right. Investors need to understand that in the long-term, the downs are temporary and the ups are virtually permanent. *The price of being in stocks is accepting the downs so you can earn the reward of being in the market for the permanent ups.* If you cannot deal with the zigzag nature of the markets then you need to reassess what kind of a return you can expect to receive in alternative investments. Stocks do not owe investors anything. As I once remarked to a client, "that stock does not love you." I was referring to Nortel after it had fallen from grace and was trading at 50% of its high and it became clear it might fall much further. Neither does a single stock care if you lose half or all of your principle. Take the emotion out of investing, diversify, and hold excellent stocks, bonds and managers in your portfolio and stop worrying about your investments. If you own a diversified basket of mutual funds, you probably own the worlds' greatest companies!

Everything is Wonderful!
Rather than picking a tragic event out of a hat to make a sensational headline, like the media, without a thorough analysis of all variables, economists and market forecasters gather the data from all sources and report their findings in a scientific and hopefully objective manner. This approach will give you a relatively unbiased and non-monetary motivation for the report either negative or positive. Unfortunately, the scientific literature rarely translates into a language understood by the layperson. Knight Kiplinger, of the Kiplinger Organization took on the monstrous task of writing and forecasting about global economics in the World Boom Ahead (Kiplinger, 1999). Written and published in 1999, he wrote that World growth would continue at a steady pace with third world countries leading the way with high single digit growth while developed nations will have a difficult time squeezing out 2% to 2.5% growth without technology and productivity gains. As of August 2016, his forecast was absolutely correct.

His premise was the world is a wondrous place, but comes with wide regional disparities. Again, he nailed the forecast and was actually too conservative. As of 2016, wide income disparities exist between the richest 1% and bottom 50%. The world has created over 2500 billionaires over the past 30 years while the incomes for average earners stagnated during the same period. The USA maintained its technological and military superiority while China and India continue to produce consumer products for the world with excessive cheap labor. This however, has changed somewhat in the past several years, to 2016, as China shifts from an industrial era to a consumer driven economy. Incomes are rising in China and India while stagnating in the developed world. Standards of living will continue to rise over the coming decades and the worlds' middle class will swell into the billions. This is true as far as we can see. The developed world will remain one-step ahead of the developing third world countries, in technological innovation, selling off old technologies that other regions of the world desperately need. Kiplinger is an optimist as are most millionaires and billionaires.

I cannot imagine a pessimist ever becoming wealthy. Perhaps a cautious investor can become "well to do", but never quite touching the stars. In reaching for the stars, you must be bold and willing to take risks. You must believe in universal abundance, in a world that has more than enough for everyone. Most of our world is infinitely free and open for opportunities to create wealth and things of value. There are 30,000 to 50,000 sku's (store keeping units), or products, on typical retail or grocery store shelves. In addition, we see thousands more products in stores in the mega malls and big box stores around the developed world. Every single product was created and designed by people like you and I, with a vision. The world population continues to rise and we continue to adapt through technology and innovation. With this constant productivity comes an infinite ability to feed, clothe, and shelter the majority of the planet's 7 billion people. In 1950, the population was a mere 2.5 billion people. As Kiplinger reminds us, there are wide regional disparities that may not diminish. Economic theory contends that in time the major wealth disparities will evaporate.

History shows us this will not happen. In fact, *income inequality* is at a historical record.

Eyes Wide Open

I choose to live my life eyes wide open. I choose to read, know, and understand the bad and horrific things as well as the good and fantastical things happening in our world. From war in the Middle East and starving children in Africa, global warming to life saving advances in medical treatments, I want to be aware. I choose to know about this information out of a quest to understand the human condition and out of a puritanical ideal of refusing to live in denial, if not in the dark. Many self-righteous individuals including religious, political, and business leaders choose to ignore, deny or distort the truth of the declining state of parts of the world. Perhaps they are smarter than I and choose not to spend energy on things they cannot change. But, I would argue that it is essential that we remain aware, at a minimum. A billion people living in poverty around the world, millions of men, women and children starving or living in sub-human conditions. Allowing people to live with no medicine or medical treatment or proper drinking water is no way to treat others.

Our leaders lack the will to help their fellow man. If it is half way around the world it is not their problem, so they keep it a thousand miles away from any political agenda they may have. Denial of the scariest issues of the day cause more stress and guilt in the end than knowing and trying to understand. Denials of the issues of the day have historically brought about the likes of Hitler, Mussolini and Stalin and now, possibly President, Donald Trump. Trump as mentioned in an earlier chapter is the result of deep seated anger with government policies and lack of dealing fairly with these issues. I do not mean that we are to obsess about these issues, because as I have acknowledged previously, they are largely out of our personal control. It is a collective and moral imperative that we as a species must transcend living our lives as though there is but a 30 mile radius and realize that there are starving and suffering people a mere 5, 10 or 15 hours away, by jet. *We are a global village.*

Beware of the Experts, Guru's and Doomsayer's

* Facts are rarely equivalent to truth *
* Facts are often biased and self-serving *
* Fund Managers have a vested interest in positive spin *
* Historical data used as proof distorts what investors receive *
* Self-Professed Financial Guru's often get it wrong *

Experts abound in every discipline. Nowhere are there more self-professed experts as in the investment industry. From Economists to Analysts and Authors (including myself!), very rarely can they agree on an explanation or theory, for a specific event. Admittedly, I am no different. If the experts speak the truth via facts derived from empirical evidence and studies, you would think that they could agree. The reality is that the facts are rarely if ever objective and more often, the interpretation slants in favor of the experts' personal bias. Case in point is with several widely publicized technology analysts, who hyped up numerous technology stocks knowing the stocks were failing miserably but continued because of the lure of absurdly rich compensation. Conflict of interest allegations were made against them, yet the alleged fraudsters walked away with millions of dollars of ill-gotten gains. As they exaggerated the value of the stocks, the prices continued to rise while they personally sold into the market making huge profits on the sale of the very stocks they promoted to the public to hold or buy more.

Much of the information distributed to the public comes from the same financial institutions that stand to gain from their expert analysis and advice. Fund managers and their firms receive compensation on the growth of larger and larger portfolios. The management expenses or fees are levied against the assets in the portfolio on a quarterly basis. They equal .5% annually on Index Funds to 2.5% on Emerging Markets and other Specialty Equity funds. The fees are charged against the assets of the fund regardless of the performance. Mutual fund investors can receive no return but the manager still needs to take the fee out of the principle to cover the expenses to operate the fund.

In all fairness, in a year the manager produces a positive return of 15% they will receive only the stated management fee, while the investor or mutual fund shareholder will receive the substantially larger remaining portion of the gain. The point being the mutual fund company must come up with a compelling if not fanciful story to persuade the investing public to invest in their particular fund or funds.

I have been an Investment Advisor for over 20 years and have observed on numerous occasions experts in financial analysis and portfolio management continue aggressively promoting their fund knowing the markets are over-valued by any reasonable measure. Is this behavior unethical, perhaps? However, it is my contention that promoting the fund and "knowing" the markets are overvalued are distinct issues. You wouldn't expect a portfolio manager to run around telling people the market is going to drop 15% based on current valuations. Firstly, most managers are required to grow the assets of the fund and invest the incoming cash according to specific investment objectives. Secondly, nobody truly knows when the markets are going to fall. Although, some contrarian managers persist in advising people the market is overvalued, based on sound fundamentals and prime for a correction.

A contrarian manager is also promoting his fund and style of management as the best way to grow the assets and build his assets under management. Therefore, my advice is to be wary of the rhetoric by all fund managers, value, and growth, as they all have their funds' self-interests in mind. It is up to the individual investor and his adviser to determine if they should hold a particular fund at any specific time. It is the managers' responsibility to achieve the highest risk adjusted returns, short, medium, and long term.

The great bull market of the 80s and 90s became the catalyst for more market gurus than ever before. There were books titled DOW 30,000, The Roaring 80's, How to Make Money in Stocks, Cash in on the Dot Com boom and many more touting how easy it was to make money in stocks and mutual funds. A quick skim through of Jeremy Siegel's *Stocks for the Long Run* provides a truckload of historical evidence for investing in stocks. However, the major failing of this type of statistical book is that it is a historical accounting, subject to many variables and conditions that may never be experienced in the future. Furthermore, historical data of market indices may easily distort what the average mutual fund investor could expect over the coming 10 years. Sure, over a 50 or 100-year period stocks will appreciate if you view only the major indexes, which drop the poorest performing stocks from the index, thus compounding the performance numbers of the entire basket of stocks. Additionally, the bulls often de-emphasize the long periods of time when equity investors make no money and take years to recover the lost opportunity.

Self-professed financial guru Garth Turner wrote in his book; 2015 After the Boom..., about the coming financial markets boom and hyped investment in equity mutual funds or risk having a shortfall of retirement resources. He wrote prophetically about running from GICs and real estate and catching the wave of equity investing. He was only partially correct. Another guru, referring to Harry Dent's prediction of a bull market from 1996 to at least 2010, he says, "The people with money will make much more money. Stock values will soar, along with bond prices and mutual fund assets. Paper gains will be substantial while residential real estate values stagnate – a reversal of the situation in which most of the Baby Boomers made their own wealth...." (Turner, 2015: *After the Boom, How to Prosper Through the Coming Retirement Crisis, 1996*). Well, the bull market lasted all of 3 years when in March of 2000 the tech bubble burst and the markets continued to slide for the next 3 years. Novice investors, first timers into the markets via mutual funds, were convinced of never ending 15% stock returns only to watch their meager returns get wiped out in the worst bear market in 30 years.

At the time of the original writing, 2008, the S&P 500 only briefly reached its peak levels of 7 years ago and the NASDAQ is still off its mark by 50% to 60%. Meanwhile to add insult to injury, Garth was promoting the stock markets while down-playing the real estate market as it went on to rise by 7% to 10% per year for the same 6 years, 2000-2006. Garth Turner writes in 1996, "WATCH OUT Real estate has no future – not for a couple of decades to come.…..After that, there will be no housing market as we have known it." He continues with more analysis, "The average house price declined by $80,000, (1988 to 1996) and it's not coming back."

Since Turner's forecast for stocks and real estate, in 1997, the US stock market (S&P500) soared 106% (December 31, 1996 to March 24, 2000); it crashed 49% (March 24 2000 to Oct 9, 2002); it soared again 101% (from Oct 9, 2002 to Oct 9, 2007); it then crashed again 57% during the financial crisis(from Oct 9, 2007 to March 09, 2009); then finally soared again over 200%(from March 9, 2009 to June 30, 2016). What is around the corner? Additionally, the real estate market took a different path. The average home price in Canada (Cambridge Real Estate Association) jumped from $164,374 in 2000, to $442,264 in 2016. Ignoring a small blip in 2008-09 to account for the made in the USA, financial crisis, that is a 270% increase in 16 years. Therefore, I would conclude that although Garth had sound logic for his predictions, "…real estate has no future…" it was based on historical data and a biased opinion. Listening to the likes of Garth Turner, Harry Dent and others cost the investing public literally trillions of dollars! In the spirit of trust, they truly believed in what they were saying. Otherwise, they could not have been so passionate about their convictions. So how can we trust the experts when they can be and often are so wrong? The bottom line: listen to them all, diversify your portfolio and make your own rational decision.

"Irrational Exuberance" was the best that Alan Greenspan could state out of fear of being the catalyst for a sharp market correction. The inevitable happened regardless of what he said. People on the inside were making fortunes knowing intuitively of the unsustainable nature of the stock market climb. Nevertheless, they deluded each other into continuing the charade. They claimed this time it was different; that technology would improve productivity in a linear fashion for the fore seeable future. What they failed to see was that capital investment was unsustainable at abnormally high rates of growth. Supply would outstrip demand and prices and growth would fall. Without any apparent revenues, earnings, or hope of profits technology stock prices would inevitably fall. Ultimately, stocks that had no earnings or profits or even physical assets, failed to produce any meaningful performance, plummeted in a matter of months if not days.

Toward the peak of the bubble, the experts were still promoting worthless stocks as being worth billions, using new and absurd formulas for stock valuation. Larger stocks such as World Com, Nortel, and Enron took a little longer to fall by 90% to 100% in large part because the executives cooked the books. Accounting scandals rocked Wall Street, Bay Street and European markets wiping out any excesses remaining in the markets in 2002, finally reverted to the mean. The mean refers to the average historical fair value for stocks making up the index. In the end, the markets were efficient in cleaning house.

During the 90s bull market, there was talk of a passive investment approach using index funds and ETFs. The experts were hailing them as the new way to invest. Because there are thousands of players, or investors in the developed markets, all analyzing the same group of large liquid stocks, the markets were deemed to be efficient. This efficient market idea implied that most investors or portfolio managers could not hope to find mispriced securities nor outperform the major indices. Active managers charge 2% to 3% so they would have to outperform the index by as much just to match the performance. With no active research or selection of specific stocks and less turnover of the portfolio, there would be lower transaction costs and therefore superior returns for Index funds and ETFs. In less developed markets such as small cap stocks and emerging markets there were considerably more inefficiencies. Therefore, investors could find and take advantage of mispriced stocks and thereby outperform the benchmark index. Largely, the majority of mutual fund managers will under-perform their benchmark index in bull markets. They have a better chance of outperforming in bear markets as they can sell out of the poorest performing stocks and hold cash limiting their downside. During a bear market, the entire basket of stocks pulls the index down while an active manager can reduce equity holdings and shift to a higher weighting of cash to preserve capital as the markets fall.

"The Bears"

Nouriel Roubini is widely known as Dr. Doom for his pessimistic and apocalyptic tone on the world economy. The New York Times, August 17, 2008, reported that "On Sept. 7, 2006, Nouriel Roubini, an economics professor at New York University, stood before an audience of economists at the International Monetary Fund and announced that a crisis was brewing. In the coming months and years, he warned, the United States was likely to face a once-in-a-lifetime housing bust, an oil shock, sharply declining consumer confidence and, ultimately, a deep recession." He was right on the money. He called the economic calamity of 2008-2009 prophetically, many months in advance. He correctly predicted rising defaults on mortgages, trillions of dollars of mortgage-backed securities falling apart worldwide, the collapse of major investment banks and financial institutions like Fannie Mae and Freddie Mac and ultimately the financial crisis that ensued throughout 2008. The public and analysts alike were skeptical if not in complete denial, but the resulting subprime mortgage meltdown vindicated Roubini.

Marc Faber, PhD. Economics, also known as Dr. Doom founder of the Gloom Boom and Doom Report. I guess the media has a hard time coming up with creative names for the select few contrarian economic commentators. Marc Faber has called for the crash of the economy and stock market many times in the past, as outlined on his website www.gloomboomdoom.com. He seems to have the macro environment nailed down. Although his timing is rarely on the money, but the macro calls on the economy are very accurate. He says the things nobody wants to hear and revels in the attention as one of the few contrarian investments and perpetual bear. Not unlike Nouriel Roubini, Dr. Faber is a realist and they are beacons of moderation, if not our voices of reason. They both see when the economy and the markets are in a period of excess. They are also not about to stick their heads in the sand like other analysts who may fear for their jobs or reputations. They are not

Portfolio Managers or investment analysts, so they do not derive their income from specific investment recommendations. Faber and Roubini have no inherent conflicts of interests as an academic and market commentator, respectively.

The new term for minimizing potential apocalyptic reporting is "career risk". That is, a Portfolio Manager or Advisor advising everyone the market is overheated and should be selling, but the markets continued to move higher, you are likely to underperform your peers. You will have one foot if not your entire body out the golden door of the proverbial ivory tower. The majority of analysts are not likely to risk it and remain neutral. On the other hand, you might get lucky with your pessimistic report and the markets fall within a reasonably short time, a superior analyst is born! My point in telling you about the bears is that we must listen to them for very rational reasons. A little digging will show that there is much truth in their analysis. All too often, the consensus finds counter arguments to suit their own self-interests. Ultimately, the bears are correct given enough time...

Jeremy Grantham "Perma-Bear"
Long-time investment manager and co-founder of GMO, a global investment management firm established in 1977, Jeremy Grantham built a reputation as a value investor and a contrarian, if not a "bear". Jeremy Grantham takes a very long-term view of the markets and very predictable valuation trends, which eventually revert to the mean. In other words, the pendulum swings too far causing oversold conditions and the opposite direction pushing prices into the stratosphere, ultimately return to fair value. According to a recent interview with Steve Forbes, transcripts reprinted on Forbes.com, Jeremy Grantham was recommending people "stay out" as early as 1999 (Forbes, 2009). This was a year prior to the technology and dot com bubble crash.

The reason for this negative recommendation was based on his and GMO's financial data and models showing that historically the market was fairly valued at a 15x's Price-to-Earnings multiple and was at 21 times earnings at the height of the 1929 market bubble before crashing, but the S&P500 was at 35 times earnings!.

They believed that the market was ripe for a sharp decline. Indeed, they were correct. Unfortunately, they pulled the plug early, underperformed their peers and lost 60% of their assets as impatient investors cashed out. In the end, they were vindicated as having made a decisive and responsible move out of equities. Steve Forbes gently made mention that it was ok to be wrong for the majority of investment participants as long as everyone was wrong. Then you could say that nobody saw it coming. Jeremy Grantham, replied, "that's what they say about today's fiasco, which actually makes me quite disgusted, because almost everyone we talked to did see it coming." The stink of it is that they did not want to risk their careers, lose assets, fees and commissions, by underperforming the market for an unknown, yet imminent period. This conflict of interest may never be fully resolved, but I believe that public pressure on the investment managers will minimize it in time.

Doomsayers
There have always been doomsayers and pessimists. Modern day doomsters come in all forms. Two of the preeminent and intelligent doomsayers of the day are Bill Bonner and Addison Wiggin, authors of the Financial Reckoning and most recently The Empire of Debt and I.O.U.S.A. On their website, DailyReckoning.com they and their team of researchers, editors and writers compose articles on every aspect of the economy and what they preach to be the truth. They purported in 2007 that the government and mainstream media were distorting the real facts about the state of the economy. They purported that inflation was substantially higher than reported, that real income and the standard of living of average workers was and has been going down for years, the housing market bubble was going to burst, gold was going to the stratosphere, the US dollar was going to collapse and hyperinflation would ensue. Well some of it clearly happened, such as the housing market and stock market crash. However, much of it did not play out as they convincingly touted. The USD did fall quite substantially in the immediate aftermath of the financial crisis, but in short order became a safe haven and strengthened against

all world currencies and the economy experienced nothing close to hyperinflation. In fact, interest rates fell every year since and the world's governments continue to fight the possibility of a deflationary spiral.

Wiggins and Bonner have hundreds of articles with catchy but dark commentary, such as "Today, with the US facing what could be the greatest financial crisis the world has ever seen..." 05/25/2006. Sensational titles of articles such as The Next Great Depression and The Real Bird Flu Danger posted daily. All of this is contrary to status quo from the mainstream media and government sources that everything is wonderful and the economy is robust. The reality is the federal, corporate and personal debt load is so monstrous the idea of repayment is moot, unless the USD is devalued, like the Mexican Peso. The USD did fall significantly against the Canadian dollar from 2002-2007, but this was largely due to the rising price of oil and commodities. Unfortunately, if the US economy experiences an economic collapse the rest of the world would soon follow.

Dozens of books written over the past several decades touting the riches and perils of the markets invariably proved wrong. One particular author, Harry Browne wrote New York Times Best Sellers, *The Economic Time Bomb*, 1989, Browne completes a thorough yet pessimistic analysis of the economy; his conclusions were far from consensual. His analysis and commentary sensationalizes basic economic facts (Browne, 1989). Yet, it is my contention that books written by Browne and others like him provide a vital alternative viewpoint at a time when the herd is prancing merrily along toward the cliff edge. With a grain of truth to each conclusion, he produces an informative and interesting read.

Ravi Batra's *Surviving the Great Depression of 1990, written in 1988,* is an even more pessimistic analysis of the state of the economy than Browne's summary. Batra could not have been more wrong about a great depression in the nineties. Like other researchers, he uses historical data to confirm his hypothesis (Batra, 1988). Again, the future will not always unfold the same as in the past. Batra is an economist and had good reason to sound the alarm about inflation, money supply, deficit and debts, based on the numbers.

My contention is that we have no way of predicting how or when these types of macroeconomic calamities will play out with any degree of accuracy. Writing a book with a title, *Surviving the Great Depression of 1990*, is sensationalism at its best. With the exception of a brief recession in 1990, the remaining nineties turned out to be one of the greatest bull markets ever!

Of course, the opposite side of the coin of hyping the markets and the economy are equally commonplace and equally irresponsible, yet necessary. Therefore, it is the case that the public read both sides and come to their own conclusions. There are clearly troubling signs in the economy at the best of times. It is often said, "The markets climb a wall of worry". Investors worry the markets are too high and overvalued, that earnings are too strong and must weaken or a myriad of other geopolitical and economic reasons. Half way through the year 2006, we experienced inflationary concerns, interest rates had been rising for 18 months, corporate earnings were rising, price of oil rising, job growth solid, but slowing. The stock markets began to peak, housing bubble looming and consumer debt at record highs. As we all know the markets crashed in 2008-2009, in what was the worst financial crisis since the Great Depression. What did it all mean? The only conclusion most of us came to was that they worried and obsessed about something they had no control over. However, with the knowledge gained from this historic event, it is my hope that you can minimize loss of capital and have peace of mind while you grow your wealth and Live for Today!

The Good Guys: William K. Black

* Rampant fraud on Wall Street *
* George Bush and N.I.N.J.A. loans *

"Bill" Black, currently a professor of economics and law at the University of Missouri, Kansas City. He is outspoken, writes and teaches extensively about fraud and authored a book entitled, *"The Best Way to Rob a Bank is to Own One..."* (Black, 2005). This particular book unravels the how and why of the Savings and

Loans scandals of the 1980s. He is more recently attacking the rampant fraud on Wall Street and the ultimate cause of the recent financial collapse. In an interview with Bill, he defines fraud as *deceit* and further states, "I create trust in you, and then I betray that trust...in order to get something of value from you..." He outlines how the 2008 near financial armageddon unfolded. In the United States, the crisis began with the Bush administration deregulating the financial industry and when nobody was looking, the mortgage brokers and the banks did junk loans (a.k.a. Sub-prime mortgages). They lent money to everyone, regardless of financial status, to anyone who wanted a new home because of the financial incentives. Compared to the lax lending practices in the USA, Canadian Financial Institutions and in particular our banks had very rigid lending practices and had only small percentage of Sub-prime Mortgages on their books. Canadian banks were seen as virtual safe havens throughout the made in USA financial crisis.

Sub-prime mortgages were aptly called NINJA loans for good reason: No Income verification, No Job verification, No Asset verification. These were very badly underwritten mortgages, basically free money given to high credit risk customers. Therefore, after hundreds of billions of dollars of these poorly underwritten loans were signed, they were then neatly packaged as mortgage backed securities by Wall Street "wizards" and stamped with a triple A rating by the major rating agencies. The rating agencies failed in their primary duty to protect the investing public. Once the Agency gave their 'AAA' stamp of approval, the investment dealers sold the fixed income investments around the world to investors looking for high yields and minimal risk. Little did they know the mortgages or mortgage-backed securities they owned would never be repaid and a falling US residential real estate prices would severely reduce their value. By the end of 2008 it all became too clear that a worldwide financial crisis was on the precipice... We all now know how this all turned out. The house of cards came crumbling down. The US Federal Reserve then printed money and dropped it from a helicopter into the hands of the very banks that created the problem in the first place...stay tuned.

By 2016, we all know that the banks were bailed out using tax-payer money and the great "Helicopter Ben" figuratively dropped money from a helicopter in a massive monetary stimulus package. Ben Bernanke was Chairman of the Federal Reserve at the time of the Financial Crisis. He was a Princeton University Professor and academic and a self-professed expert on the Great Depression of the 1930s. In 2008, President Obama had said that Bernanke had averted another Great Depression. Ben Bernanke's studies and theories had led him to believe the cause of the Great Depression of the 1930's was due to tightening the monetary supply. Disruptions in lending to individuals and small and large business all but stalled the economic growth machine. He convincingly argued that monetary expansion would stimulate the economy and avert a recession or depression. He ultimately convinced the President, the Federal Reserve and the Senate to a massive monetary expansion to put money back in the hands of the banks and business. It has appeared to work. The US stock market has risen over 200% since March 2009 and the jobless rate fell from 11% to 5%. That said, the economic miracle was not without its costs, which I will speak to in a later chapter.

The Greatest Ponzi Scheme of All Time

Shortly after the financial crisis hit the newsstands, I read about an alleged, now proven, $170 billion fraud, on one of the financial websites that I frequent. At the time, I was somewhat indifferent as the bad news was coming at us fast and furious during those first days of the financial crisis on Wall Street. Over the coming weeks, further details came out about the fraud this kindly old man had pulled on 1300 close friends and family, multi- billion dollar trusts, foundations, hedge funds, movie stars and movie directors. I was again indifferent as the news coming out at the time was overwhelming in terms of the trillions of dollars wiped out on Wall Street in a matter of months.

At the time of the sentencing, March 2009, several victim impact statements highlighted the calamity that he bestowed on his trusted investors. The Globe and Mail reported, "I was introduced to Bernard Madoff 21 years ago at a business meeting....I now view that day as perhaps the unluckiest day of my life....This beast who I call Madoff. He walks among us. He dresses like us... but underneath the façade is a true beast...He is an equal opportunity destroyer." – Sheryl Weinstein. "He stole from the rich. He stole from the poor. He stole from the in-between. He had no values. ...His was a violent crime without the use of tangible weapon. ...My life will never be the same. I am financially ruined and will worry every day about how I will take care of my wife." – Tom Fitzmaurice. "Life has been a living hell. It feels like the nightmare we can't wake from." – Carla Hirshhorn (The Globe and Mail, 2009). Justifiably, he received the maximum 150 years for his crime. Victim impact statements only begin to reveal the pain that such a financial loss brings. People in our society require financial resources analogous to pre-modern man needing fire to survive. They were stripped of the comforts of life, not life itself.

Financial Shenanigans

Portfolio managers and their team of financial analysts are required to conduct their own independent research before making specific investments or recommendations. They should tear apart quarterly and annual reports looking for "hidden" items in the footnotes that may indicate trouble. Accountants may, if incentivized, distort company financial statements, income and cash flow statements using *legal* accounting methods. Portfolio Managers and their analysts can be fooled into thinking the company is stronger than it is. In an appropriately named book Financial Shenanigans, (Schilit, 2002) the author outlines countless ways some accountants and financial executives distort or attempt to hide potentially damaging information. For example, management can decide to record revenue early. A sale is made on March 15th, but is only partially delivered or not expected to be completely delivered for 3 more months. Management can still record the revenues for the quarter ending March 31st, inflating revenues and earnings. This practice is even more deceitful when the sale was of questionable quality in the first place. Another example of financial shenanigans applies to company's recording revenues on sales to customers that have questionable repayment history and that have been extended outrageous credit terms in order to take more of their product. These types of practices pump up the price of the stock in the short run, but ultimately the true value comes out. As you can see from a few examples, without detailed analysis and dissection of management practices, annual reports and financial statements and footnotes investors can easily make costly investing mistakes.

Value or Growth

Investors implementing a growth style of investing will often perform *top down* or macroeconomic, industry and sector analysis, as well as individual company analysis. Once a portfolio manager identifies the macroeconomic variables, such as GDP and productivity measures, he will focus on the leaders in a particular sector and conduct detailed company analysis. The manager or analyst will visit with management for in-depth interviews to determine the quality and strategic approach of the executive team. Analysts will then visit plants and other facilities as well as customers and suppliers to get a feel for the quality of the business as a whole. It is not good enough to read an annual report passively, as noted above they can be riddled with less than accurate information. Finally, the earnings growth rates and stock performance speak for themselves and a decision made to buy, sell or hold a stock in the portfolio.

Does it not make sense that you would want to own shares in a company or portfolio of companies that have very little debt, steady revenue and earnings growth and a well-established product or service? Growth managers are always looking for companies with the fastest rate of earnings growth and subsequently the fastest stock price appreciation. At the first sign of a slowdown in that earnings growth, the big growth fund managers dump the stock and the price falls. Comparatively, value managers have a different approach to their stock selection.

Value managers, like growth managers, are looking for companies with solid financial statements, balance sheets and income statements and growth. These portfolio managers and analysts perform many of the same due diligence exercises as growth managers. However, they tend to ignore or pay less attention to the macroeconomic environment or momentum in earnings growth. Value managers are often strictly looking for excellent companies at discounted prices, regardless of the economic conditions. Value managers like unloved companies with great long-term record and superior financial fundamentals. Having more patience results in holding companies longer or until they appreciate to their *intrinsic value* relative to similar firms. Intrinsic Value can be contrasted with current market value, current price to book. Intrinsic value is what the company's actual value is, based on its *book value,* its assets less liabilities, strength of financial statements, etc. Unfortunately, in the case of a bull market at its peak, market prices are very high and if your manager is the last to leave the party you stand to lose a great deal of your principal in a correction. Bottom line, find a trusted financial adviser, portfolio manager that has the same philosophy as you whether it is value or growth and that the adviser knows the difference in the management styles of the funds he recommends.

PART III

PLANNING

CHAPTER VII

FINANCIAL PLANNING

"Have a well-thought financial plan that is not dependent upon correctly guessing what will happen in the future."
Barry Ritholtz

- ➤ Financial Planning Defined
- ➤ Finding and selecting a Financial Planner
- ➤ Financial Planning vs. Retirement Planning
- ➤ Financial Planning as a process

What Is Financial Planning?

First, I will tell you what financial planning is not. It is not simply about buying a stock and bond portfolio or a mutual fund or insurance policy. *It is a process of discovery, knowledge, planning, and action to accomplish specific goals.* Personal and financial information, including investment statements, tax returns, and insurance policies are gathered, and organized as well as making a determination about any problems that may be at hand. Based on this detailed information the financial planner develops one or more of several different possible plans. The professional will then present a specific plan such as a Cash Flow, Net Worth, Investment, Retirement, Tax, and Estate Plans. If the client approves of the plan, the planner would then implement it. Therefore, the financial planning process is ongoing and monitored and adjusted if needed on a periodic basis. It is as simple or complex as each situation warrants.

Here are a few of the statements and plans that a professional planner would provide as part of the service:

Financial Planning Statements and Plans

- Net Worth Statement
- Cash Flow Statement
- Investment Analysis and Plan
- Insurance and Protection Analysis
- Estate Checklist and Plan
- Retirement Goals and Income Projections
- Credit or Debt Analysis and Restructuring
- Tax Analysis and Plan
- Wealth Preservation and Generational Wealth Transfer

Retirement Planning vs. Financial Planning

Financial Planning is a comprehensive process that involves every aspect of your personal finances throughout your adult life. It is a process of defining what you want and setting goals and strategies to achieve them. Estate Planning, Education Planning, Investment Planning and Retirement Planning are all component parts of Financial Planning. Retirement Planning for example is very specific to planning for retirement. Detailing where you are today in terms of your financial resources and envisioning and projecting out to where you want to be at retirement.

Financial Planning involves going through a net worth, income and expenses exercise to start, in order to determine your current financial position. This would involve taking a snap shot of all of your assets including house, cottage, cars/trucks, furniture, savings, investments, RRSPs, pensions, and life insurance policies. A net worth statement also includes liabilities, such as mortgages, loans, credit card debts, and taxes owing for example. The snap shot also includes looking at household income and expenses, utilizing Tax Returns or Notice of Assessments from recent years. Upon completing the net worth statement and house hold cash flow statements, retirement plan and income projections are produced using powerful computer software and showing if there will be a shortfall or surplus at a specified retirement age and if so how this situation could be reconciled. Retirement planning is more specific to retirement savings strategies and retirement income; whereby, financial planning is a more comprehensive look at your finances.

What to Look For In a Financial Planner
Seek out an accredited financial planner that is willing to understand your personal financial position, your risk tolerance, and your short, medium and long-term goals. Your financial planner must have at a minimum the Certified Financial Planner (CFP) designation awarded by the Financial Planners Standards Counsel of Canada. You can find all of the pertinent information on the website www.fpsc.com. Of course, the confusion does not end here. There are dozens of other designations to sort through, but learn about the CFP as a starting point. Again, my goal is to simplify your life not make it more complicated.

Financial Planners
What does a financial planner do? What are his credentials? Which organization regulates financial planners? Is a financial planner just a mutual fund or insurance sales representative? My hope is to address the many common misunderstandings about what a financial planner is and what he does. *A financial planner is a professional that assists people in achieving their personal and financial goals through specific investment, cash flow, insurance and protection advice and service over their lifetimes.* Regulation of accredited and licensed financial planners, selling investment products as well as advice, comes through their specific licensing such as the Investment Industry Regulatory Organization of Canada (IIROC), for example. In order to hold the CFP designation, the professional must successfully complete a rigorous course of study and examinations and then adhere to professional standards and a code of ethical conduct, set out by the Financial Planners Standards

Council. The CFP holder must also complete 30 hours of continuing education each year. Most importantly, you require a Financial Planner for his or her expertise in the many areas of personal financial matters.

The Canadian Securities Administrators defines a number of types of Firm Registration types which can be held. An Investment Dealer is a business that sells stocks, or shares, bonds, mutual funds and exchange traded funds for example. This type of a business often hires Certified Financial Planners licensed as a Registered Representative. This permits the Investment Advisor to provide advice on all of the available investments as well as provide financial and retirement planning advice. In contrast, a Mutual Fund Dealer is a business that sells only mutual funds. But, they will also hire or employ Certified Financial Planners to also provide financial and retirement planning advice and service to their clients. A Portfolio Manager is a business that gives advice and manages client portfolios according to the instructions or discretionary authority you have given the Advising Representative.

Financial Planner as General Practitioner

A Financial Planner is like a family Physician, a general practitioner. A financial planner will provide general advice in the area of insurance, but may need to refer their client to an insurance broker or specialist to buy the actual insurance and obtain accurate advice if not insurance licensed. Similarly, a good planner can provide valuable general tax advice but will refer his clients to an accountant or tax specialist to get the most accurate advice and have the tax return completed. Additionally, financial planners provide general estate planning advice, but ultimately a lawyer will have to draft the Power of Attorney, the Last Will and Testament and Trust documents, for his clients. Some Financial Planners will specialize in one or two areas such as retirement planning while others might focus on investments or taxes. Therefore, financial planners can be a generalist or have multiple areas of specialization.

The Financial Planner's role then, is to coordinate and manage the entire process for the Client. In many parts of Canada, to use the title *Financial Planner* the individual must have achieved one of only a select few professional designations. The Financial Planners Standards Council of Canada grants the Certified Financial Planner (CFP) designation. It appears to be the most sought after designation in the industry. There are others, such as the Registered Financial Planner (RFP), the Personal Financial Planner (PFP) and the Chartered Life Underwriter (CLU). Nevertheless, the industry is going through the process to have one primary designation that can be promoted and bring awareness to the public of a regulated industry that carries with it professional standards and ethical conduct.

The products that financial planners sell and recommend are simply the tools to help clients achieve their goals. Financial Planners provide advice on every aspect of personal finance, including credit, cash flow, investments, risk management and taxes. For instance, a financial planner may be providing advice in the area of credit and suggest that his client restructure their debt. Consolidating high interest credit cards, a high interest loan, and an existing mortgage into a single re-financed mortgage, amortized over 15 to 25 years with a lower interest rate that could possibly save thousands of dollars in interest costs. This results in reduced monthly payments freeing up cash flow for other priorities such as education savings or even groceries. Therefore, the product, a mortgage is merely the tool that will provide the client with lower monthly payments and save interest costs.

The recommended product is often how the financial planner earns his living, through commissions or service fees, as discussed in a previous chapter. However, financial planners at the major banks are paid salary and bonus. The industry has not reached the stage whereby the public or advice seeking client is willing to pay a set hourly fee as they would pay a lawyer or accountant. Although advisers are not charging their clients, a set hourly fee they are moving to a fee based structure of payment. A fee-based program sets out the annual fee up front, as a percentage of the assets under management and there are no commissions on a specified number of trades, nor is there a deferred sales charge (dsc). This type of fee eliminates the possibility of a conflict of interest in triggering a buy, sell trade on a stock, or bond just to generate a commission. Under the fee-based program the client will pay, for example a 1% annual fee for a set number of trades, ongoing service, regular monitoring and management of the account.

Financial planners use mutual funds, stocks, bonds and guaranteed term deposits as tools to help his client reach his financial goals. The goal may be short, medium, or long term. The goal may simply be to build a cash reserve to provide for 3 months income if a job loss or layoff occurs. In that case, he would recommend a money market instrument for safety and short-term liquidity. Perhaps the client wants to build his wealth over the long term, 20 or 30 years. A recommendation to invest into a diversified portfolio of mutual funds, stocks and bonds, is a solution to achieve the desired goal by age 65. The financial planner can choose from any of the hundreds of different alternative investments available to him depending on the clients' investment objectives, risk tolerance, knowledge of investing and timeframe for the money. The professional financial planner follows a prescribed process before drafting recommendations or plans.

Financial Planning As a Process
According to the Canadian Institute of Financial Planners(CIFPs) there are six steps to the financial planning process.

Step 1: Establish the terms and scope of the engagement and set out the details in a Letter of Understanding.
Step 2: Gather Client Data, determine the client's goals, needs and priorities.
Step 3: Analyze the Client's financial information as it relates to their goals, needs and priorities and evaluate the probability of those objectives being met.
Step 4: Develop and Present a financial plan which identifies and highlights the strategies to achieve the client's stated objectives.
Step 5: Implementation of the financial plan upon agreement of the actions to be taken and time frames for achieving the stated objectives.

Step 6: Monitor and Review the financial plan on an agreed schedule and time frame. Re-evaluate the plan based on progress.

I have re-written the 6 steps to provide a slightly different perspective.

Step I: Discovery
The first step in the process is to get to know each other in an interview. Disclose as much information as the Financial Adviser asks for to determine specifics about personal goals and financial situation of the client. A financial adviser cannot provide recommendations without knowing what the client wants to do or what his personal and financial circumstances are. So information about the clients' name, age, home address, annual income, marital status, job status, assets and liabilities, knowledge and experience in investing and how involved the client wants to be in day to day management of the money are all critical before putting recommendations together. During this initial step, the professional will review the financial position or net worth and cash flow of the client. He will consider their goals and priorities and determine how realistic they are. Once the FP makes a determination about the current situation and any existing or potential problems or constraints he would then communicate the reality of the situation to the clients. He would present to the client, the probability of reaching specific goals in terms of a short fall in projected retirement income or ability to pay-off debt in a set period-of-time. A plan and solution would follow.

Step II: Planning and Recommendations
Once any financial problems and personal goals are isolated, the planner can develop a custom plan to fine-tune the client's situation. The plan may be a general financial plan or a complex investment analysis and plan or strategy. An Investment Policy Statement (IPS) may be done for larger accounts. This document outlines the clients' time horizon, investment objectives, risk tolerance and constraints to be followed while under the advisors

management. The Advisor will also describe the assumptions made for rate of return, inflation and specific security selection. Dates and or circumstances for asset allocation rebalancing will be documented as well. Although, the client may already be doing many of the right things, they may be missing a few key essentials. For example, "savers" do not have a problem putting money away for their future, but are often unaware of investment alternatives that will yield higher returns with less risk and that are tax efficient. Therefore, the professional once again is providing valuable advice and using certain investments as the tool to help his client achieve a particular financial goal, such as reducing taxes and saving for retirement.

Step III: Action
By setting up the appropriate investment accounts, loans, mortgages, or insurance policies you are having the plan implemented as agreed. A financial planner or broker may execute buy and sell trades to design the portfolio of investments using either stocks, bonds or a diversified portfolio of mutual funds that will help their client achieve wealth creation goals. A mortgage broker may take his cue from a planner and complete the mortgage application then submit it for approval. Additionally, a bank financial planner may set up a consolidation loan or line of credit to help their client achieve credit goals. The client may be required to meet with a lawyer to set up estate or trust accounts, to incorporate or meet with an accountant to seek expert tax advice.

Step IV and V: Monitoring and Periodic Review of the Plan
You and your planner will monitor the plan for progress and make adjustments on a quarterly, semi-annual, or annual basis. This part of the process is just as important as or more important than the previous steps. It is too easy to let the plan slip. So, it becomes more and more critical that a partnership develop between you and your financial planner to stay the course and make changes throughout all of the various life stages. Initially young couples, buying a home, establishing a career, and beginning a family are priorities. The focus for a couple in their 40s might be putting their teenage

children through College or University rather than contributing to RRSPs and Pension plans. Furthermore, couples in their 50s and 60s focus is on retirement planning and ensuring they have enough income to maintain their current lifestyle. Finally, a couple in their 70s and 80s will be thinking more about end of life or estate planning needs such as their Will or Powers of Attorney and who their beneficiaries will be. It is essential that between you and your financial planner you monitor the progress of the plan and stay on target. Financial Planning is a lifetime process and not merely a one shot investment in a mutual fund.

Financial Plans

- Eldercare Planning
- Tax Planning
- Retirement Projections
- Investment Analysis
- Risk Analysis
- Education Planning

CHAPTER VIII

NET WORTH & BUDGETING

"A budget tells us what we can't afford, but it doesn't keep us from buying it."
William Feather

"Your net worth to the world is usually determined by what remains after your bad habits are subtracted from your good ones."
Benjamin Franklin

➤ Calculating and monitoring your net worth
➤ Determine your cash flow and set up a budget
➤ Forced savings and borrowing
➤ Getting out of debt
➤ Why we feel the need to buy more stuff
➤ Good debt vs. bad debt

Net Worth

* Assets minus liabilities = net worth *
* Grow your assets and pay down your debts *
* Build your wealth by systematically building your NW *

Your *net worth* number is likely the single most important document in your financial plan. It summarizes where you are today and every year thereafter. It also tells you how you are progressing towards your goals with a single number, in dollar terms. Do you know what your net worth is? Net worth is the value of all of your major fixed and liquid assets, such as your house and investment savings and minus all of your debts, like your mortgage and car loan. Statistics Canada found, 'the median net worth of Canadian family units was $243,800 in 2012..." (StatsCan. gc.ca, 2014). I have chosen to report the median rather than the average because the average is not as representative of what most Canadians net worth is. The wealthiest top 10% significantly skew the averages. According to a Globe and Mail article, June 3, 2015 the average net worth of a Canadian family grew 73% to $554,100 in 2012 from 1999. In another article in Canadian Business, November 25, 2013, a survey found that the top 10% own or control 70% of the wealth in Canada, with an average of $1.4 million net worth; the next 10% of households have an average of $633,000. The bottom 10% has an average of $57,000 net worth. The richest 10% own $774,000 in liquid assets and another $800,000 in real estate. It is clear how there is a growing perception of the wealth inequality and significant income gap.

You probably know in general what you own and what you owe. However, if you have never done an official net worth statement on yourself I have provided a basic statement below. This is the single most important exercise you can do to understand your personal financial wellbeing. This exercise is intended to give you an inventory of everything you own (ie. your assets) and a list of all of your debts (ie. your liabilities). Subtract your liabilities from your assets and you will arrive at your net worth. You may have a very comprehensive net worth statement, including house, cottage, business, investments and insurance policies, cars, household furniture and antiques. Alternatively, you may have a basic net worth inclusive of your house, savings account and a mortgage for example. The primary goal of developing and maintaining a personal net worth statement is effective management of your financial affairs. A primary role for a financial planner is to help you to grow your net worth, build your assets and pay down your debts over time.

You can monitor your net worth year over year and determine if your personal financial situation is improving or deteriorating. You can then make necessary adjustments. If you are unaware of what your net worth is, there will be difficulties achieving your goals. As a result of not knowing your current financial position you will not know what it is going to take to get you to your target. A primary goal people have is to retire comfortably and maintain the same or better standard of living they have always enjoyed. Nevertheless, if debts are piling up and there is nothing to show for it, no assets, net worth is probably falling. For example, using credit cards to take expensive trips, buy clothing or dining out does nothing to build your wealth. In all likelihood, net worth is going down and there will be no increase in assets, only an increase in liabilities. In addition, you will have higher interest costs on the credit card balance, which implies less disposable income for future purchases. Here is a sample of a very basic net worth statement for an individual or family. A great deal of detail can be added to each section, but to get a handle on how to begin I have provided this outline.

NET WORTH STATEMENT DECEMBER 31, 2016

ASSETS	$ value
Liquid Assets	
Bank Accounts	$ 2,500
Money Market Investments	
<1 year maturity	$12,000
RRSP	$24,000
Stocks/Bonds/Mutual funds	$25,500
GICs <1 year maturities	$10,000
Insurance: Cash Surrender Value	$2,000
Total Liquid Assets	**$76,000**
Fixed Assets	
Residence	$485,000

Commuted Value of Pension	$75,000
Cottage	$000,000
Vehicles	$24,000
Total Fixed Assets	**$584,000**
TOTAL ASSETS	**$660,000**

LIABILITIES
Short Term Debts

Credit Cards	$ 12,500
Short Term loans <1 year term	$ 5,000
Total Short Term Debts	**$17,500**
Long Term Debts	
Loans <1 year term	$ 10,000
Car loan or lease <1 year term	$ 32,000
Mortgages	$ 205,000
Second Mortgage: Secured Line	$ 000,000
Total Long Term Debt	**$247,000**
TOTAL LIABILITIES	**$264,500**
NET WORTH	**$395,500**

Monitor your progress quarterly or annually to fit your interests, but remember your goal is to increase your assets and decrease your liabilities each year to improve your net worth. This is a tool to assist, not consume you in your life. If your goal is to achieve financial independence, this exercise will provide the feedback to determine if you are on track. As a financial planner, I see many people that are not aware what the value of their assets are, how much debt they have, or how much they can comfortably afford to carry as part of monthly expenses.

Cash Flow and Budget
Now that you know your net worth, we can now determine cash flow and disposable income in order to develop a plan that you can

use to modify, but not significantly affect, your current lifestyle. Of course, there could be a few sacrifices, but all good things come at a price. Stats Canada reported July 14, 2016, the median total annual income for a family unit in Canada was $78,870. Using a combined family income of $75,000 annually as an example of a common household, see income and expense report below:

CASH FLOW STATEMENT

Gross Monthly Income	$6,250/mth
Debts	**Monthly Payment**
Mortgage of $125,000	$800
Car Loan of $20,000	$469
Credit Card of $4500	$135
Expenses	
Income Tax/CPP/EI(35%)	$2,187
Property Tax	$250
Hydro	$125
Gas Heating	$100
Gas and auto repairs	$300
Home/Auto Insurance	$325
Telephone	$75
Cell phone	$45
Cable/Internet	$100
Life Insurance	$35
Groceries	$800
Total Monthly Expenditures	**$5,746**
Disposable Income:	**$504**

Disposable Income
Disposable income is the most essential number that we need to get a handle on. It tells us if we have borrowed and spent beyond our

means and if our fundamental life style expenses have exceeded our income. Reducing your monthly expenses may require a change in lifestyle. Fixed expenses are the price we pay for living in a typical suburban setting. What we can change is how we allocate the surplus cash to further our plan. In general, saving 10% of our net income is an accepted rule of thumb. Trading Economics.com reports that the Canadian savings rate for the first quarter of 2016 was 3.9%. Looking over the past 35 years, the savings rate fell from the highs in the 1980s and early 90s and then the trend continued lower until the mid-2000s. Canadians began to save a little more over the past decade, but at an anemic rate. As time goes on and your debts are paid down the 10% savings goal can be increased by the equivalent and proportionate amount paid down.

Practicality & Thrift

* Getting creative to save money *
* Saving thousands of dollars in interest *
* Thrifty, cheap or shrewd? *

The aim of this book is to mix a philosophical ideal with the reality of the challenges of modern society. Reality hits home for many retirees when they no longer get the big Christmas bonus or regular income. It comes as a disappointment when the retiree has to stop the weekly $100 dinners for two at the local steak house. But wait a minute, here is a wonderful idea: buy 2 – 6 ounce steaks $12, 5lb sack of potatoes $5, a bag of frozen peas or head of broccoli $4, a fine bottle of Cabernet Sauvignon $10 at the local grocery store for a grand total of $30, no tip. Light the candles and enjoy the quiet time with your soul mate at a fraction of the cost. Same pleasure, but a great deal of money saved. There are many other ways you can save money, by taking a few moments to consider your options. Financial Planners can offer many ways to save you money and grow your wealth. On the credit side of the equation, mortgage holders can save thousands of dollars in interest costs over the life of a mortgage by simply accelerating the payments. That is, instead of making monthly payments, change the frequency to weekly.

Because there is 4.333 weeks per month, on average, your effective monthly amount is higher. For example, if your monthly payment is $1,000/month, divide by 4 and your weekly payment becomes $250. Multiply $250 by 52 weeks and your annual payments total $13,000 compared with $12,000 on a monthly basis. This will be equivalent to making an extra month worth of payments each year and effectively reduce the amortization, saving hundreds of dollars each year in interest. As you can see, on a monthly basis it is higher dollar figure. Make sure it is affordable. If so, you will not miss the extra amounts coming out of your account.

Similarly, if you have acquired high interest credit card balances and other personal debts consider consolidating these debts into a mortgage refinance option. Using the equity or collateral in your home will give you the advantage of lower interest rates the banks have to offer. Interest rates on credit cards are often in excess of 18%, while the current 5 year fixed mortgage rate is 3.0% at the time of this writing. On $25,000 of personal debts, the 15% difference equates to over $3,000 in saved interest on an annual basis! If you are unable to use the equity in your home or you do not own a home, negotiate a consolidation loan with your bank or credit union and shop three financial institutions for the most competitive rate. Failing your ability to negotiate a consolidation loan, pay off your highest interest credit card debts then high interest loans, leaving lower interest loans and lines of credit to be paid last. Moreover, there are good debts and bad debts to be paid in priority. Bad debts refer to consumption-based debts such as furniture, stereo, and clothing and entertainment debt. Good debts as will be discussed later are debts that are investment, business, or education related. The interest on these loans is tax deductible, so the net payment is lower after tax.

Budgeting vs. Forced Savings

* Budgeting is tough medicine but sets you straight *
* Forced savings to achieve your financial goals *
* Awareness of where you are spending *

Budgeting is a very systematic approach to managing your money on a week-to-week basis. Budgeting is the process of looking at every detail of your spending, itemizing each area of spending and deciding what percentage of your disposable income (ie. after tax) to allocate to fixed, variable or discretionary monthly expenditures. Expenses such as mortgage payments including principle, interest and taxes or monthly rent, heat and hydro bills, telephone, cable television, car payments and loan payments are all considered fixed expenses. Expenses such as groceries, clothing and gift purchases, car maintenance and repairs, and house maintenance and repairs are all required expenses but will be variable on a monthly basis for most of us. Discretionary spending will be everything else such as piano or figure skating lessons for the kids, a trip to Mexico, or a new piece of furniture for the house. Discretionary spending is also part of planned or forced savings. You will have to decide whether the money is for retirement, education, travel or to start a business.

The key is not whether you are very detailed about sticking to the exact dollar amounts on a week-to-week basis. Rather, the importance of this exercise is about your awareness of where your disposable income goes. Through this awareness, you can begin to recognize how you might begin to live within your means or acquire the funds required for retirement or a trip for example. Bank statements will itemize all of your spending if you have used a convenience card, while a single credit card will itemize your credit purchases. Keep your banking streamlined and stick to a single bank account if possible to have a better handle on monthly cash flow in and cash flow out. If you do not have a computer, draw a pie chart on a piece of paper and use color or patterns to illustrate your spending habits. If your total deposits to your bank account equal $5,000/mth and your mortgage payment is $1500/mth this will equal 30% of the pie. Try it; you will have a great time with this exercise.

If you are still having difficulties with the budgeting idea, try forced savings. In other words, add another fixed expense you have on a monthly basis, such as saving for that special trip or toy you have always wanted. Alternatively, another idea for retirement savings is to set up a RIP or regular investment plan.

This amount should begin as the minimum allowed until you get used to the money coming out of your bank account. This will leave you with less disposable income and a reduced temptation to spend on discretionary items. You will still need to know where your money is going and how much disposable cash you have on a monthly basis, but you will then be restricted to a smaller amount of monthly spending on frivolous items. I personally have used this strategy in my household and I have paid down debts quicker than I would have otherwise. As a caveat, it is essential that you are not robbing Peter to pay Paul. That is, make sure you are not accelerating paying off your mortgage while racking up the balance outstanding on the credit cards. So, keep an eye on your total debt month to month to adjust your spending if you are spinning your wheels on the debt front.

Reducing Financial Stress: Saving vs. Borrowing

* Era of easy credit and discretionary spending *
* The *Walmartization* of Society *

People lived within their means for centuries until the advent of credit and then easy credit. Saving was probably not an option for the masses, as money that came from employment would barely cover food and shelter. I can imagine the thirties during very tough economic times when jobs were scarce for the masses and they had no social net or social programs. People had to make do. Taking part time and odd jobs to earn a few dollars to buy a few loafs of bread and milk or butter to feed the family. There have been times in the not so distant past when the most people had no hot running water, refrigeration or heating because it was too expensive or there simply was insufficient money.

Where would the middle class be today if it were not for easy credit? We would quite simply not have the material stuff that we all so very much enjoy. The *Walmartization* of North America and the cheap imports from China and other parts of the world are having a dramatic effect on our lives. Along with the mega malls and big box stores like Costco and Home Depot or Best Buy we are digging ourselves into early graves just to have bigger homes, 2 or 3 big screen television sets and another pair of shoes. In 2016, we can scarcely imagine living without warm running water, efficient gas heating in the dead of winter, air conditioning in the sweltering heat of the summer, 2000 square feet of living space, 2 cars in the driveway, 5 or 6 pairs of shoes and fine dining every weekend. We have become *Consumerhabilis Immediagratificatius (Consumer-hab-a-lis Immedia-grati-fi-kay-shus)* a new specimen in the evolution of man. Yes, I made up this silly word, taken from the world of Anthropology. It means that we are superficial and materialistic in every sense of the word. When the urge hits and we need or want anything, we buy it immediately, to satisfying our desire to possess it. The happiness or joy that results is temporary gratification at best.

Saving Money

* Pay yourself first; set up monthly payment to savings *
* Learning how to be thrifty *
* Get three quotes for every major purchase *
* Shop at discount stores and save *

Although we all have high monthly costs, to cover, even to maintain a relatively moderate lifestyle there are ways to save. Use a forced savings or the "pay yourself first" program. This may sound cliché, but when you think about paying yourself like any other bill it begins to make sense. We have dozens of bills to pay each month and still manage to make it month to month. Does it not make perfect sense to create a monthly payment to you, for short term, medium term and long-term goals? You and your spouse may want to travel but do not have the cash readily available. Generally, most people will reach for the credit card to purchase the trip. This strategy implies no planning or thought, just immediate gratification. Then upon returning, the reality sinks in that a $5,000 balance remains on the card. For short-term goals write them down and determine how much you will need and when you may require this money. The next step is to implement the monthly pay yourself plan of $100, $200, or $500 per month into a separate account. This strategy will give you personal power and independence.

Being called cheap, frugal or a tightwad is all negative connotations for aspects of being shrewd. If being a tightwad offends your friends, you either need to either re-evaluate your behavior or your friends. Generally, there is nothing wrong with being thrifty, but sharing with your friends once in a while is ok too. Some of the wealthiest people in the world live very modestly by any standard. If we slow down and think about what we are buying, perhaps do a little research on the product or service we could all come up with a wealth of money saving ideas. We can save money on everyday items by taking the time to understand what it is that we are buying and why we are buying it and doing price comparisons. Simply calling your local hydro company and asking how you can reduce your monthly bill will probably give you enough information to save hundreds of dollars each year.

Get three quotes if you are purchasing any major product or service. Car insurance premiums fluctuate widely between competing companies. If you are making a major purchase of furniture, electronics, windows, or kitchen cabinets get three quotes and compare quality of materials used as well as experience of installers or trades people in the case of home renovations. I have always talked to my clients about a major purchase like a car. Buying a car is indeed a major expense that can run into the tens of thousands of dollars. If you play your cards right you can save literally thousands of dollars by taking your time. Before jumping in to buy a used car, find out about the make and model, its record of maintenance or breakdowns, the year, the mileage, red book value, etc. This information can be found in a book called the Lemon Aid Guide Used Cars and Minivans or Consumer Reports magazine. To own or lease, is an age-old question. Ask your insurance broker how much the insurance will cost on specific makes and models before you purchase or lease. For example, insurance on a 2-door sports coupe will cost hundreds of dollars more than a four door family sedan. Unless you plan on racing at the local raceway, why would you want to buy a high performance sports car if you are simply using the car to get to and from work? You might say that having a sports car is a personal dream. This is perfectly fine as long as you are willing to give up or sacrifice an equivalent lifestyle expense in order to make it affordable and it fits into your overall plan.

Get creative about saving money, bag the guilt, and dump it in the lake. If you feel like you are offending the clerk, the waitress, the car salesman or a friend or family member, think to yourself that you are simply being shrewd. That is how the rich get richer. Wal-Mart parking lot is full of BMWs, Mercedes and Toyotas. Smart wealthy people know they can buy quality at a discount at Wal-Mart. Buy quality and spend a little more initially but have years of additional use from the product. Bag your feelings of public embarrassment and dump it in the lake with the guilt. This is for your own self-preservation. Live for today!

Borrowing

> *"A Bank is a place that will lend you money if you can prove that you don't need it."*
> *Bob Hope*

* The costs of borrowing *
* Tax deductible debt vs. consumer debt *
* Advanced planning for major purchases *

Borrowing money has been around for centuries and has always fulfilled an important need. The easy credit that we are privy to today is a recent phenomenon. A loan or mortgage gives us the funds to make a large purchase such as a home or a car, but also may provide the money needed to start up a business. The interest on a loan for business is tax deductible. This is what I consider good debt. The interest on personal debt such as mortgages, lines of credit and credit cards is not tax deductible and will almost invariably cost you a great deal if not paid down in a reasonable time. Interest rates on credit card balances are exorbitant and are typically in the range of 15% to 28%. The cost of borrowing takes away from many of life's little pleasures such as going to a movie or buying a couple of hotdogs at the park. A one-thousand dollar balance on a credit card will cost you about $25/ month in interest if not paid in full. Moreover, a $200,000 mortgage amortized for 25 years at 6% interest will cost approximately $385,000! At 8% interest the $200,000 mortgage will cost $460,000. Unless you plan to sacrifice many of life's little pleasures, I would suggest keeping debts to a minimum.

I discussed in previous pages the importance of budgeting and determining the amount of discretionary dollars remaining at the end of each month and possibly reducing some of your discretionary expenses. Then you can begin to "pay yourself first". Allocate a dollar amount or percentage of your disposable income to each of your various goals on a monthly basis. With a disciplined approach, short, medium, and long-term goals to pay down debt can reduce your level of stress and give you a sense of control. The idea is to reduce stress while actively trying to achieve your goals and to eliminate the stress that will surely come from using your credit card or refinancing your mortgage. It flies in the face of immediate gratification to save for 48 months to buy a car or other major purchase rather than borrowing to make the purchase. Nevertheless, it can be done with advanced planning and systematically saving a monthly amount in a high interest savings account that will earn you interest. Each individual will have different goals depending on their personal financial resources, income, and stage in their life. It all boils down to the same message of living within your means and being mindful of the costs of debt.

How to Get Out Of Debt

*Cut up all your credit cards except one *

You will need to have a very close look at your monthly take-home pay, your fixed monthly expenses (i.e. bills, food, rent/mortgage, current debt obligations...) and determine how fast you would like to pay off your debts, excluding mortgage. You may need to complete the cash flow statement provided above to assist you in calculating an amount that is affordable on a monthly basis for debt repayment schedule. If your debt situation is relatively complex, visit your local bank where a personal banking representative can help to consolidate your multiple debts and come up with a repayment plan that is right for you. *Cut up high interest credit cards and keep only one major credit card, no frills, lowest interest rate possible and a low or no annual fee.* It is essential that you have a goal to pay off the personal debt in 3, 5 or even 10 years. By beginning the process now, you will immediately see the results in your net worth statement as you pay down the principle on the loan.

Spending Habits Die Hard

One of the most basic observations I have made as a financial planner for the last twenty years is the amount of discretionary money people spend on a monthly basis. Statistics have shown that on average, people will spend exactly what they earn, living paycheque-to-paycheque. Even if their income increases, they will spend that much more. In the third quarter of 2015, Statistics Canada estimated the savings rate in Canada at 4.2% and the US is 5.5%. That is, on average people are spending almost everything they make. Most Canadians are saving very little for their retirement or for an emergency and always counting on credit to bail them out of an unforeseen event. Low savings rates are not indicative of the masses spending recklessly. Historically low interest rates are a disincentive to save in the traditional manner, by tucking it into a bank account or GIC. Another large percentage of population spends substantially more than they earn because of the high costs of living and therefore remain perpetually indebted to the banks, credit card companies, automobile finance companies, and department stores. You will know if you are a saver or a spender if you have been following your net worth or cash flow over the years.

A quick look at the assets and the debt obligations of my clients tells me whether money is coming in the front door and saved or going out the back door to buy more "stuff". Alternatively, in the case of savers, money is coming in the front door and going to savings and investments for their future. Gross income, investments, Pensions and/or RRSP balances and bank account balances, as well as the amount of debt and monthly obligations provides me with this insight. For example, if a client has a combined household income of $125,000, a $150,000 mortgage, $43,000 in credit card and personal debt, a $2,000 RRSP and a house valued at $375,000, I would probably jump to the conclusion that they are spenders and are in need of a plan to pay down personal debt over the next several years.

The only way to change the behavior is force the change, short of going bankrupt. That is, restructure the debt to reduce interest costs, determine an affordable fixed monthly payment for a specific term, and accept only a limited amount of credit. This would force them to rethink each purchase, as they are limited to how much access they have to credit. Far too often, we have several credit cards in our wallets (purses) and it is simply too easy to buy on impulse. By having a specific plan of action and a commitment to sacrifice, anybody can reduce their debt load and stress, build their net worth, and build confidence. Instead of buying another pair of shoes, clean up the old ones with shoe polish or other cleaner, unless of course there are holes in them. Replacing worn out shoes would constitute a need and not necessarily a want. Make sure your next purchase is a need and not a want.

Why We Feel the Need to Buy More Stuff

* Media bombardment *
* Peer pressure and "keeping up with the Jones's" *
* Immediate gratification and temporary happiness *

We are literally surrounded with retail malls, big box stores, big houses, luxury automobiles, and shows like "Lifestyles of the Rich and Famous" and "Keeping up with the Kardashians" enticing us to go out and emulate these spending habits. Having nice things is not a bad thing per se, unfortunately, not everyone can have everything on demand. Mega malls have thousands of items for sale on any given day. We live in a consumer society in which the consumer drives 70% of the economy. It is essential, according to the economists that we continue to grow the economy and that can only take place if we are all buying more stuff. Current growth is unsustainable for our environment and our mental well-being. Western society is consuming natural resources at an astounding rate, and now there is exponential growth in consumption by the Chinese and Indians. Sadly, this accelerating pace of growth is virtually unstoppable, until we deplete every drop of oil, cut down every tree, and net every fish in the oceans while simultaneously destroying our planet's climate. Therefore, we will continue with the bombardment of newspaper and television advertising telling us that we will look better and feel better about ourselves if we own a particular luxury car, wear the latest new perfume, or take a Caribbean Cruise. It is true that these items make you feel better, but the feeling is only fleeting. Buying more stuff will only be a temporary solution to making you feel better for whatever ails you.

We do not need any more stuff to be happy. As I mentioned in an earlier chapter, happiness has its limits and money can only provide it to a point. From that point, it is up to each one of us to develop an attitude of happiness and gratitude. Stressing about our monthly debt payments and feeling guilty for out of control spending habits or your latest purchase of a top of the line smart phone or Nike running shoes is no way to go through life. Until we can let go of the obsession to make more money and buy more stuff, finding meaning and purpose in our lives will elude us and our unhappiness will remain. Happiness comes from inside us and not from material goods. It is ok to appreciate the finer things in life but not at the expense of your own personal health or happiness. It is ok to strive to be your best and even be the best! In addition, it is okay to want these things but not if it means a life of stress and sacrifice. Build and acquire if you must, but not if you feel empty or guilty upon receiving them and then immediately wanting to acquire more for another happiness fix. More stuff can never fill an empty heart and aimless or meaningless life. *Go back to your goal plan and get busy. Forget the stores and new clothes, shoes, computers or electronics gadget. It will always be there for you if you must have it. Live for Today!*

Chinese, Japanese, and American manufactures are not going away. They will continue to ship tons of retail products to all your favorite stores for you to live out a hedonistic life if you wish to. Wal-Mart has several thousand stores around the world, their shelves holding 50,000 to 100,000 sku's in some of the superstore locations. Wal-Mart now has groceries, bakeries, auto services, travel services, and McDonalds Restaurants in each of their locations, in addition to all of the regular department store items. Hundreds of retail clothing franchises, electronics franchises, auto dealers, sports equipment, jewelry stores and restaurants litter every community and large city in North America and Europe. Every year Entrepreneur Magazine publishes a listing of 500 Franchises available for sale in North America. Franchises offering everything from lawn care and ice cream parlors to tax preparation services. There will never be a shortage of material goods to buy. Stop thinking you are missing out if you do not buy the latest fad. Sometimes adults regress to the mentality of a young child afraid they will not get their fair share of chocolate cake at a birthday party. Learn to come from a feeling of abundance rather than a place of impoverishment.

Easy Credit; Short Term Pleasure, Long Term Pain

"Don't Pay a Cent Event!" "Don't Pay til 2021!" The advertising campaigns work like bears to honey. Low interest rates, 0% financing schemes and delayed payment programs by retail are wreaking havoc on our personal finances. This is a disturbing trend brought on by the obsessive need for sales and economic growth. Canadian and U.S. governments continue to keep a relatively loose monetary policy to stimulate the economy. However, both governments always have the option to begin tightening. The Bank of Canada's overnight rate and the major banks and credit unions lending rates remain at historical lows. Paradoxically, while interest rates remain low people are reluctant to save and lured to buy products or services they could not normally afford. Real estate and the new housing market have seen double digit growth for several years due in large part to the lowest mortgage rates in 50 years. We all know firsthand, with huge appreciation in the value of real estate, people feel richer, and have been refinancing at a staggering rate. Homeowners are usurping the equity in their homes to build additions on their homes, pools in the back yard, to take trips to consolidate high interest credit card debt.

Commercialization has taken over our psyches. Forever buying more stuff, luxury cars, leather furniture, jewelry, trips, but never quite feeling satisfied. Maybe for a few days, but the novelty and excitement quickly wear off and then again, within a few weeks, the unsatisfied, unfulfilled shopper concludes that a new stereo is what they need.

Good Debts vs. Bad Debts

* Good debts give you tax deductible interest *
* Bad debts generally bought some consumer product *
* Pay off "bad debts" first *

Pay your bad debts first. Any discretionary consumer purchase of new furniture and appliances, luxury items and depreciating assets like cars and boats will rarely build your wealth. Good debts tend to build wealth and reduce income tax over the long run. Borrowing to invest in real estate, a portfolio of stocks or mutual funds are examples of good debt. The interest is tax deductible for income properties and non-registered investments and the investments are generally going to appreciate or grow in value. Borrowing to buy a second or third property can help build your wealth. However, there is a cost to manage and maintain the property as well as capital gains tax on any appreciation in value on any property other than your primary residence, such as a cottage or rental property. If the second or third properties are rental or investment property the interest on the mortgage is tax deductible, as are any expenses to maintain the property over time. In addition, if all goes well and the investments appreciate over time, the gain is tax-preferred income from capital gains.

In Canada, only 50% of the capital gain is tax-exempt leaving only 50% taxable at the investor's personal marginal tax rate.

Currently, for 2016 tax year, the highest marginal tax rate on capital gains is 26.76% and 53.53% on regular income in Ontario. This is on taxable income over $220,000. This is how the rich get richer. For an income of $73,145 or less, the capital gains tax is only 14.83% and 29.65% on regular income. While many equity investors are getting tax breaks, many more savers are putting their hard-earned savings into guaranteed investment certificates or GICs paying double the tax on the historically low interest income. Therefore, if you are confident in the stock markets, leveraging or borrowing to invest is a tremendous strategy to pay less tax on your personal income today and build your nest egg for the future.

CHAPTER IX

RETIREMENT PLANNING

"How many millionaires do you know who have become wealthy by investing in savings accounts? I rest my case."
Robert G. Allen

> Calculate your retirement income needs *
> Start a monthly savings plan *
> How to invest your savings *
> Borrowing to Invest vs. RRSPs *
> RRSP Tax Trap *
> Pensions *

How Much Money Will I Really Need At Retirement?

* You will require a percentage of your current income *
* Inflation and rate of return assumptions are critical *
* Begin saving today *

People ask this question every week and I have a relatively simple answer. It will be a percentage of what you are comfortably living on today. Fewer assumed expenses will reduce the amount of income required. Planners assume that you will no longer have a mortgage or costs of child rearing or education costs in retirement. However, a wide range of scenarios develops for each individual or couple. Financial Planners have powerful software that will accept all of the data you input and provide a customized and comprehensive retirement income projection. It is important to note that it is not prudent putting left over income into an RRSP the last day of RRSP season, to get a tax deduction. A long-term savings plan is required. You need to look at your entire financial situation and all sources of expected retirement income before deciding how much money to put into an RRSP. Tax consequences should be of secondary importance.

First, we need to know where you are financially, so take a financial snap shot of your current situation. What is your individual income or combined income if married? What is the age of the eldest spouse and what year would you like to retire? Determine what your net worth is in terms of assets such as your house, registered and non-registered investments and cash savings minus your liabilities or debts. Base the formula on requiring 65% to 75% of your current gross income at retirement, assuming you are mortgage free. Planners also need to introduce inflation into the formula. Financial planning software includes these numbers, although they are historical in nature, so more current data and forecasts can be integrated. Currently in 2016, the Canadian core CPI is 2.2 percent and the US is about the same, from the double-digit highs in the 70s and early 80s. Bond yields are the lowest we have seen in decades. A 30-year Canada Government bond currently yields 1.09 percent and the US at 1.63 percent. There are a number of possible explanations for low rates. According to Dynamic Funds (UN, Haver Analytics, 2016), "...aging populations, weak productivity growth, excess capacity and chronic disinflation." are possible factors. I typically work in current dollars and assume savings amount and rates will increase annually with inflation as will CPP and OAS. However, we cannot make these same assumptions with certainty, so re-evaluation is required annually. For illustration, I will use data compiled from Mr. And Ms. N. Vestor, 2016.

N. Vestor's Financial Data

Current Combined Income	$110,000(maximum pensionable earnings; each $54,900)
Current after tax income	$82,500(assuming 25% average tax)
Current RRSP	$100,000
Current Age	42/43
Age of Retirement	65/65
Projected (after tax) income needed (75%)	$61,875

Sources of Income at Retirement

Combined Pension/RRSP Income $00,000	
OAS x 2	$13,692
CPP Split	$26,220
Total Government Support	$39,912
Projected after tax	$31,930 (assuming 20% average tax)
(approximate amount based on 100% of CPP for both spouses)	
Income Shortfall at Retirement	$29,950 (after tax)

How do we make up the $29,950 shortfall? Financial Planners will make assumptions about rate of return, years to retirement and calculate the lump sum amount of money required. Furthermore, this amount must be able to provide that amount of income on an annual basis from 65 to the end of life. You will also want to determine your personal life expectancy to build a plan most accurate for your situation.

Assumptions

Desired after-tax Income (today's dollars)	$29,950
Initial Investment	$100,000
Monthly Savings Amount	$1,242

Monthly Savings Index Rate	2.00%
Savings start age	42
Retirement year(age)	2039(65)
Life expectancy	90
Rate of Return	5%
Average Tax Rate	20%
Retirement Income Index Rate	2.00%
Delay RRIF minimum payout until	71

- Note: Retirement income of $29,950 today, indexed at 2.00% is the equivalent of $47,228 in 23 years, at age 65.

Important: these calculations were generated by NaviPlan® version 16.0 and do not reflect actual investment results, and are not guarantees of future results. They are shown for illustrative purposes only because they utilize return data that may not include fees or operating expenses, taxes.

Using time value of money calculations, in current dollars we will require $29,950 annual income, after tax, for 25 years, from a combination of pensions, registered or non-registered investments. Assuming a $100,000 initial investment and 5% average rate of return, we would be required to save $1,242 per month (indexed at 2%). The market value would be $1,069,501. At age 65, $1,069,501 lump sum would pay $47,228 after tax income, indexed to inflation to cover the shortfall.

How Will You Invest Your Savings?

* A diversified basket of stocks and bonds *
* Assumptions about rate of return, taxes, age
of retirement and income projections *
* Use the expertise of a financial planner to build the portfolio *

Answering this question is essential if you wish to fully understand how much you will have at retirement. Moreover, you need to understand how to invest the money at retirement in order for you to determine how long the money will last. Understanding what type of investments to use during retirement is essential to determine if your goals are reasonable. In a previous chapter, I discussed and outlined various types of investments of various levels of risk and return and complexity. Create a retirement nest egg amount X by making assumptions about inflation, monthly or annual savings, or contributions, rate of return and number of years to retirement. Similarly, calculating how long that nest egg will last also requires us to make assumptions about rate of return, inflation, etc...The rate of return assumption refers to understanding historical rates of return on various investment classes such as stocks, bonds or cash and even real estate. Since these historical rates of return may not be the same in the future we will need to use best estimates based on current economic conditions such as interest rates and inflation. Once these assumptions are determined, retirement income projections can be calculated.

Ultimately, Financial Planners use their knowledge and expertise to design a portfolio based on your personal investment objectives, risk tolerance and timeframe for the money. A diversified approach is often a primary recommendation. I often suggest investing half of the money into fixed income or bond type investments and half into stocks or equity type investments. Depending on your adviser's investment philosophy and your risk tolerance, he may allocate 50% into Canadian stocks or break it up into geographical regions for global diversification. Nevertheless, it is your money and if you are uncomfortable with the recommendation seek another opinion.

Borrowing to Invest a.k.a. Leverage
Many readers will have heard of RRSP loans and some, if not all, have heard or read about leveraging and investing into non-registered investment portfolio. I will outline the pros and cons of these strategies and the investor profile of the ideal candidate. This strategy will potentially magnify your returns, but also magnify losses in the short run. I will use an example of the ideal candidate for borrowing to invest outside an RRSP vs. contributing to an RRSP. The individual is earning in excess of $100,000 and has $50,000 carry forward contribution room. The $50,000 deposit to the

RRSP will immediately yield approximately 35% tax credit. That is, the $50,000 will reduce the investor s taxable income to $50,000 resulting in $17,500 tax return. Assuming the proper amount of tax had been paid throughout the year.

Example 8.1

RRSP	Non RRSP Investment
$50,000 borrowed @6%	$50,000 borrowed @6%
$17,500 tax credit applied to the RRSP Loan	
Interest on $32,500 = $1,950/yr Less tax credit of $1,050 Net Interest Cost = $1,950	Interest cost: $3,000/yr
Interest cost over 25 years = $48,750 = $48,750	Interest cost over 25 years
$50,000 Invested @ 8% = $342,423 $342,423	$50,000 Invested @ 8% = $342,423
* Now assume a full redemption after 25 years	
$342,423 less 45% tax = $188,332	$342,423 less $50,000

Less $32,500 loan repayment	capital invested = $292,423 x
	50% taxable capital gain
= $146,211	
Less 45% of $65,794 = $226,629	
Less $48,750 net interest cost	Less $48,750 net interest
= **$107,082 net return**	= **$177,879 net return**
214% total return or 8.56% /yr 14.23% /yr return.	355% total return or

If you had difficulties following these calculations, *the main point to the illustration is that there are greater long-term rewards from investing in non-registered investments than RRSPs.* The big discrepancy comes from the after-tax return between the two strategies. It stems from the tax-deductible interest cost on the non-rrsp investment loan and the tax-preferred income from the 50% capital gains exemption and dividend tax credit on equity investments in Canada under the CRA rules.

The RRSP strategy can work more efficiently if the tax credit of $17,500 is invested into a non-registered equity portfolio. Assuming an average annual return of 8% after 25 years, you would have a pool of $120,000. Assuming a full redemption after tax of $23,062 your net would be = $96,937 add to the $82,082 net return on the RRSP investment and the total return would be $179,019. Dividends and capital gains from stocks and equity mutual funds in a non-registered are tax efficient and will pay for taxes on the RRSP.

The RRSP Tax Trap
The government, the media, and financial institutions tell Canadians to put money into RRSPs for tax savings and deferral and of course your retirement income. What I am seeing in my practice is extremely large RRSPs for both spouses and then one spouse dies unexpectedly. Now RRSPs combine for one gigantic deferred tax hit waiting to happen. What many people fail to consider is the loss of multigenerational wealth. Wealth transferred

193

to the government, Canada Revenue Agency rather than the beneficiaries of the surviving spouse. For example, an average working class couple earning $35,000 each put their maximum of 18% of earnings into their RRSPs for 25 years. They will have received a meager 20% tax credit on their annual contribution. The surviving spouse has the entire RRSP in his or her name. They will pay a higher tax rate on the mandatory withdrawals. In addition, their estate might pay the highest marginal tax rate of 53.53% on the entire amount on death. Therefore, the government will take almost half of the estate, leaving significantly less wealth to the children or beneficiaries.

The solution: If you are going to contribute to an RRSP, it is essential that you invest the tax credit into a taxable or non-RRSP investment portfolio building up a pool of money to pay the taxes on the RRSP when withdrawn, as a RRIF or at death.

Pensions: Defined Benefit vs. Defined Contributions

* Defined Benefit = Guaranteed retirement income *
* Defined Contribution = Retirement income
based on investment returns *

We need to distinguish between Defined Benefit and Defined Contribution pension plans and how they are different and similar to RRSPs. A defined benefit pension plan (DBPP) can be contributory or non-contributory by the employer. Using actuarially developed tables and complex formulas a guaranteed retirement benefit is determined based on years of service, age of retirement, level of annual salary the employee earns in his last 3 or 5 years or some variation best or average salary in last several years. The employer guarantees the retirement benefit, which implies the employer bears the liability or risk if the investments do not perform.

In contrast, the defined contribution pension plan (DCPP) the employee bears the risk of investment performance and consequently retirement income. The employer may contribute to the plan, match what the employee contributes, but the final benefit is contingent upon how well the investments perform over time and the total value in the pension at retirement. In addition, pension plans are restrictive in how much can be withdrawn in any one year. The maximum allowable withdrawal is based on government legislated schedule, approximately 6% to start, increasing according to the schedule, or the higher of the long-term bond yield. That said, the rules for withdrawals have now been relaxed and if the employee transfers the pension into an LRIF or Locked in Retirement Income Fund with a qualifying financial institution the ceiling has been raised to the highest of 6% or the previous year's return on the fund. For example, if the fund had a total return of 12% on capital appreciation, dividends, and interest, the pensioner could withdraw the 12%. In addition, the Ontario and Federal governments allow for a 1-time 50% lump sum unlocking of funds for withdrawal or transfer to RRSP, effective January 1, 2010. Speak with a Financial Planner, like myself, about the "New LIF" to determine if you should take advantage of this program.

Individual Pension Plans

* High income owners and key employees *
* Popular alternative to RRSP's *
* Significantly higher contributions *
* Effective way to transfer assets to second generation *
* Notable disadvantages and costs *

Individual Pension Plans or IPP's are specialized defined benefit plans. They are employer-sponsored plans for owners of incorporated business and key employees with employment earnings of at least $122,200 annually. Similar to regular DBPPs, IPPs are creditor protected and also provide for guaranteed income at retirement, so the performance of your particular investments are not going to dictate your retirement income. Clearly, investment performance will be important to the employer contributing and funding the shortfall if performance is poor.

IPP's are becoming a popular alternative to RRSPs since they allow for greater contributions for high-income earners and a guaranteed income at retirement. According to 30 year veteran Louise Guthrie of Manulife Investments Tax and Retirement Services department (Guthrie, 2009), "An IPP for a family business can be an effective way of transferring registered assets to the second generation on a tax deferred basis." How does this work? Typically, on the death of a surviving spouse, of a pensioner, registered assets are taxable at the individual's marginal tax rate; the balance after tax going to the estate. In the case of an IPP set up for a family business, a son or daughter can be added to the plan; thereby transferring the assets to a second generation without tax consequences. This becomes a significant advantage over regular RRSPs and Pensions as it provides valuable tax deferral and benefits for a significantly longer period.

The primary advantage of an IPP is the significantly higher contribution levels for high-income earners. The calculations are somewhat complex but the general idea is that the contributor can apply past years of service, since 1991, plus RRSP contributions since 1991 to fund a new IPP. For example, a 50-year-old individual having maximized his RRSP contributions and having earned $122,200 annually, since 1991, could transfer up $347,800 plus an additional $134,400 employer contribution for a total $482,200. Funding an IPP for a key employee or owner may provide a great opportunity for a corporation to move excess cash to a tax-sheltered plan. Annual contributions starting at age 50 are also $6,800 higher than for RRSPs and increase annually. At age 65, the contribution difference is $15,800 higher for an IPP than an RRSP.

Disadvantages of IPP's should be noted here as well. Several professionals are required to administer and register the plans and initial set up fees, annual fees and triennial actuarial fees can be several thousand dollars. Unlike RRSPs, funds are locked-in and until retirement. An employer must clearly understand that it must provide additional funding if the performance is below a threshold and must also forego funding if the returns are higher than the set target return. In this case, the corporation would miss anticipated tax deductions from contributing to the plan. Due to the many intricacies of IPPs each plan must be carefully considered before it is set up. If the plan is properly set up for the ideal candidate, the rewards will follow.

Government Pensions: Old Age Security (OAS)

This government pension is paid to all Canadian Citizens starting at the age of 65. Effective January 1, 2016, it is paying $570.52 monthly and indexed to inflation. A few guidelines about eligibility: In order to qualify for OAS benefit you must be 65 years of age, lived in Canada for 10 years after turning age 18 and must be living in Canada, Canadian citizen or legal resident at the time of approval. Old age security benefits claw back benefits at certain net income levels. OAS benefits are clawed back, .15 cents per dollar (15%), over an individual net income of $73,756. At a net income of $119,398 the OAS is completely eliminated. For low income earners the Government introduced the Guaranteed Income Supplement, which tops up your OAS amount. It is determined by single or married household income.

Canada Pension Plan (CPP)

Unlike the OAS, Canada pension benefits are not paid to all Canadians automatically as a privilege of being a Canadian. The pension benefit is a calculation of all of your years of employment and contributions a percentage of your income, as a CPP premium, up to the maximum pensionable earnings of $54,900 less $3500 exempt amount. This amounts to 4.95% of $51,400 or $2544.3 CPP premium in 2016. For Self-employed individuals the premium amounts to 9.9%, or $5,088. Effective January 1, 2016 the current maximum benefit at age 65 is $1,092.50 monthly, $13,100 annually. The pension benefit can be received early at age 60, but at a 30% reduction. The pension is reduced by .5% per month. Similarly, if you delay receiving the pension to age 70 you would receive 30% more than the max. My recommendation is to take early payment at age 60, upon retiring from full time employment. The rationale for taking the early pension is that you have contributed to this pension and should begin to benefit from your contributions. If you die prematurely, the remaining benefit will transfer to your surviving spouse but only to the maximum for an individual, or $655.50 per month, minus 30% for early take out. If you die without a spouse, your entire benefit is lost and it will go back to the CPP pool. Therefore, I recommend most people take it early, if you are not working.

The OAS and the CPP is a wonderful, globally respected retirement income program. The CPP contributions and benefit amounts are hotly debated. Retirement savings rates are quite dismal in Canada, 50% having virtually no savings. The government is reviewing whether the contributory amounts should be increased. Currently, they provide for a guaranteed minimum income for all Canadians and working Canadians can expect even more if they have contributed through payroll deductions, currently 4.95% of your income up to the maximum pensionable earnings. Your employer also contributes an equal amount. According to some, this initiative has virtually guaranteed a long and viable retirement pension plan. By contrast, the OAS is paid out of general revenues and is the more likely program to be squeezed in the end. Of course, with all things government, there are many rules and regulations with respects to living outside Canada, splitting pension benefits upon divorce, etc... In addition, what happens on death or disability of an annuitant? For specific details on your situation, I would refer you to the nearest pension office or the Government of Canada website, choosing the Canada Pension Plan option in the site index.

CHAPTER X

END OF LIFE PLANNING

"Estate planning is an important and everlasting
gift you can give your family.
And setting up a smooth inheritance isn't
as hard as you might think."
Suze Orman

- ➤ End of Life Planning as a process
- ➤ Will preparation and checklist
- ➤ Types of Life Insurance and Inheritance
- ➤ Types of Trusts and trust taxation

A Planning Process

* Determine your goals and final wishes *
* Take an inventory of assets and liabilities *
* Considering your Beneficiaries, Executor and Trustees *

Most of us are uncomfortable with the discussion of death and disability or wills and powers of attorney. It is part of the *estate planning* process. As important as it is, the law does not require us to prepare a Will or a Power of Attorney (POA). However, if you die without a Will, intestate, the courts will decide how your wealth is distributed and to whom it is bequeathed. *The Family law act* and the *law of consanguinity* will determine how your money is distributed. Moreover, if you become incapacitated without a POA the courts again will determine who will manage your affairs. In practice, as a financial planner, I recommend everyone have at a minimum a basic will prepared by a lawyer. More importantly, I recommend that spouses have Powers of Attorney prepared. POA's provide for the legal authorization for spouses to act on each other's behalf if they become physically or mentally incapacitated.

Estate Planning or end of life planning is much more than preparing a Will and Power of Attorney. It should involve making advanced funeral arrangements and understanding the cost of the service and some of the options available depending on funds available. Estate planning is a process that should at some point consider *gifting* to family, friends or church; *charitable giving* should be considered if there is significant wealth; setting up trusts for spouse, children and grandchildren. In terms of health care issues, it is more likely that as we age we become afflicted with a physical or mental ailment that debilitates us. A stroke or other crippling disease can block our ability to speak or sign financial documents at the bank or other institutions. This could lead to serious delays in the flow of funds to your spouse or household. Thus, it is important to discuss what needs to be done and who will make decisions on behalf of the elderly individual if afflicted. Who will decide which long term care facility? If palliative care is required for a terminally ill family member, who will decide? A will is essentially a written document that will execute your wishes once you are gone. A will does not take care of the above-mentioned health concerns while you are alive.

Having estate planning goals is no less important than retirement goals, unless of course you have no concern for the well-being of your survivors or loved ones. One essential question that I ask of each of my clients entering retirement with substantial excess wealth is what their intentions are with respects to their legacy wealth. Do they intend to spend it all, gift the surplus money to children and grandchildren before they pass-on or leave the surplus in the estate for distribution after their death? These are thought provoking questions for the family to discuss in advance of incapacity or death. With a little bit of forethought many good things can be finalized. If the money is to stay in the family, trusts can be set up and taxes on the wealth minimized or at least deferred to future generations. Charitable donations can be made and again the estate can benefit from tax credits. Even if you do not possess large wealth right now, you can begin the planning process, which will ensure that all of your wishes are carried out to the letter. I have included a few items below for consideration when preparing for a will.

Will Preparation and Checklist

✓ Personal Information
Name, Date and Place of birth
Marital Status
Marital or Other Agreements
Former Spouse and offspring
Dependents names

✓ List of Personal Assets
House value and address
Cottage value and address
Cars,
Recreational vehicles,
Furniture, household items and Jewelry
Books and CD's, Electronic equipment i.e. Computer, TV's, Stereo
Photo collections, Antiques/Art/

✓ List of Financial Assets
Registered Retirement Savings Plans (RRSP): account #s, value$
Registered Retirement Income Fund (RRIF); account #s and value$
Group RRSPs; name of employer and plan sponsor

Investment and Brokerage account #s and value$
Bank accounts #s and value
Life insurance cash values: policy #s; amounts
Stock and Bond Certificates and location of certificates and amounts.
Pension Plans: statements, name of employer and plan sponsor.

✓ List of Debts
Financial Institutions and list of:
Mortgages
Loans/Leases and Lines of Credit
Credit Cards
Debts to family or friends
*copies of statements should be included with copy of will and kept
in a safety deposit box

✓ Life Insurance Policies
Group Life policies with employer: account # and value$
Personal Life policies with specific Life Insurance Companies: account # and
value$

✓ Name of Executor
An Executor is the person that will be responsible for carrying out the instructions written in the will.

✓ Name of a Trustee
A Trustee is the person that will be responsible for managing the estate according to the will. If you leave large amounts of money to your beneficiaries, you can have a trust set up and the money distributed to them over a 10 or 20-year period. This will give you control over the money long after you are gone. Create a "Spend Thrift Trust" for a beneficiary that has a history of spending money frivolously does not have access to

the entire lump sum all at once. The lump sum remains in the trust and provides a steady income to them over many years.

✓ Name of Guardian
Guardians are the person or persons that you have appointed to take care of your minor children in the event of death.

✓ Names of Beneficiaries
The names of your beneficiaries, those who are receiving the inheritance and your bequests to them should be stated clearly and concisely. You should also note specific details about what you wish to leave in kind (leaving an antique chair or piano for example to a specified person or charity) and gifts in cash. The beneficiary can be a person, business, or charity. State your funeral arrangements. Otherwise, the courts decide where you have a plot and who does the ceremony if any. There are many more things that can be included in a will but the preliminary collection of information needs to be put together prior to meeting with an estate lawyer. The lawyer will then put your wishes into the jargon of legalese. The reason for the legal jargon is the avoidance of misinterpretation of your wishes. You may have a basic list and few demands or a large list of assets, investments, debts, business assets, a large family, and a long list of beneficiaries. It is up to you and your lawyer to decide what will go into the will. A basic will should not cost more than $500; while a more complicated and involved will may cost a few thousand dollars.

Inheritance

I could not discuss the end of life planning, or estate planning, without a discussion about being on the outside of the casket and the receiving end of the estate. A lump sum from a loved one is the greatest gift you could receive. It is a testament to their love and appreciation for you. What you do with this money or other assets will be your response to the gift. If it is unappreciated and wasted, you are sending a message of disrespect. Ideally, you would first carry out the wishes of the deceased, if any, and possibly imagine what they would have wanted, based on how they lived their life. More importantly, allocating part of the money to do some good by giving to a charity, foundation, or the less fortunate is something to consider. Finally, it is your money and you have choices to spend or invest. If you are investing for the long run seek out a qualified financial planner with the appropriate qualifications and experience, as well as a personality and investment style that you can be comfortable with. Live for Today! Plan for Tomorrow.

Life Insurance
Life insurance is part of the estate plan and something people do not like to talk about. If they do finally discuss it they want it done and over with quickly and painlessly. Purchasing life insurance is a very personal thing and everyone you talk to will have a different view on it. As a father and husband to a wonderful wife of 30 years, I believe insurance is a gift for your loved ones. Life insurance proceeds will never benefit us personally. In the builder stage of our lives, we have young children and spouses to take care of, mortgages and possibly other major obligations so we require higher amounts of life insurance. We have to think what would happen to our surviving spouse and children if we were to pass away early. Our income would be gone and the bills would go unpaid. How would we provide for our family? Life Insurance can provide for your family when you are gone. Similarly, considering disability insurance is even more critical as we are statistically more likely to have a disability than to die prematurely. Disability insurance provides income replacement while we are sick or disabled and unable to work. Many employers have plans but experts recommend having insurance with outside insurance companies, not tied to your employer. If you were to lose or change your job, or become self-employed you lose the employer sponsored insurance.

Types of Life Insurance: Whole Life vs. Term Insurance
* Whole Life = level premiums throughout your life *
* Term Insurance = "Pure" - no savings component *

* Universal Life = Insurance plus Investment component *

Old-timers in the insurance business would argue that Whole Life policies, permanent insurance, are the best type of insurance available. The premise behind permanent life insurance is the premiums are level throughout your life for a given death benefit. This implies that the premiums are greater for a given amount of insurance in the early years, but with each passing anniversary, and in later years, the premium is lower than for comparable term insurance. In addition, there may be some secondary cash surrender value depending on the degree to which the premium exceeds the cost of the insurance. If the truth be known, the premiums are very high in the early years, comparatively, when you can least afford it, but tends to reverse as the policyholder ages. In contrast, Term Life policies ("Pure" Life Insurance with no savings or Investment component) offer lower premiums and significantly higher death benefits when the policyholder is young, but higher premiums as the policyholder ages. For example, a 25-year-old married couple might be able to buy a $250,000 10 year joint term policy for $30 per month, but after 10-year term is up for renewal the premium will jump to $40 per month for example. Whole life premium may begin at $125 per month for $250,000 death benefit but the premium remains the same throughout the policyholder s life. Of course, there are literally hundreds of variations of these primary types of life insurance but this is the general idea.

Term Life has 5, 10, 15, 20-year terms and term to 100 available and it seems to offer the cheapest solution while providing for the highest death benefit. I call term life "pure life insurance" as it does not commingle future life insurance with current needs nor does it commingle life insurance with investments, as we will see with Universal Life. Another side feature of Term Policies is the option to convert to Permanent insurance at any time up to age 60 or 65. Although you may not know the future cost of conversion, it is available. This gives added sense of security if there is still a mortgage or other income requirements to cover. Whole or Permanent life offers a sense of security over your entire life in terms of level premium and guaranteed life benefit. A third major type of insurance has come into play that has appealed to many people is Universal Life. It is a combination of term life and investments. This is a very interesting insurance product in that it allows the investment portion of the investment to increase the tax-free death benefit within the policy, with some limits on deposits to the investment side.

How much should the death benefit be?

This amount will be different for everyone, but there are standard questionnaires to calculate what is required. For instance, income replacement models help to determine how much money would be required to provide an income if the major bread winner or one spouse was to die prematurely. Young families with greater financial obligations and responsibilities as well as less savings or assets will require the largest death benefit. A $500,000 death benefit, for example, would provide an income of $40,000 for 18.5 years assuming a 5% investment return. As young families reduce their debts and increase their savings, investments, or assets and the children have completed their education the large death benefit may not be required. Furthermore, seniors may not require any life insurance if they have adequate savings and investments. Ultimately, the amount of insurance we buy is going to be a gift and more importantly a way to take care of your family if you are gone.

Most insurance agents will perform a *Needs Analysis* to help determine the approximate amount of life insurance required. I have provided a summary of a typical information-gathering tool used in the analysis.

Needs Analysis Checklist

   ✓ General Information:
   Name:_____
   DOB:_____
   Smoker/Non-smoker: Y/N
   Have you smoked in the last 10 years: Y/N

✓   Estate Assets:
Quick Cash:_____
Investable/liquid or marketable securities such as t-bills, bonds, stocks:_____
Existing life Insurance policies(personal/group):_____
Mortgage insurance:_____
Business assets(simple or complex):_____
Government death benefit:_____
Total Estate Assets: $_____

Subtract.....

✓   Cash NEEDS on death
Taxes due on death:_____
Property taxes owing:_____
Income taxes owing:_____
Capital gains/losses accrued_____
Final Expenses: funeral costs, legal and probate, executor/ admin fees, accounting/tax preparation:_____
Emergency fund; repair/replace car, roof, appliances:_____
Special Bequests: charitable donations, dependent parents, gifts to children, grandchildren:_____
Non-Insured loans;_____
Credit cards, lines of credit, auto loans:_____
Education Fund; education costs:_____
Business liabilities;_____
Total Immediate Cash Needs: $_____

✓   Income Needs
Monthly Income needed (calculate 75% of current):
Monthly Government benefits:
Total Monthly Needed: $

✓   Cash Fund Required
Rate of return assumption_____%
(Divide "total annual need" by rate of return assumption, multiply by 100 and enter here_____) For

example, $40,000 total annual needed divided by 5% = $800,000. You could add in an Inflation factor of 2% for 25 years (2.16) and your Gross cash fund required is $1,728,000; **less:** your net Estate Assets(ie. all assets from existing life insurance policies, investments and savings and other personal and business assets...) is the cash fund required from a new Insurance policy death benefit.. Note this is the maximum amount if you didn't want to deplete the principle over the 25 years.

You can see from the above basic information required that it is prudent to speak with a qualified insurance broker or Financial Planner about your specific needs and options. He can input all of your personal information into a software program and estimate the amount of the required benefit.

Disability Insurance

Disability insurance (DI) (PlanPlus Inc., 2009) is another risk management tool that Financial Planners utilize and recommend to their clients. DI provides replacement income in the event of a disability, physical or emotional. Most employers provide DI as part of a group benefits package. Large Insurance corporations provide for the many features of a group benefits plan, including life insurance, health and dental plans and DI. Typical Group DI includes a short-term disability component as well as a long-term disability component. The short-term component, also called weekly indemnity, will cover a percentage of weekly salary for up to 1 year. The long-term component will begin when the short-term benefits expire and the employee's disability qualifies according to stringent definitions and criteria set out in the employee benefits manual. Once approved for long-term benefits the employee will still only receive 50% to 75% of his wages depending on the program. The limits to disability income benefits are in place so there are no long-term incentives to avoid going back to work. Receiving 100% of your income would clearly tempt even the most honest employee to malinger!

Private DI programs offered through Insurance Companies provide many variations for the multitude of different needs of workers. Insurance companies created a few major types of coverage with a variety of features. Owner Occupation Coverage designed for white-collar professionals and self-employed individuals who would cease earning money if they became disabled. The basic concept provides for a disability benefit if the individual can no longer perform the duties of their job. In a larger corporation, the employer will often find a replacement job or modify the job duties so the employee can continue to produce at some level. Insurance companies created a variety of features and variations of the Own Occupation coverage, such as Proportionate Disability protecting the insured from a partial loss of Income due to disability. For example, if the insured lost 30% of his revenues due to disability he receives the percentage lost.

A second major type of coverage is the Two Year Own Occupation Coverage, designed to protect the business owner and employee for 24 months if he is unable to perform the substantial duties of his regular job. After 24 months, a strict definition of disability must be met in order for benefits to be paid.

Additional riders and provisions can also be added to private DI policies. A cost of living allowance (COLA) rider provides for a raise in income every year matched to the CPI or some other indexing method. A future earnings protector rider can be added to the policy which provides for set increases in disability for a young individual with expectations of large increases to his income in the future. For example, professional athletes such as hockey players or football players, or doctors, accountants or lawyers anticipating partner offers in their future would all consider this rider. The innovation and creativity of the insurance companies is never ending. DI is just as important as life insurance if not even more important as the statistics are quite clear that you are more likely to suffer a disability than death during your career.

Tied to life and disability insurance is Critical Illness insurance. With an ageing population and health care budgets tightening at the government level, baby boomers are thinking more and more how they will obtain the best medical care if they were to suffer a serious illness. Critical illness benefits provide coverage for a number of serious and debilitating illnesses, such as heart attack, stroke, paralysis, organ failure, but will only pay a lump sum after meeting specified criteria. A waiting period of 30 days, whereby claims adjusters review the doctors' notes for the legitimacy of the illness and then the various features of the policy triggered. Whether it is Life, Disability, Critical illness or Long-term care, insurance is a very important part of a financial plan that requires serious thought and advice from a Financial Planner or Insurance Specialist.

Trusts

* Relationship between 3 parties create a trust *
* Complex rules govern trust taxation *
* Three Certainties must be met *

The nature of a trust is based on a relationship involving 3 parties: the Settlor, the Trustee and the Beneficiary. This relationship creates a trust. The Settlor is the party that is gifting or transferring property of some value to a trustee for the benefit of and use by the beneficiary or multiple beneficiaries. The Trustees accept the responsibility to administer the Trust as detailed in the Trust Deed. The Beneficiaries are the recipients of the assets held within the trust.

Trusts are not recognized as legal entities such as Corporations or individuals, although they are recognized as separate entities for tax purposes. The trustee may be sued for mismanagement or some other breach of fiduciary duty. The CRA has created many complex rules around the taxation of Trusts, which are beyond the scope of this discussion. For the purpose of this discussion, it suffices to say that Trusts are useful in specific circumstances to achieve certain objectives. Please seek the advice of an accountant or Lawyer prior to establishing a Trust of any kind.

Trusts are created for many reasons that bring tax and estate planning benefits to an individual or family. Organizing family affairs and controlling multigenerational wealth can be accomplished through a trust document. Saving taxes and probate fees on death of the settlor are two monetary reasons for setting up a trust. Controlling assets without ownership for many years into the future as well as distributing and protecting capital and income contribute to long-term wealth preservation. Trusts can be very general in nature or infinitely complex depending on the needs of the settlor. The many types of formal trusts each bring with them a variety of unique features and tax benefits. A lawyer, with the Settlors wishes in mind creates a Trust Document. The Trust specifies how the income and capital and ultimately how the assets are distributed to the beneficiaries. Many people may have set up an informal trust account at their local bank branch for their children or grandchildren, aptly named "in-trust for little Johnny", ITF, for example. However, Three Certainties are required for this account to be qualified as a trust for taxation purposes (Poyser, 2005).

The first of the three certainties is the *Certainty of Intention*. The person creating the trust, the Settlor, must expressly declare intent to create the trust, held by one party for the benefit or use by another, the beneficiary. *Certainty of subject matter* refers to the explicit knowledge of the property transferred from the Settlor to the trustee for the beneficiary. *Certainty of object* refers to an express knowledge of the person and purpose for which the trust created. If these 3 criteria are met then a trust can be said to exist, for taxation and/or other purposes. A lawyer typically establishes trusts through a trust agreement or declaration of trust. Without formal documentation, the CRA can still declare that no trust existed.

Types of Trusts

There are two basic types of trusts: the *inter vivos trust* or the living trust and the *testamentary trust*, initiated after the death of the settlor. The settlor will establish an inter vivos trust by transferring property into the trust while alive. The settlor writes into the trust agreement how the beneficiary is to receive the property, either through capital or income distributions at some point in the future. Therefore, the Settlor can continue to exercise control, as the trustee, without ownership, over the assets throughout his lifetime.

The Trustee, if not the settlor is required to carry out the wishes of the Settlor, governing the trust as detailed in the Deed.

The reasons for the transfer of property are many, but typically, there would be a gifting nature to the transfer, which often triggers taxes, but simultaneously freezes further taxation to the settlor. With the estate freeze of assets transferred to the trust, future growth and income taxed in the beneficiaries' hands. The property can be shares in small, medium and even large sized corporations, real estate, stocks, bonds, farm property or other appreciating assets. A more commonly known trust is the testamentary trust, which arises on the death of an individual. According to the wishes of an individual, the Last Will and Testament creates a testamentary trust on death.

Lawyers establish, various types of testamentary trusts each used for specific reasons. A primary reason for a testamentary trust is to maintain control of wealth from the grave, after death. Additional reasons for setting up a testamentary trust is to preserving capital and minimizing and deferring taxes on the estate, especially in the case of a spousal rollover. If a substantial amount of assets or wealth are involved and the beneficiaries are ill equipped to manage money then it makes sense to establish a spousal (sometimes referred to as a "spend thrift trust") or family trust.

"Families create trusts to shift income from a high tax rate individual to a lower tax rate individual." (Wilson, Gwen, & Bullis, 2003). To illustrate how a family with a corporation can take advantage of establishing a Family Trust I will describe a typical situation. Generally, one individual builds a small to medium sized business. He or she will have significant income compared with other family members. Income splitting can be done by hiring family members but it has its limitations. Creating a trust by issuing special shares to the business owner ensuring he maintains and retains a fixed income and control over the business. Additional shares issued to the newly created family trust where his lower income family members receive future growth and some earnings from the business as beneficiaries. The net result is lower taxation on the earnings of the corporation and income splitting between family members.

An RRSP trust is not considered by many to be a trust in the traditional sense, but it works the same way as a testamentary trust. Having the Settlor's estate, trustee and/or designated beneficiary receive or manage the value of the property on death of the annuitant. In the case of a minor child, the trustee would manage the RRSP paying out the value over the following years leading to the minor's 19th birthday. This provision reduces the tax burden on the estate, as the child will be in a lower tax bracket than an individual on death.

Taxation of Trusts

Inter-vivos trusts are generally not tax advantaged entities. The income earned inside the trust will be subject to the highest marginal tax rate. However, if certain conditions are met, income distributed to beneficiaries can be taxed in their hands. Attribution rules come into play if beneficiaries other than those specified receive trust income. Therefore, the settlor would be no better off if he received the income into his personal income tax return. So, why have an inter-vivos trust? Again, a few primary reasons are to implement an estate freeze. This effectively transfers property to designated beneficiaries well in advance of death of the Settlor. At the same time, the Settlor can maintain control over the assets. For example, a business owner can exchange his common shares for preferred shares and issue new shares to be held in trust for his children. The preferred shares will continue to yield a dividend from the company and any future growth or capital gains will accrue to the children. This effectively freezes the estate to any further capital gains.

Another example for uses of a trust is for income splitting. If your income producing assets are in the highest marginal tax bracket, but other family members have lower tax rates, you could transfer the income-producing assets to a trust. Family members will be tax at lower rates. Capital gains may be triggered on the transfer and other tax consequences such as taxable dividends and capital gains tax may be subject to the kiddie tax. That is, a child receiving dividends and capital gains from private corps will pay tax at the top marginal rate. This effectively eliminates tax avoidance used in income splitting strategies.

Testamentary trusts are tax advantaged entities and structured for reasons other than tax minimization. They are created to setup multigenerational family wealth and retain control of substantial assets and income to beneficiaries over time. Testamentary trusts are subject to a graduated tax structure like individual taxpayers. So, the types of investments and securities inside a testamentary and inter vivos trust may look different if minimizing taxes is an objective. Similar to inter vivos trusts income paid out to the beneficiary the charity owns the property and taxed according to tax rules applied to its structure, is a deduction to the testamentary trust. A charitable remainder trust has the primary advantage of securing an immediate tax receipt for the charitable donation. The settlor or some other designated beneficiary continues to receive income from the capital within the trust, but the capital accrues to the trust. So, ultimately the creation of the charitable remainder trust and subsequent gift can potentially result in substantial tax credits. Finally, taxation of trusts can be complex and costly errors can be made if not structured properly. Seek professional advice from a lawyer and accountant with expertise in Trusts.

Summary of Trusts
The two primary forms of trusts are the testamentary trust and the inter-vivos trust. There are a number of types of trusts within in each. The former arises on the death of the Settlor, while the latter is in affect while the Settlor is alive. Some trusts such as a spousal trust can initially be set up as an inter-vivos trust, then, on the Settlor's death, rolled over to the testamentary trust. A primary benefit of the spousal rollover provision is the deferral of taxes. Property is transferred at the original cost base deferring capital gains tax until the death of the surviving spouse. Family trusts can yield numerous advantages in terms of reduced income taxes through income splitting and probate fees on death as well as retaining control of family assets over time. Charitable remainder trusts are created to provide for an immediate tax

receipt for a charitable gift, while still allowing the Settlor or other designated beneficiary to receive income from the trust property until a stipulated date. Testamentary trusts allow for the control of significant wealth, appreciating and income producing assets, after death. Managing multigenerational family wealth, tax deferral and tax minimization and capital preservation are the primary reasons for Testamentary and Inter Vivos Trusts.

CHAPTER XI

THOUGHTS ON INCOME TAX

"In this world nothing can be said to be
certain, except death and taxes"
Benjamin Franklin

➤ Differentiating between tax avoidance and tax evasion
➤ Tax efficient investing through capital gains and dividends
➤ Taxes and death of a tax payer
➤ Taxes on Pensions
➤ Tax strategies for every Canadian

Tax Avoidance vs. Tax Evasion

Tax avoidance is the legal way to minimize the amount of tax you pay on your income. Tax evasion is the illegal act of hiding income from the CRA or failing to disclose accurate amounts of income or deductions. Numerous legal strategies are available and known to Accountants and Tax Specialists, large corporations, small and medium size business owners, and individual taxpayers. The Income Tax Act provides for specific provisions available to every Canadian to benefit in an effort to be fair to honest hard working and entrepreneurial individuals. The ITA offers incentives and rewards investment in self and country.

The RRSP is a perfect example of rewarding individual taxpayers to save for retirement and reduce their current level of income tax paid. In 2016, a taxpayer earning between $90,564 and $140,388 per year will be in a 43.41% marginal tax bracket (mtr), in Ontario. At an income of $96,000 an RRSP contribution of $5,000 will reduce taxable income and reduce taxes by 43.41% or $2,170. Similarly, a taxpayer earning between $41,537 and $45,282 will be in a 24.15% mtr. A $5,000 RRSP contribution may be a challenge, but the taxpayer would reduce taxes by $1,207.75. The most important point to remember is that it is unlikely the individual taxpayer would be earning $96,000 at retirement. Therefore, when the RRSP rolls over to a RRIF (Registered Retirement Income Fund) that same money can be withdrawn at a substantially lower rate. For instance, if the retiree has an income of $45,282 his marginal tax rate is only 24.15%. Hypothetically, the taxpayer could withdraw a supplemental amount of registered income of $10,000 to bring his income to $55,282 and pay only 29.65% tax vs. 43.41% tax, saved on the contribution. See table below.

ONTARIO	Marginal Tax Rates (%)			
Taxable Income ($)	Interest & Regular Income	Capital Gains	Eligible Canadian Dividends	Ineligible Canadian Dividends
0 to 10,011	-	-	-34.53	-17.33
10,012 to 11,474	5.05	2.53	-27.56	-11.42
11,475 to 41,536	20.05	10.03	-6.86	6.13
41,537 to 45,282	24.15	12.08	-1.20	10.93
45,283 to 73,145	29.65	14.83	6.39	17.37
73,146 to 83,075	31.48	15.74	8.92	19.51
83,076 to 86,176	33.89	16.95	12.24	22.33
86,177 to 90,563	37.91	18.95	17.79	27.03
90,564 to 140,388	43.41	21.70	25.38	33.46
140,389 to 150,000	46.41	23.20	29.52	36.97
150,001 to 200,000	47.97	23.98	31.67	38.80
200,001 to 220,000	51.97	25.98	37.19	43.48
220,001 and over	53.53	26.76	39.34	45.30

Source: Manulife Investments, Tax Rate Card for 2016

The government created the RRSP in the 50s as an incentive for Canadians to save for their own retirement income needs. RRSP contributions effectively level out the amount of tax we pay on our income over our lifetimes. During our peak earning years between 35 to 55 years of age, we can defer taxes through the RRSP. We will typically pay less tax during retirement, not receiving employment income and will be in a lower tax bracket when we begin to withdraw funds from our Registered Retirement Income Fund (RRIF) or pensions.

Tax Efficient Investing

* Three general types of investment income *
* Capital Gains taxed lower than Dividends *
* Dividends taxed lower than Interest *
* Leveling out your income throughout your life *
* Pension or RRIF income taxed at highest rate *
* Preferred Shares for dividend income *
* Corporate Class mutual funds *

In order to understand how to save or defer income tax you will need know about the three basic types of personal income tax. The first type is tax on ordinary income or salary, pension income, and interest income. This type of income falls into your highest marginal tax rate. The second type of income is capital gains income. It is the most tax-preferred income. A provision for a 50% exemption means only 50% of a capital gain is taxable at your marginal tax rate. This equates to exactly 50% less tax payable on this type of income. Capital gains accrue on investment property such as rental units, apartments, commercial property and secondary personal properties such as a family cottage. Additionally, capital gains accrue on investments like stocks, bonds and mutual funds to name a few. The third type of income is dividend income from Canadian corporations. It becomes tax preferred through the Dividend Tax Credit provision of the tax rules. Dividend Income comes from mutual funds holding dividend-yielding stocks, or from individual stock ownership.

To illustrate the significance of tax preferred income, an individual earning $73,145 would have a 31.48% marginal tax rate(mtr) and pay $31.48 on the next $100 dollars earned; a 15.74% mtr on the next dollar of capital gains; and 8.92% mtr on the next dollar of "eligible dividends" as defined by CRA. The difference between mtr on interest and regular income and dividends and capital gains, in all tax brackets, shows the tax benefits of investing in stocks and tax preferred investment vehicles. Keep in mind that registered investment accounts will not receive tax-preferred income. To coin a popular cliché: "It is not always about how much you make, but how much you keep!"

With a little basic knowledge of the income tax brackets in your province, it is possible to maximize the tax credits you receive for RRSP contributions. In other words, it may not make a whole lot of sense to contribute to an RRSP to reduce your income below $45,283 to save 24.15% when you might have an income between $45,283 and $73,145 at retirement. You will be simply paying the same or more tax on the withdrawal as you saved on the contribution and consequently missing more tax efficient methods of saving for retirement, outside of a registered plan. Although arguments for tax deferral are solid, arguments for long-term capital gains accrual can be equally compelling. In some cases, it might make more sense to invest in a non-registered savings or investment plan holding individual common or preferred stocks or mutual funds that would yield a significantly higher after tax return than if they were held in an RRSP. Withdrawals or income from an RRSP is taxable as interest or regular income. There is no preferential tax treatment of income in an RRSP regardless of the type of investment income, capital gains, or dividends from Canadian corporations. The concept of tax-preferred income is one of the most important lessons I wish to convey at this point in tax planning.

At the risk of belaboring the issue of tax-preferred income, I've provided an illustration: **Non-registered vs. Registered portfolio.**

| Investor A; buys $50,000 Equity Mutual Fund (RRSP) | Investor B: buys $50,000 Equity Mutual fund (Non-Registered) |

No further deposits made to either account.

20 years grows to $200,000   20 years grows to $200,000

Tax credit on the $50,000 RRSP Contribution: bought and spent on appliances, furniture and a trip to Hawaii.

$25,000/year withdrawal: investor is at a marginal tax rate of 31.48%

Taxes paid: $25,000 at 31.48% = $7,870	Taxes paid: ACB: $6,250
	Capital Gain: $18,750
	50% Exemption = $9,375
	Tax on $9,375 at 31.48% = $2,951

A variety of scenarios can change the results, but this shows the significance of tax preferred income as part of your long-term investment strategy. Had Investor A invested the tax credit into a non-registered investment account it may have grown enough to pay much of the tax on the future RRSP withdrawals. I did not include annual taxes owing on dividend income earned on the mutual fund in the non-registered account. This also would have affected the results, so it is not always as simple as illustrated above.

Death of a Tax Payer

In Canada, we do not have death taxes as they do in the US. However, we have other punitive taxes on RRSP's or RRIFs and Non-Registered Investments in the form of capital gains taxes. Fortunately, we can transfer our RRSPs to our surviving spouse tax-free. However, this often creates a potentially bigger deferred tax on the death of the surviving spouse. We are taxed on the entire value of the RRSP plus all other income earned in the year of our death. So, if you are going to die with a large RRSP, make sure you die January 1st, as you will only have 1 day of income to add to the value of your RRSP. We pay no tax on our personal residence no matter what we paid for it. A secondary property such as a cottage or rental property will be subject to capital gains tax on the increase in value. Small, medium, and large incorporated businesses are subject to a comprehensive set of taxes, beyond the scope of this book. In addition, preventative strategies can be put in place decades in advance to reduce estate taxes through succession planning and estate freezes. Lawyers and Accountants specializing in succession planning are required at every step of the process so it is not a strategy for smaller businesses or estates under $2 million, due to cost.

Taxes on Pensions

The Federal Pension Legislation regulates pensions for Federal employees and the Provincial Legislation the provincial employees. In most cases, Provincial Pension Legislation governs corporate pension plans. Members of Federal Pension Plans include, Crown Corporations, RCMP, Defense or Military employees, and Federal Government employees. Pensions are complex and multi-featured creatures, variations built in to almost every case. They are different in plan administration, such as the investment management, options for employees and contribution levels. However, the legislation states what is required in terms of locking-in agreements, transferability, protection, provisions for withdrawals, marital breakdown, tax consequences of withdrawals and what happens on death of the annuitant. Most pensions will have a survivor benefit payable to the surviving spouse. In many cases, it will be a percentage of what the annuitant was getting or going to get at retirement. However, if the surviving spouse dies shortly after the annuitant, the pension benefits drop to zero for the estate and beneficiaries. In the case of single pensioners, the story is even more scandalous.

To illustrate, a pensioner receiving $50,000/yr indexed to inflation dies prematurely at 63. He has no spouse and no beneficiaries. The pension, which could possibly have a commuted value of $500,000, goes back to the pension plan! This is tragic. However, there are options to avoid this scenario, but must be done at the time employment is terminated and retirement commences. Transfer the commuted value of the pension to another financial institution, such as a Bank Brokerage or Investment Dealer, not another pension and into a Locked-In Retirement Account (LIRA) or a Locked-In Income Fund (LIF). The married annuitant can transfer the entire value of the plan into his wife's name on death with no penalties or reductions in benefits. If the surviving spouse then dies shortly thereafter, the estate will receive the entire amount after taxes, for their beneficiaries. The benefits of this strategy are clear.

The risks are then borne by the pensioner, now the investor, as the benefits become uncertain due to the selection of securities in the LIRA or LRIF and the fixed or guaranteed pension income is lost. The locked in plan also restricts how much can be withdrawn on an annual basis. Although, effective January 1, 20010, if money is transferred into a "New LIF", the government allowed a one-time 50% lump sum cash withdrawal, or transfer to an RRSP or RRIF. Similar to RRIFs there is a schedule of minimum and maximum withdrawals from LIFs and LRIFs. Registered Retirement Income Funds (RRIF) differs in not having an annual maximum on the amount withdrawn. You can withdraw the entire amount from a RRIF, subject to tax. You will have a number of things to consider, so I suggest seeking advice from a financial planner, like myself, before making a decision to keep or transfer your pension.

Tax Strategies for Canadians

Average people of all incomes can benefit from knowing and understanding the tax system. The tax system works to reward entrepreneurs and risk takers as well as those willing to invest in themselves, self-employed. For example, the most basic of all tax shelters the RRSP, registered retirement savings plan, provides for tax sheltered savings and investing as well as an immediate tax deduction against current income. Earned income in excess of $86,177 is taxable at a marginal rate of 37.91%, while income in excess of $220,001 is taxable at a marginal rate of 53.53%. An RRSP can level out income over a 35-year career as well as during an additional 35-year retirement. Typically, your highest income years are between the ages of 35 and 55. Subsequent years' income will often fall as we wind down the number of hours worked and the responsibilities taken on. It would make sense to shave off a part of the income in the high-income years and move it to the lower income semi-retirement or retirement years. This simple strategy results in paying less tax throughout our entire lives. Every working Canadian can learn about the tax system and how to use it to their advantage.

There are several wonderful books written for the layperson that will help give you the understanding and knowledge that the richest Canadians already know. For example, basic knowledge about the taxation of investments can mean a significant difference in how much of your income you keep and how much tax you must pay the government. Investment income from such securities as bonds and term deposits, interest is taxable at the highest MTR. While dividends and capital gains income from eligible Canadian corporations are, tax preferred. That is, the CRA has reduced the taxable amount on capital gains to 50%. Therefore, the maximum MTR on capital gains is 26.76%. In addition, the highest MTR for dividends is 39.34%, given the generous dividend tax credit. Of course, many wealthy Canadians take advantage of these basic preferential tax treatments. In truth, any and every Canadian should be aware of this opportunity to pay less tax and build their personal wealth.

When it comes to seniors or those with disabilities and lower incomes knowing the tax system can pay dividends. At age 65, there is much tax relief from age, pension, and sales and property tax credits that can add up to thousands of dollars. You can claim medical expense deductions from income as well as charitable donations and costs of supporting a loved one. Educate yourself to know what is available to you. Nobody is going to volunteer this information, so it is up to every one of us to learn. Spend a few hours reading government brochures or tax-planning guides published every year by Chartered Accounting firms and the CGA, Certified General Accountants. They have a wonderful little booklet, Personal Tax Planning, which provides us with dozens of hints and tips for filing a tax return.

Self-employed Canadians enjoy numerous tax benefits for the risks and entrepreneurial spirit they embrace. Deductions for expenses incurred to run a small business are endless and extremely generous. Any purchase or lease of equipment for the office or factory is tax deductible. Moreover, you can purchase a personal computer and printer for the business as well as for personal use as long as you document how many hours for business and personal use. Similarly, you can claim business use of a personal vehicle as long as it is clearly documented what percentage is personal and what percentage was business. Clearly, the small business owner must spend money (i.e. expenses) to make money and to earn the tax credits. However, there are many benefits to the small business owner and his family when it comes to reducing taxable business income.

At some point, small business owners need to determine if they should incorporate. The small business deduction (SBD) is a primary reason to incorporate. Canadian-controlled private corporations (CCPCs) are entitled to claim the SBD on the first $500,000 taxable income earned on *active business income.* This income will be taxed at very low corporate rate of 15% combined (10.5% Federal plus 4.5% in Ontario), for 2016 vs the regular income rate a sole proprietor would pay. Active business income is income earned from any business adventure or concern in the nature of trade. Non-Eligible, *passive income* comes from a business that derives its income from personal services with fewer than 6 employees or specified investment businesses earning interest, dividends or rent. Additionally, the regular federal corporate tax rate that applies to Investment, Mortgage and Mutual Fund corporations is 28%.

The business owner also has the option to add members of his family to the payroll for the benefits of income splitting. As long as the pay is reasonable for the work done by the family member, income splitting is permitted. The business owner can also decide if he should pay out salary or dividends to himself or family members. Salary or regular income is taxed at the highest level to the employees, but benefits, such as CPP and RRSP contributions are not available on dividends. On the other hand, the corporation receives a tax deduction on salary paid. However, dividends received are tax-preferred income to varying degrees depending on the province and whether the corporation was designated to pay eligible or in-eligible dividends. In order to pay *eligible* dividends to shareholders a CCPC must qualify according to a complex formula and "…..to the extent it has a balance in its "general rate income pool" (GRIP) (Grant Thornton, 2015). This implies that the dividends be paid out of income that has not benefited from the SBD or other tax refund mechanisms. Additionally, the corporation must have designated the dividends eligible in writing and have notified the CRA and other interested parties. Although there are massive amounts of information on the internet and in books it is advisable to seek the advice of a Lawyer and Accountant for professional legal and tax advice for your situation.

Eldercare Planning
Tax Planning
Education Planning
Financial Plans
Risk Analysis
Retirement Projections
Investment Analysis

CHAPTER XII

FUNDING EDUCATION

"An investment in knowledge pays the best interest."
Benjamin Franklin

> RESP Rules
> Contributions and Grants
> Withdrawals
> Informal Trusts

Similar to funding your retirement you must set a goal when planning for education costs. For example, assuming your child or grandchild is 5 years old and will be attending post-secondary education at age 18, you have 13 years to save a set amount of money. A financial planner can help you determine how much money to invest on a monthly and annual basis. Your adviser will also help you determine personal investment objectives and risk tolerance. He will build a suitable investment portfolio and determine an assumed rate of return to calculate the amount of money needed to invest over the 13-year period.

RESP: The Rules

Most Financial Institutions across Canada promote and offer Registered Education Savings Plans (RESP). The major banks, Independent Financial Service companies, and the major brokerages will all assist in opening these accounts for named beneficiaries, your children or grandchildren, under the age of 21. The plan matures on the 35th anniversary of opening the plan and no further contributions after the 31st anniversary of plan opening. The CRA registers the plan as an Education Savings Plan. A Family plan allows for multiple beneficiaries while a Specified plan permits only a single beneficiary to receive. The Subscriber, such as a parent, guardian, or grandparent enters into the RESP contract and contributes up to limits specified by the Income Tax Act. The Promoter or financial institution administers the plan, accepting contributions and making payments to finance the beneficiaries' education, while the CRA provides the grants as laid out in the guide (www.cra.gc.ca).

The rules are somewhat confusing. In fact, September 1, 2016, David Hodges of the Investment Executive wrote that, a CIBC survey recently found that "four out of five parents can't estimate tuition costs and don't fully understand how RESPs work". The poll also found that parents should count on $25,000 per year for College or University. This amount will be required for tuition and non-tuition expenses, such as books, food and accommodations and extra-curricular activities. In addition, 75% of parents had set up RESPs, but did not clearly understand them. Understanding the basics before opening an account will allow parents to take advantage of various grant moneys and other features. Brochures are available from the major banks, credit unions, investment and mutual fund dealerships. The government created new rules for the RESP, which included the education savings grant in 1998 and can be applied for and deposited into the RESP.

Contributions and Grants

In 2004, the Government of Canada introduced two additional RESP grant programs (www.hrdc.gc.ca). Under the original Canada Education Savings Grant (CESG) program the beneficiary qualifies for the 20% grant, on the first $2,000 saved, providing the contribution is made no later than the calendar year in which the beneficiary turn's 17. Effective January 1, 2007, the maximum annual RESP contribution eligible for the 20% grant was increased to $2,500 from $2,000. In other words, the maximum annual grant increased from $400 to $500 per beneficiary. In addition, effective 2007 or later, the rule provides for $500 grant room for each child, each year, for carry forward. If one year is missed, the maximum of $5,000 contribution could be made to qualify for $1,000 grant. The lifetime maximum contribution increased to $50,000 from $42,000 and the maximum CESG is $7,200.There is no income requirement to receive the Basic CESG.

Under the two new grant programs, there are income requirements for eligibility. The Additional CESG provides 40% (20% extra) on the first $500 saved, provided the net family income is below $44,701, for 2015; 30% (10% extra) provided the net family income is above $44,701 but below $89,401, for 2015. The second addition to the grant program is the Canada Learning Bond (CLB). An initial, one time grant of $500 is available for eligible beneficiaries born January 1, 2004 or later, as well as an annual $100 subject to meeting income guidelines. The income criteria require the family must be in receipt of the National Child Benefit Supplement. I would recommend a review of the program details provided in the CRA RESP Guide and the RESP booklets provided by The Department of Human Resources and Skills Development as well as guides offered by most financial institutions.

Withdrawals (Payments)
To make a withdrawal or receive payments from your RESP, the promoter requires proof of acceptance or enrollment in a qualifying or specified educational program. A qualifying education program is a Post-secondary school level, a University or College Program and a program of 10 or more hours of course work per week for a minimum of 3 weeks. A specified education program is at a post-secondary school level lasting minimum 3 weeks and 12 hours per month on course curriculum. The academic program will not qualify if the student is receiving full-time employment

income, although part-time employment income is acceptable. Therefore, any major training courses and College and University programs are all eligible institutions. Once proof of enrollment in an eligible academic program is provided, the promoter may then make the various types of payments to the beneficiary. The payment is made up of a refund of contributions (made by the subscriber), educational assistance payments (EAPs) and after 1997, accumulated income payments (AIPs) (ie. growth of the investment if any). Some restrictions on the amount of withdrawal may apply. Nevertheless, generally, the rules are lax.

If your child decides on another path and does not go to school the plan must be collapsed within 35 years of the plan opening date. The education savings grant portion must go back to the government and the interest, dividends, and capital gains would then be taxable in the hands of the contributor. This could be a substantial amount of taxable capital gains if the investments grew in value over a period of 15 to 20 years. Therefore, this is a possible downside of this type of plan. However, under the new rules the contributor can transfer the plan assets, minus the education savings grant portion, to his RRSP. Providing the subscriber had the contribution room as stated on their individual Notice of Assessment.

Informal Trusts
An RESP may not always be the best solution as a savings vehicle for education funding. It may be somewhat restrictive in how the money and growth are ultimately allocated. Setting up a trust account for your child or grandchild is a flexible alternative. Many financial institutions will set up informal trusts. This essentially signifies the money in the trust belongs to the beneficiary, your child or grandchild. The informal trust is not a legal trust in terms of using a lawyer or having notarized by a lawyer. However, it is always prudent to seek independent legal advice prior to setting up a trust for little Johnny's education fund. An informal trust then has no specific clauses to direct how or when the money is to be distributed. There are no restrictions on using the funds only for

education, a down payment on a house or starting a business. It is a flexible alternative to the restrictive rules of an RESP. However, there are no government grants for contributions made to informal trusts.

PART IV

ACTION

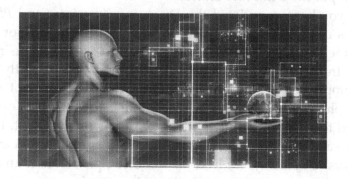

CHAPTER XIII

LIVE FOR TODAY!

"Live your life. Take chances. Be crazy. Don't wait.
Because right now is the oldest you've ever been
and the youngest you'll be…ever again."
Suzanne Collins

- ➤ Putting the Plan into Action!
- ➤ A Cerebral Life: Using Your Brain
- ➤ A Physical & Healthful Life
- ➤ An Experiential Life
- ➤ A Financial Life
- ➤ Get Creative!
- ➤ Spectator or Participant? * Make It Happen!
- ➤ Facts of Life
- ➤ What to Do?
- ➤ Needs & Wants * Recreational Activities*
- ➤ Art, Science and Music * What Is Really Important to You?
- ➤ Who Says Money Doesn't Buy Happiness?
- ➤ Everything In Moderation
- ➤ Life-Long Learning* Continuous Pursuits
- ➤ Lifestyle*
- ➤ Live For Today! Plan For Tomorrow

Time to put the Plan into Action

Bravo, you have completed the *Discovery, Knowledge* and *Planning* sections of the journey it is now time to begin to live for today. It is time to set the ball rolling and get on with the business of living. In the *Discovery* section you learned how broadly based and complex our lives can be. Without full awareness of money, social, philosophical or spiritual or financial aspects of our lives we tend to go through life a little like robots on autopilot. I prefer to be awake and fully aware like a deer or small animal evading predators. Obviously, we lead far more complex lives than a deer. Nevertheless, it remains an essential part of our survival and success in this world to be aware of how money works, how best to socialize and network in your "village" and equally crucial, to take care of ourselves and others.

I brought you up to speed regarding investing, economics and the business cycle and how they may impact your personal investments. The meaning of life delved into practical topics of life choices, education, career and jobs. Additionally, you learned about life expectancy and the health adjusted life expectancy numbers and how they may impact your immediate life choices and consequently your longer term plans. In the last part of Discovery, I stress the importance of developing short, medium and long term goals. Without goals, you will be living an aimless and life absent of purpose.

The *Knowledge* section may have been a little tedious for non-financial readers, but I felt it to be an important part of your education. An in depth discussion about the different types of mutual funds, stocks, bonds, preferred shares and several other essential marketable securities. I discussed *exchange traded funds*, the latest trend investments as well as alternative investment strategies using *options, futures* and *forward contracts*. The markets can be a mysterious world for some people, so I have provided you with ample ammunition to ask the right questions of your advisor or financial institution.

The *Planning* section may be the most pertinent to what you wanted out of a book such as this. Finding out what a Financial Planner is and what products, advice and services are offered will bring you that much closer to your objectives. I highlighted the importance of a Net worth statement, budgeting and cash flow and how this is a starting point and way to keep score. I reviewed and contrasted Financial Planning with Retirement Planning and highlighted the most important aspects of retirement planning, how much to save and how much you must save for your particular situation. I also included a few notes on government pensions which supplement personal savings in RRSPs and Group Savings Plans, or pensions. I summarized estate planning and how this is part of the process and another component part of financial planning. I noted the importance of wills and powers of attorney, life and disability insurance and understanding various types of trusts for larger estates. I touched on tax planning and how to reduce income taxes and estate taxes using a variety of *tax avoidance* strategies. And I also touched on a very important topic of funding post-secondary education through the Registered Education Savings Plan.

The *Action* section is where you begin to live the very things you have learned in the previous pages. You are armed with knowing how to find a financial planner, what to ask, what to expect and you will understand the investments they are recommending. Your financial planner will learn about you and your objectives and set you on the path to financial independence. You will be at peace knowing how investments function as a result of the economic cycles and stay the course until you reach your goals. You will then be free to live, learn and enjoy every part of your world.

A Cerebral Life: Using the brain you never knew you had
The cliché, *"You Only Live Once"* is a phrase referring to the fact that we are not making the most of our time on earth; nor are we using our minds to its full capacity. Leonardo da Vinci, inventor and creative genius of the 14th century, had interests in numerous disciplines. He is widely known for his artistic endeavors and particularly his portrait of the Mona Lisa. However, his intellectual pursuits, such as his contributions to medicine, science, physics, art, philosophy, and engineering, out-weigh his art. He worked

and exercised his mind like an athlete works his body and it was utilized to its fullest, with astounding results. He pushed his logical and analytical left hemisphere and his creative right hemisphere to capacity each day of his life. His passion for learning, designing, creating, and painting immortalized and captured in copious notes of his observations, thoughts, and opinions daily.

We cannot all be Leonardo da Vinci, but we can get the most out of our brain and enjoy a rich cerebral or thoughtful life. If you doubt you are capable of learning at a high level, *think again*. Napoleon Hill, a Depression-era author interviewed more than 500 successful men to determine the keys to their success. He then summarized their thoughts and published them into a best-selling book, *"Think and Grow Rich"*. Although this books focus is on being successful, it can also be used in everyday life to think and critically analyze the world around you. There are brain building strategies and information available to help us reach for the stars. I have provided a few titles of books in the references that can help you think like a genius.

Case in point, Michael Gelb writes about Leonardo da Vinci's *seven principles* (Gelb, 1998). He writes about how to live with the insatiable curiosity of a child. He would say to keep asking questions of the world you live in; make notes and describe everything you see, hear or perceive like flowers, buildings, computers and people then ask more questions. Ask those questions that begin with who, what, where, how and why.

Consider the amazing transition of a caterpillar to a butterfly. *How* does this happen? *What* is the trigger that starts the metamorphosis from caterpillar to butterfly? *Why* does this occur? There are complex scientific explanations at the biological and chemical levels. However, what directs and initiates the change from a multi-legged larva to a beautifully colored flying insect at the molecular or even sub-atomic level? At the subatomic level, we have scientific theories and growing evidence for what triggers the atoms and DNA molecules to act in a way that will cause the cells to grow into a wing instead of a fin.

A Physical & Healthful Life

I can honestly say that I have not always been physically fit. After playing hockey for 15 years, running and swimming as a youngster, I switched to a more cerebral life. I attended University in the early 80s and for the first time in my life, I became immersed in my studies and the quest for knowledge, neglecting my level of fitness. On graduating, I obtained a highly stressful management position, which again was more intellectually challenging than physical. For a period of several years in my mid-twenties, the balance between physical health and mental health in my life was out of balance. Having read several books about the state of the average adults' health, I should have known better than to neglect my own health. I learned about the Canada Health Food Guide, Carbohydrates, Proteins, Fats, vitamins and minerals through self-study. However, I had failed to act on this knowledge until years later. I finally saw the light and began to eat right and go to the gym a few days per week to start, persevering through several episodes of vomiting after exercising and pushing the weights a little too hard. Lactic acid and other metabolic wastes build up in your muscles and blood very quickly, as your body performs aerobic or anaerobic exercise. Your muscles work in a very narrow range around 7.0 ph. As the muscles begin to work they break down muscle glycogen and the cellular environment quickly goes relatively acid and you feel sick and nauseous. This metabolic process interferes with the chain of physiological events that produces energy and muscle contraction. Thus, the burn and fatigue that comes with exercise (Cogan, 1993).

As I learned my limitations and improved my strength and endurance, the nausea and vomiting dissipated. I discovered the *runners high* from my workouts and currently exercise for 40-45 minutes 3 to 4 times weekly. I do not wish this initial negative reaction to exercise on anyone, but just as we fall a hundred times before learning to walk this may be a small price to pay on the path to good health.

With the exception of only a few fad diets most are quite ineffective and possibly dangerous. The Canada Health Food Guide is your best source for proper nutrition and guidelines for intake of adequate calories, carbohydrates, fats, and proteins on a daily basis. Based on what you are eating the dietitian will calculate exactly the amount of carbohydrates, proteins, fats, calories in your diet. Dietitians also provide a little, or a lot of fine-tuning of the amounts and how to count and measure on your own. Reading labels of food packaging gives us most of the essential macronutrient information required to minimize portion sizes to our particular needs. More activity or physical work done in a day requires more calories from carbohydrates and fats; while less active or sedentary office workers need far fewer calories. In addition, a registered dietitian helps set up a schedule of what to eat for breakfast, lunch and supper with snacks in between meals. I recommend that anybody with a weight problem, or risk of heart disease or anybody wanting to be in optimal health to seek out a registered dietitian and eat according to the guidelines. Your heart, brain and body will love you for it.

An Experiential Life

Aside from becoming more open to learning, outside your occupation or taking care of your health, you may have a passion for helping others. Whether it is orphaned children, seniors, the infirm or victims of crime, disease, or poverty make a commitment to taking responsibility for others. Refuse to bend to the pressure of doing the same things repeatedly simply because you have always done it. Branch out, experiment, and experience all of the wonderful activities in your community. Volunteering for various community programs, participate or attend local sporting events, museums, art shows, travel shows, home, and garden shows. Life is for the living. Get excited. Get involved. Once you begin to get involved, you become addicted to living. Not to mention you will sleep well each night. In my meetings with seniors with substantial amounts of wealth, I am witness to married couples who have been together for 40 years, lived, saved, and sacrificed together so that they might have a comfortable retirement filled with travel, leisure and relaxation. Couples who on the surface had it all only to have one of the spouses fall ill, become immobile, or pass away. Then the tragedy really begins. The surviving spouse usually loses motivation and enthusiasm for their dreams of travel and life of pleasure because there is nobody to share those dreams. Such is the main reason for this book. *Live for Today!*

Make a bucket list of things you would like to do. I am not referring to climbing a mountain or embarking on a 3-month adventure through the Amazon jungle. I am talking about visiting your local zoo, museum or city hall. How about visiting 12 different restaurants of various ethnicities over the next 12 months and writing to tell your family about your experiences? How about taking an adult education course to learn a new language, cook or bake or a survival course? If you enjoy attending a local church, perhaps break out of your comfort zone and attend another church, which provides a different perspective on your beliefs? Go to your local market and try buying local vegetables, fruits or meats. Traveling is at the top of many bucket lists, but it is also an expensive wish that not everyone can afford. Perhaps, shorter local trips are the answer, or study the place you would like to go and use your imagination to take you away. Learn about the culture, the food the language and play the music in the comfort of your own home. Besides, it's much safer to visit deepest darkest Africa or Antarctica from the comfort of your living room than actually traveling to these destinations. In a society of high technology and vast information at our fingertips, we can literally experience anything our hearts desire.

It is a statistical fact that tomorrow may not come for many people who are looking forward to a comfortable retirement. I provided life expectancy and the *health adjusted life expectancy* statistics to help you determine and consider your own longevity. Life Insurance actuaries have all the numbers you can imagine and they tell us repeatedly that many people with heart disease, stroke, cancer and other age related tendencies will not reach retirement in comfort or at all. Look at your own health and family history and you may get a hint about your personal life span.

A Financial Life

Learn all that you can about money, the economy, investments, interest rates and personal income tax. Our world demands that you have a basic understanding of personal finance. Just as you require a doctor for your physical health, I would suggest that you seek the expertise of a Financial Planner, like me as the "Quarterback", for your financial health. An accountant and a lawyer also play important roles in your financial life. With knowledge, you benefit financially and in terms of peace of mind by controlling your own personal financial future.

Regardless of your age, if you are saving and investing in the stock markets remember to dollar cost average. That is, set up a monthly investment plan, *pay yourself first* and consider the payment like any other household bill. Secondly, diversify your assets into various international and domestic stock portfolios, bonds and preferred shares as well as a percentage in short term savings instruments. If you are to live and thrive in modern society, you must participate in it economically either by investing in world stock and bond markets or real estate investment properties.

Assuming you have invested in a prudent manner, either in a company pension plan, mutual fund or stock and bond portfolio, I am as certain about your money growing over the long-run, as I am certain about the sun rising tomorrow morning. History has shown that over the long run stock markets continue to rise. It is important to note that not all investments appreciate in value like the indices as discussed in previous chapters. It goes without mention the great disparities between the vast numbers of investment products available today. So learn as much about investing as possible and find a trusted Financial Planner, to help guide you.

Get Creative!
Have we lost the imagination and creativity that produced many of our great discoveries and fundamental academic disciplines, such as medicine, science, mathematics, art, and philosophy? Not everyone, but our jobs have become highly specialized and sometimes routine, often leaving us with a tortuous and repetitive experience. We go home after a long day and we are seemingly incapable of creative endeavors. We succumb to numerous distractions and find every excuse in the book to avoid being creative. Because it is hard and takes some effort! Our children and grandchildren are addicted to high energy yet brain numbing

electronics and an unreal life through video games and television. The few children that escape the vacuum of the video life are actively involved in sports and recreation, studying at school and playing other social games. Adults that have escaped routine are involved in the community, taking night courses or passionately involved in hobbies or personal endeavors, such as arts and crafts, coaching sports or swimming and the like. If your job is routine and borderline boring, seek outside creative endeavors.

Spectator or Participant?

Those who have not yet succeeded in breaking away from the spectator role to the action role can rewire themselves for change. I am an advocate for active participation in life and not just passive participation watching television, or reading the newspapers believing you are a part of it. I am referring to becoming active whether it is a cycling, singing in a choir, golfing, walking, or any sport or activity. An essential part of a healthy lifestyle is physical activity. Strong bodies outlast physically weak, sick and frail bodies. A fit body allows you the freedom and independence of movement and the freedom to choose where you go and whom you can be with, for life. "Use it or lose it", is as true today as ever. A fit body translates into a fit mind. Break away from the television or the video game and get involved. Get involved outside of work if you want to break away from the confines of your employment.

Make It Happen!

Throughout this book, I have talked about writing goals and planning. There is a very good reason for this. Setting goals, targets and planning are an integral part of a management team within any large organization or corporation. Without this exercise, there is no direction for employees or managers. There would be no way of measuring how well individuals or the company are doing. The company or organization whatever it may be will be winging it day after day with no real idea of what the sales revenues should be; how they are to achieve them; or, which products and services will succeed. How then would any company succeed if they were uncertain about their costs and their sales targets? How would they succeed if they did not know who their customers were? Individuals must also set goals, targets and plans.

Without setting out the strategy or plan in advance and monitoring the progress periodically, there is no chance of success. Similarly, individuals need to develop their own short, medium, and long- term goals. Personal and financial goals may overlap but generally, personal goals should not be contingent on the availability of financial resources. Although in western society, this scenario may be somewhat idealistic, there are countless things people can do with little or no money. Create a plan and work it with passion and perseverance!

Luck does not just happen to people. Perhaps on the odd occasion some people will win a lottery or inherit a fortune. These are anomalies in making money and of getting lucky. Most self-made millionaires, billionaires, and successful athletes, for example have discovered their personal niche in life, utilized all the skills and talents available to them and then manufactured their own luck. They made it happen through sheer determination, perseverance, and a vision of what it is they wanted.

I do not know if anybody can explain how it is that if you visualize exactly what you want, it materializes in the real world, but it works. Every detail of every building, electronic component, car, and car parts, consumer product and piece of clothing and furniture began in the human mind as a thought or visualization! This fact is mind blowing to me personally. They all miraculously materialized in our world for all to see, feel, and experience. "Whatever the mind of man can conceive and believe it can achieve." (Hill, 1960). Napoleon Hill wrote these inspirational words almost 50 years ago and gave thousands of followers thought and visualization a new power. *Think and Grow Rich* will change your life.

Facts of Life

Statistics Canada shows the average time spent on physical activities being very low. I have noted a few of the highlights of an average Canadian. Not surprising, hours spent on "Total Work" per day was reportedly 7.8 hours. "Household Work and Related activities" was 3.2 hours per day. Cooking and washing was measured at .8 hours;

shopping for goods and services .8 hours; meals 1.1 hours. "Free Time" jumped out at me at 5.8 hours per day. This statistic begs the question: How are people utilizing this valuable free time? The statistics report that people are spending 1.9 hours socializing and eating in restaurants. Television watching is another brain sucking activity of Canadians' time. Almost 3 hours per day watching TV and the saddest statistic is that Canadians spend less than 1 hour per day on active leisure activities. Canadians spent even less playing sports actively.

Baby boomers, born between 1946 and 1964 are beginning to turn 70 this year, some comfortably retired. Many more are entering retirement and not all in comfort. They are surely feeling the effects of aging and their life's financial indulgences. They have had material wealth and influence like no other demographic group in modern history. It has also resulted in this group being arrogant, self-entitled, demanding and desensitized to the ill effects of a sedentary and indulgent lifestyle. They are more likely to be obese and prone to heart disease, diabetes and stroke than previous generations. Fast food restaurants, high stress jobs and lack of exercise have put them on the fast track to cardiac wards throughout North America. As this group heads into retirement, the reality of their mortality will hit home.

The leading causes of death, as reported by Statistics Canada (1997 statcan.ca) are as follows:

* 27.2% die of Cancer
* 26.6% die of Diseases of the Heart,
* 7.4% die of Cerebrovascular diseases,
* 4.5% die of Chronic obstructive pulmonary diseases and allied conditions,
* 4% of unintentional injuries,
* 3.7% of Pneumonia and influenza,
* 2.6% of Diabetes Mellitus…

These numbers have changed slightly for Canadians, since 1997. The World Health Organization (WHO) lists the top 50 causes of death, as reported in 2014: Coronary Heart Disease (16.8%) was listed as the top cause of death in Canada followed by Alzheimers/ Dementia (11.52%), Lung Cancer (9.88%), Stroke (6.59%) and Lung Disease (5.43%). Other causes of death on the list; Breast Cancer (2.64%), Falls (2.29%), Hypertension or high blood pressure (1.26%), alcholol in 32nd place (.67%) and violence in 39th place (.31%). For a full and complete listing of life expectancy and cause of death statistics by country and world rankings, visit www. worldlifeexpectancy.com.

What is the probability that you or a loved one will succumb to one or more of these disorders? Cancer is the one thing that we all fear and justifiably. Thirty-two percent of all deaths, annually in Canada are caused by the major cancers combined. Under the age of 40, there is less than 1.6% chance of developing and dying from Cancer; Up to the age of 50, 5.6% chance of developing and dying from Cancer. We see a relatively large jump to 14.2% probability of developing and dying of Cancer by the age of 60, 20.9% by the age 70 and 17.8% by 80. Therefore, as we age we begin to see our friends, neighbors, parents and grandparents die of Cancer. Heart disease and stroke takes similar numbers as we age.

The point to all of the above morbid statistics is to highlight the fragility of life and treat it as a precious gift. What do you want to do with your life? How do you challenge yourself? What really makes you happy? What would you like to accomplish? How do you wish to spend your leisure time or equally important your work life? How do you experience all that is out there? How do you live every moment to its fullest? Live and breathe as if it was your last. Tony Robbins talks at length about the pain and pleasure principle (Robbins, Unlimited Power, 1986), in his book Unlimited Power. We are often motivated to act, by the promise of pleasure or the horrifying possibility of pain. Pain can be either psychological or physical. The prospect of emotional and psychological pain is equally terrifying. For instance, many people will not ever fall in love or get married because of the fear of being hurt or let down. Statistics Canada reports in 2001 that 13.8 million Canadians are single, not ever married. This number is staggering in terms of the 12 million Canadians that are married out of a total population of 32 million, now 36 million, 2016. Add to these numbers, the pain and anguish experienced by the 4.12 million Canadians legally separated, divorced, or widowed. Such is life. The relationship, for one reason or another did not work out. That said, it is important to recognize the reasons for our inaction and even if somewhat outside our comfort zone we need to think about the reward. A bad experience should not be an excuse for never opening up to love or an intimate relationship with another individual.

Canadians enjoy an incredible standard of living and financial wealth, yet many people experience depression, anger, alcoholism, drug abuse, psychosomatic illnesses, high blood pressure, obesity and other stress related diseases. According to StatCan.gc, September 2016, Canada has a population of 36 million. Approximately 19.5 million people eligible to work yet only 14.6 million have full-time jobs, 3.5 million part-time. The other 1.4 million, unemployed are experiencing the pain and suffering of low income, low self-esteem, and hopelessness. The average net worth of a Canadian is substantial. Although averages sometimes skew the picture, the median income in Canada is almost half of the average. The median takes the income in the middle. If there are 19.5 million incomes listed, 9.5 millionth persons income will be the median income. Since there are fewer high incomes and substantially more lower and middle-income individuals, the median income number will be lower. The point here is Canadians enjoy a very high standard of living compared with many other people around the world. We are generally free to travel anywhere within our borders without interrogation or special passes. We are free to think and write whatever we feel as long as we are not inciting hate, racism or making other defamatory statements. Within the framework of a moral society we can dress, act, speak, and conduct ourselves in many culturally diverse ways without fear of conviction or discrimination. With all these freedoms, why are we becoming more and more like robots? Why are so many depressed or bored or simply doing what society expects of us. Be good upstanding citizens, go to school, get a job, get married, have children, buy a house in the suburbs, work for 40 years and drop dead of a heart attack? Is that what it is all about? I do not believe this to be the case. There is so much more life has to offer.

Sports

Active participation or even watching and learning about sports is incredibly enriching for young and old. I played organized hockey from the age of 5 to 20, continued to plan as an adult for another 15 years and loved every minute of it. I received huge gratification from the exhilaration of the speed and scoring or assisting on a goal. The team spirit and camaraderie, the "thrill of victory and the agony of defeat" will never be forgotten. Watching the game versus playing the game is no less of thrill, although the health benefits effects are clear. How many sports events have you watched whereby you were virtually lost in the game, cheering for your team in the final minutes. If you cannot recall a sports event that you were so caught up in that you were excited for days after words, you will need to build this into your goal plan. Your goal might say something like, "I commit to be a spectator or participant of 5 different sporting events over the next 2 years and lose myself in the excitement!" The five sports that I would choose are hockey, baseball, downhill skiing, NASCAR racing and soccer. Pick any five sports or activities that you are interested in or attracted to and make them a part of your goal.

Travel

As a financial planner to many wealthy individuals, I often observe many people postponing what could be done today, for tomorrow. People in their sixties and seventies become unable to travel because of an illness or physical problems. My suggestion is to travel while you are young, healthy, and mobile. Do not wait until you retire or when you "have the money". In all probability, you have the money now, but have chosen to spend the money on "other priorities". You might be saying to yourself that saving more for my retirement, buying a new car, bigger house, or new HD TV is more important. This might be true but make sure that you have your priorities straight. In fact, if we were to sit down and take a good hard look at the things we want the most, we may realize that many of the things we have spending our money on are not truly the most important things to us.

Travel need not be expensive. Weekend hiking, camping, canoeing or visiting local sites in your own or a nearby city can be an eye opening and fun experience. My wife and I just began over the past several years visiting Toronto, Ontario. We live one hour from every major site in the city and there are many, as we are discovering with every "trip". When was the last time you ventured off your typical route to the cottage, trailer or boat? Try a different route next time and move your trailer or boat if feasible and see your environment from a slightly new perspective. A boat cruise to the Caribbean, Mediterranean or down the Danube River in Eastern Europe may not be in the budget for everyone. However, it also does not exclude you from canoeing down a local river or across one of the thousands of lakes in Ontario with a few knap sacks full of food and enjoy the scenery and experience.

Needs and Wants

I have personally done this exercise and written down in two columns: WANTS AND NEEDS. Draw a line down the middle of a page and begin to list your wants and needs. Then have your spouse or significant other do the same. In most cases, you will find an immense difference between your list and your spouse list. If not then consider yourselves fortunate that you have similar fundamental life goals. Once the list is on paper, prioritize the "wants" as this will give you an important insight into where to spend your money.

Here is a sample of a Wants and Needs list.

WANTS	NEEDS
3 New Sports Car	Transportation
2 New big screen TV	A television
5 New furniture	A couch and chair
6 Cottage	A vacation
1 Trip to Egypt, Mexico…	An experience
4 New suit, dress, pants….	New clothes
7 Bigger house	A home

Recreational Activities

I have provided a list, below, of activities as long as your arm, so let's get busy! Depending on the climate and the weather on any given day you may wish to go outdoors with nature camping, cycling, jogging, walking or hiking, cross country skiing, downhill skiing or lawn bowling. Indoor activities may include swimming, tennis or racquetball, aerobics, weightlifting, or playing cards to name a few. The point is to stay active. I have asked this question of many seniors in their 80s and 90s what is their secret. The reply is the same every time I ask, "I stay active and keep busy". My grandmother lived to the age of 80 never having a serious illness until an unfortunate stroke killed her. She always had a large garden with a variety of vegetables, and a wide variety of flowers that she tended to on her own, spring summer and fall. She tended this garden, until the day of her un-timely death. Her secret was about living and staying active in the community, the church and family. She also had no TV, no washer, or dryer, choosing to listen to the radio, read, and wash her clothes by hand. This lifestyle is unheard of today. We often choose to lay on the couch with the remote control for the TV in one hand and junk food in the other. Yes, undoubtedly our fast-paced lives dictate that we have modern appliances in our home for washing dishes, clothes and cutting the lawn. Nevertheless, is it not also true that we have vast amounts of free time because of these efficient machines, to participate in many activities? Let's get busy!

Art, Science and Music

Artists throughout the ages were never driven by money or acquiring more stuff. Not like most in our fast-paced Western Society today. Michael Angelo, Leonardo da Vinci, Picasso and most recently Canadian Artist, Robert Bateman all had a passion to express themselves on the canvass. Their creativity and need to fulfill their personal destiny is within us all. We cannot all be a Mozart, Bach, Beethoven or Bateman, Picasso or Madam Curie, but we can all find our own personal level of excellence. It is inside and only you can find it, pursue it, enjoy, and embrace it with your whole being. Otherwise, we are not taking out of life, which is rightfully ours. I am not referring to striving to achieve a promotion or an MBA from college, or to make a hit record. These are all incidental to living with passion. I am referring to finding your personal path and if you happen to be the best and actually win trophies, adulation, recognition, or money along the way that is all good too. Having a passion for the arts or becoming a dedicated scientist searching for a cure for cancer, diabetes or cystic fibrosis are worthy paths to follow. A long-term commitment to be a volunteer in the community is a generous and rewarding path. Learning to play the piano, guitar, or some other instrument is also a part of our human nature to make music. I would contend that it is virtually impossible to be depressed, tired, or unhappy while participating in these activities. We are all here for a brief moment in time and once we are gone, having three Mercedes in the driveway of a large mansion is inconsequential.

Boredom

How anybody can be bored in our society is completely beyond my comprehension. It may be that we are simply overwhelmed and paralyzed with the vast number of choices of things to do in our free time. There are so many things to do, activities to participate in, sports to play, games to play and things to get involved in. There are literally hundreds of books written on "Things to Do". I recently had a vacation at Wasaga Beach, Ontario, situated along the longest freshwater lake in the world. The sand is white and as soft as silk to the touch. The water is clean, fresh and free of any rocky or environmental dangers. Moreover, of course there are no sharks, poisonous jellyfish, or other salt-water predators. I picked up the Wasaga information booklet from the local information center. The brochure listed dozens of activities to do, sites to see, restaurants to eat in, and many places to go. Here is the amazing list that I viewed in the booklet:

Fun Things to Do
- Sightseeing Flights
- Fishing and Sailing Charters
- Casino Tours

- Go-Karts
- Tennis
- Racquetball
- Rollerblading
- Swimming
- Bowling
- Miniature Golf
- Fishing
- Water Slides
- Billiards
- Antiques
- Hockey
- Cycling
- Hiking
- Skiing
- Art Galleries
- Rent a Jet Boat
- Wagon Rides
- Rock Climbing
- Dog Sledding
- Snowshoeing
- Golf
- Tubing
- Soaring
- Baseball
- Outdoor Skating
- Snowboarding
- Beach Volleyball
- Snowmobile Tours
- Craft & Pottery Studios
- Rent a Snowmobile
- Tree-Top Walking
- Zip Cable Gliding
- Suspension Bridge

The above list is merely the beginning of the many wonderful recreational activities and sports we can participate in. A short list, of the many hundreds of things we can do on any given day. Admittedly, money is a requirement for almost every necessity in our society. Having limited disposable income will always put restrictions on what activities are reasonable to consider. Do not let money be an excuse to avoid participating in your world. Prioritizing the things we spend our money on is the key to *Live for Today!*

Obviously, having large financial resources, high income, will allow for more options, but does not imply activities that are more exciting or more fun and enjoyable. How can you put a price on hiking through the bush and experiencing the fresh air, the birds, trees, animals of the forest and above all the exercise? Would this be any less of an experience than to charter a yacht for the day and paying $1500 to go around the lake looking at the shoreline? Alternatively, is it more exciting spending $150/ticket to watch a professional sports match versus going to the local arena to watch an amateur hockey game? I honestly do not believe this to be true. We have gotten away from all of the free things in life in pursuit of the many highly advertised and marketed activities and sports events that cost more than the average person can afford. So, many, not all, individuals become paralyzed by their inability to think of other things to occupy their time. We simply need a gentle reminder.

What Is Really Important To You?
I have referred to the importance of making a list of your goals. Ascertaining your goals is the result of a systematic and thoughtful effort to determine what is of value to you. If you want to save and buy a cottage you must ask, "What is important about buying a cottage? Why do I really want a cottage? What is important about saving a million dollars? What would I do with the money? What is important about retiring at 55?" Ask yourself what it really means to you. In other words, what does the cottage give you in terms of making your life more pleasurable? Does the cottage mean quiet, peaceful living, at one with nature, freedom? Does it allow you to go fishing, be alone with your spouse or family? Drill down and ask yourself during a quiet peaceful moment what it really means

to have the 40-foot yacht, the million dollars saved, or the financial resources to start your own business. You will be wonderfully surprised why you want or do not want these things. You will discover that you may not even want to achieve these goals after you truly understand why you want them. You will discover that in your heart you know what is important to you. You may discover after every effort, your family, spouse or significant other, your health and your own back yard give you ultimate happiness. We get caught up in wanting without knowing why we desire these things.

A parallel to goals are your values. Ideally, your goals should complement your personal set of values if there are no obstacles in your way. Ask yourself if there were no social or monetary constraints, what type of career or job would you want to have and why. What types of activities or hobbies would you participate in? How would you describe the ideal relationship with a spouse or life partner, friend, family member; describe what you feel is being a good friend; describe how you would like people to behave toward you and your fellow human beings locally and globally. This type of exercise gets us looking inside at our innermost desires and our innate personality without societal pressures affecting our decisions. Most of us are in a job that we have simply acclimated. Rather find the job where you say if you love your job, you never work a day in your life!

Marriage & Relationships
Marriage and relationships with family, friends, coworkers, loved ones and intimate partners are an essential part of living for today. Finding a life companion or intimate partner is a gift and unfortunately, too many souls never find what they are looking for. In our hectic and hurried lives, we are not always paying attention and may miss the opportunity for a life companion. Before you know it, you are beyond safe child bearing age for women, or too set in your ways to form a cooperative and sharing relationship. So if you are to experience the full spectrum of life as a social-sexual being determine what kind of individual you would like to have a relationship with and start looking. Your ideal mate will not fall

out of the sky and into your lap. You will have to make an effort. Animals will roam through hot dry deserts or muddy swampland for hundreds of miles to find a mate. You too may have to put in a concerted effort. Although, your quest for a mate will probably not be so dramatic it still requires some work. There are many ways to find love. The internet has online dating services, the newspapers have love wanted ads and the local colleges have adult education classes where you may have some luck finding someone with similar interests.

Who Says Money Doesn't Buy Happiness?
Many people may argue with this phrase, especially if they have no money. People living in poverty with low income, no access to good food, clothing and safe living arrangements may still be happy although it is *more* likely they are in a constant state of despair or stress. As I mentioned in an earlier chapter, happiness does not correlate very well with higher and higher income. Several studies found that measures of personal happiness will only increase up to an $83,000 level of income. Although the extremely rich and sometimes famous seem to be supremely happy, we read in the papers every day that another as died because of a drug or alcohol overdose. These individuals clearly have champagne problems compared to most. Never the less, the problems are deep internal sadness and emotional conflict despite having money. With the exception of people living in stark poverty, happiness and contentment are ultimately a choice. A mental and psychological decision to be happy with whom you are and accepting your lot in life is yours and yours alone. Having money to buy more stuff is not the answer. It is an ongoing challenge to ignore the advertising from retailers trying to sell more. True, it is difficult to ignore pictures and images of luxury automobiles, yachts, big houses, top of the line appliances and big screen televisions. Keeping busy with your own passions and personal activities are the path to living happy and free. Happiness comes from what you enjoy in your life, not what is external to you. Having a new SUV simply does not give you a deep appreciation for life; it merely gives you a short jolt of pleasure and false feeling of respect and recognition. Believe

in yourself and that you are always a worthy individual with or without the SUV.

Pets

Many people would never give up the experience of an animal in the home. Dogs and cats are the most common pets and bring immeasurable companionship and pleasure to the household. I personally grew up with a dog and a cat, together. They brought a huge entertainment value to my family. The sly cat would often hide behind the corner of a chair or couch, in ambush, waiting to pounce on our poor unsuspecting dog. Jump on his back, nip at the back of his neck, and run before the dog knew what hit him. At other times, they would both lie at our feet content to know they were part of our family. We could always count on being greeted at the front door by one of them. Other family members were too busy to come and say hello. Nevertheless, we were always welcomed home and made to feel wanted by these warm and social animals.

Dogs in particular have a keen and intuitive sense and awareness of our moods, health, and physical wellness. There have been many reported cases where dogs have sensed their masters were in physical distress or danger and either began barking or awoken them to a close call with fire or other impending health hazard. Lead dogs for the blind are truly the most amazing animals on Earth. Trained to be the eyes of their master, they lead them through busy streets, buildings and in their own homes. The fact they do this in relative safety day after day is an awesome feat.

The point being is that animals bring an additional level of pleasure and happiness to our existence. If you have wanted a pet dog, cat, or other social animal, then do not delay. There may not be another time. Yes, you need to carefully think about getting a dog for instance as they do require a higher level of care. There might be other sacrifices involving the feeding and care of these loyal creatures, but the value added to our lives is priceless. I for one highly recommend a pet for children and adults alike.

Choosing a pet needs careful consideration depending on budget, time, knowledge, and personal tastes. The type of pet you choose will be followed by a big personal and financial commitment and the choice should not be made in haste. There are currently more pet cats than pet dogs in North American homes. Cats require less hands-on care. They can be left for 2 or 3 days at a time if necessary as they do not have to be let outside like a dog and can be given 2 or 3 days ration of food without concern that they would eat it all in one sitting. Cats will use a litter box and will snack on the larger quantity of food over the few days. A dog would seriously mess the carpets, would eat all the food in first day, and likely chew up all of the shoes and furniture while you were out. So, think about how you might be involved in taking care of specific animals.

My Personal Credo: "Everything In Moderation"
Americans in particular are statistically one of the most obese populations on the planet. Over fed and undernourished by any nutritional or dietary standard. Everyone has eaten in a sporadic fashion, going all day without eating, then gorging on the most accessible junk food available. Many of us require a life-altering event to change our diet and outlook on many aspects of health and ultimately, longevity. Living in moderation will include everything from career, food and diet, sports and activities, goals and aspirations, chocolate bars, and drinking. Measured intake of alcohol will not harm anyone, nor will eating junk food in moderation make you obese or sick.

Aspiring to be the best you can be is a noble desire. However, far too many people are neurotically attached to an obsessive desire for success and goal oriented promotions and money. Being passionate about a life goal is not the same as being obsessive about achieving a particular success. Being obsessive about anything is generally not going to be healthy as the balance in your life is going to be tilted one way or another. Too often, family, relationships and health suffer and the ultimate goal to achieve will eventually collapse if you go beyond your limits.

How will you know if you have gone beyond your limits? There are many red flags and symptoms of physical and emotional stress. You may be getting sick or tired more often, missing work or family gatherings, having sleepless and restless nights, gaining weight, irritable, angry, or unusually depressed. Many successful individuals have worked to the point of exhaustion to achieve their dreams only to realize they have no friends or family and failing health. There is nothing wrong with having dreams or aspiring to have or build your own business, become a doctor, lawyer, engineer, financial wizard, teacher or world-class athlete, for example. The point to remember is to achieve these dreams within a balanced lifestyle and without becoming sick or so stressed that everything collapses.

Life-Long Learning

I am a huge proponent of education and learning as an ongoing part of your life. Learning is not just for kids in grade school, high school, University or College. Life-long learning should be a part of everyone's life beyond traditional avenues of education. Work toward a passion for understanding and an awareness of your world. Live every day in awe! I have a personal library with over 800 books. I have an insatiable appetite for knowledge and always want to learn more. Every time I open one door and learn something new, I find another door that I had never considered. The more I learn the more I realize how little I know. I had difficulty in grade school, not because I could not learn the material, but because I was not ready to learn a particular part of the curriculum. When there was something that interested me, like science or history my eyes were wide with wonder and excitement. I guess I did not want to be told what I had to learn. Unfortunately, until you have graduated from our modern system of education everyone will have to learn the curriculum to achieve the desired diploma or degree. Fortunately, this part of the learning process usurps only a quarter of your life. For the remainder of your life you can read and study whatever you want!

Many of us make the mistake of taking courses to achieve a degree or designation for the letters behind your name only. Do not let the end be the goal, missing the excitement and awe of learning. Ideally, we should be curious about the topic and even better have a passion for the subject and not simply learning to obtain a prestigious job or promotion. If the truth be told. The degree or diploma that you achieve may put you into a miserable, albeit a prestigious job. In our society, letters and degrees are however, one of the most important ways employers can weed through hundreds of applications and candidates.

So, let us not forget or misconstrue what I am saying, that if we are to be happy and content in our lives we should be mindful of the subject or discipline we are studying. If money is an issue and the job puts food on the table, keep the job and seek the alternate route in your spare time of lifelong learning. When your workday ends, you can begin your own quest for discovery. Your local library has thousands of books to read and study. Big city libraries have hundreds of thousands of books available for a few weeks at a time. Areas of study include everything from the study of Apples to Zoology for a few dollars. Local colleges and universities have hundreds of free online courses available. The courses are available for audit, which means you can sit in on the classes free, but your essays and exams are not graded. Major Educational institutions like MIT and Universities across the United States are now posting entire course curriculums online for the taking so people can learn for free anywhere in the world! MIT is offering courses in Engineering, Computer Sciences, Physics, Biotech and Sciences and Electrical and Mechanical studies. All free for the taking. I feel very strongly that each of us needs to work toward this passion and desire to learn. Perhaps with heightened knowledge and awareness of how our world works our species will survive for another 5,000,000 years.

Climate Change or Climate Catastrophe?
David Suzuki and Al Gore, former Vice President of the United States, Nobel Laureate and founder and Chairman of the Climate Reality Project along with the scientific community have been sounding the alarm for global warming for several decades, yet world leaders in the industrial developed nations fail to act. Weather is becoming more erratic, with greater and greater fluctuations in temperature, rainfall, and severe storms. The rapid rise in global temperatures over the past 50 years are causing glaciers worldwide and specifically at the north and south

poles to recede and melt at accelerating rates. This will raise the level of oceans to catastrophic levels by the end of this century, if not sooner. The nightly news and the media show us massive destruction by tornados, hurricanes, and flooding on a weekly basis, yet we do nothing.

The latest catastrophe, Hurricane Katrina, made a direct hit on the city of New Orleans, Louisiana, while simultaneously leveling major parts of 3 states. New Orleans was living on borrowed time, built below sea level. With this knowledge, city planners had built a system of levees on the chance that a storm surge hits the area. What the city had never quite prepared for was a level 5 Hurricane. Sustained winds of 150mph and storm surge of 20 feet plus 15-foot waves, which ultimately caused a major break in the levees, flooded 80% of the city. Thousands of homes leveled, thousands of homeless, and a FEMA scandal that will be hotly debated for years. It was estimated to have caused $200 billion in damages. Easily the greatest and most costly disaster of the century, New Orleans is a wake-up call. Cities below sea level and many low-lying areas around the globe are imminently at risk of flooding. Geographic locations such as the West Bank, Israel, Bangkok, Thailand, parts of Greece, Netherlands, Denmark, Germany, France and Sweden are all in danger. Many parts of Western California, New Orleans and Miami are all at elevations at or below sea level. Large regions around the world are or will be experiencing similar flooding and weather related disasters on a more frequent basis over the coming years and decades, unless governments have the will to make radical changes to reduce greenhouse gases.

What is causing global warming and climate change? Quite simply the answer is the burning of fossil fuels to power cars, trains, planes, factories and to make electric and other sources of energy. Additionally, one of the most potent greenhouse gases comes from a surprising source: cattle. Many people around the world are demanding beef and with more cattle, more land is required, reducing forests that actually suck up excess CO_2. Cows and bulls burp and excrete methane. Methane is 20-30 times more potent greenhouse gas than carbon dioxide from burning fossil fuels. With 1.5 billion head of cattle burping and farting methane plus the clear-cutting of trees for grazing land we end up with a lot of greenhouse gas!

The gases and pollutants that result from burning coal, gas and oil produce billions of tons of Carbon Dioxide (CO2). These gases rise into Earth's atmosphere where they remain for centuries trapping heat in, while letting the sun's heat penetrate the planet's land, air and water. How do we know for certain, the earth is heating up? Scientists have been measuring the CO2 levels in the atmosphere for over 60 years from the Mauna Loa Observatory, Hawaii and have precisely observed the measurable increases annually. Scientists perform countless experiments scientifically validating the reliability of the measurements. Further analysis indicates very high correlations with the rising global temperatures and trends. Based on these precise measurements, the planet earth is now hotter than it has been over the past several million years. At the beginning of the industrial revolution, from about 1760 to 1840, CO2 concentrations were around 280ppm (ie. parts per million), where it had been for 10,000 years. Currently, the CO2 concentration has surpassed 400ppm. If nothing changes to reduce carbon emissions and we continue with business as usual, the earth will be unrecognizable in 25, 50 and 100 years.

Climate change affects everyone to a degree and some a very large extent. If you live in a high- risk city like Los Angeles, you are aware of the risk of a cataclysmic earthquake. Many people living in the area deal with this possibility every day. For the most part it is not something anyone can prevent, nor does it directly affect their daily lives, until of course they are sitting down to dinner and the house begins shaking, dishes start rattling and pictures begin falling off the walls. In moderate climates such as Southern Ontario, Toronto to Windsor for example we have 4 seasons. We have the odd blizzard, the odd tornado, and even the odd torrential downpour causing some flooding. However, there is never the risk of a hurricane, or massive flooding of the sort we hear about in the news from other parts of the world. Our summers are typically warm, occasionally reaching into the thirty-Celsius range unlike the Southern States reaching daily temperatures over 40 Celsius.

However, we have all read the headlines about major typhoons and hurricanes in the northern and southern hemispheres, monsoon rains wiping out entire villages and crops in northern India, drought and lethal heat in the Middle East and Africa topping temperatures of over 50 Celsius. Even in the Southwestern United States, heat and drought are becoming annual occurrences. Flooding in some parts of the world is offset by drought and depleted water reservoirs in others. Glaciers are melting at accelerating rates leading to rapidly rising ocean levels, endangering millions of people living in coastal areas. Warming oceans contributes to rising sea levels as water expands when it warms. Increased CO_2 absorption is also leading to massive acidification of perfectly balanced ph levels of seawater. Acidification of our oceans is causing a mass extinction of coral reefs and the thousands of species making it their home. Dumping chemicals, fertilizers and toxic pollutants into our oceans like flushing a toilet with no thought to the consequences needs to stop. The consequences are dire for the major food source, fish, for 50% of the world's population.

To end this brief commentary on climate change I will quote a few people on the topic of global warming and climate change beginning with Christine Lagarde, International Monetary Fund: "The science is sobering-the global temperature in 2015 was among the hottest since records began in 1880. Make no mistake: without concerted action, the very future of our planet is in peril." "Globally-averaged temperatures in 2015 shattered the previous mark set in 2014 by .23 degrees Fahrenheit. Only once before, in 1998, has the new record been greater than the old record by this much.", stated by NASA Goddard Institute for Space Studies, January 20, 2016. NASA wrote on July 19, 2016, "The first six months of 2016 have been the warmest half-year on record."; since modern records began in 1880 (NASA, July 2016). At the same time, scientists found measurements of the Artic sea-ice extent to be significantly less than in the late 1970s and 1980s. With less light refraction from the snow and ice the sun relentlessly heats up the darker Arctic waters, accelerating the sea-ice melt. I think we can all see were this is headed if we continue on this path of burning fossil fuels. I provide this commentary not to have everyone running and screaming in terror, but to bring awareness and hope that business and government leaders are working very hard around the world to find solutions, but every must do their part.

Income Inequality

Income inequality is a term that many of us intuitively know about, yet brought to conscious public awareness over the past several years by the media, economists and human rights advocates. I will begin with a few facts about the United States. Income inequality has fluctuated for the last hundred years with peaks in 1920s and 2000s. Income growth for all ages and income levels remained stable from 1950-1980 (John Cassidy, 2013). The lion's share of income growth began to funnel into the hands of higher income earners. Significant income increases began in the 1980s and has remained the trend to this day. The Organisation for Economic Co-operation and Development (OECD) is a group of 35 member countries using its data gathering powers "to help governments foster prosperity and fight poverty through economic growth and financial stability" (OECD.org). The OECD Gini coefficient for income inequality in the United States is 37 in 2012 compared with Norway, 25.6 and Sweden, 25.9. The higher the Gini number the greater the inequality.

The United States ranks around the 30th percentile in income inequality globally, which implies 70% have more equal income distribution (World Factbook, CIA.gov). The US well known for having low tax rates on upper income earners along with many loopholes for corporations to significantly reduce taxes. This results in less government revenues, less infrastructure spending, less for education, health, and social programs. Many progressive countries like Finland, Sweden and France have exceptional health care and educational programs for every citizen. Yes, they all have higher levels of taxation. However, these countries also grant significant freedoms to create, innovate, build large business and prosper, while paying a fair portion of their incomes to the government.

Governments provide many of the services that private enterprise simply should not, because there is an inherent conflict. For example, in the United States the prison system has been privatized. There is an incentive for prisons to have more souls incarcerated and to keep them longer. This is completely unacceptable treatment of prisoners who will have paid their dues and put in their time. Private prisons receive compensation or fees for each prisoner kept in their jail. Do think unscrupulous prison managers will be offering fine dining and quality health facilities for prisoners, no, of course not. It costs money and lowers profits to provide better services. Do private hospitals in the United States accept individuals without some sort of health plan, not likely if there is a chance of not getting paid. There should always be a financial incentive to innovate, create and provide a great service or product, like Facebook, Amazon, Apple, Microsoft and Google. However, we should not overlook how unfettered and unrestricted growth can become a serious problem in the public sector.

Companies begin to abuse their power at the slightest hint of competition they buy out the competition remaining a monopoly. In a stable and civilized society, government plays an essential role that led to the great prosperity many of us enjoy today. Sometimes the pendulum swings to far one way or the other, as with communism where the government became overly corrupt and implemented restrictions that impeded any incentive to create, innovate or build. While at the other end, capitalism corrupts as well with vast monetary powers to lobby in their own self-interest, literally writing the laws to protect the path they might be on. Government regulation is clearly an annoyance and like any good thing can go too far. So, we will continue to debate and fight those regulations that are unnecessary and likewise fight for the regulation that benefits everyone.

The "trickle up" effect is the word of the day. Trickle-down theory promoted by a handful of economists, politicians and corporate elite simply did not work. In the last thirty years, the middle class shrunk the lower income class numbers grew and the rich got richer, much richer. There are more than 2,700 billionaires in the world today. Corporations are hoarding billions of dollars in cash or stashing it offshore, rather than investing in research and development, growth projects and human capital. Workers and owners have always fought over a piece of the pie, but unions and labor movements have been shrinking for decades, while pro-capital legislation has crept in to fill the gap. Anecdotally we can see that income inequality may be contributing to the massive household debt loads of average citizens, governments and corporations and potentially lead to financial crisis. Nobel prize winner for economics, Robert J. Shiller has called rising economic inequality "the most important problem we are facing now today" (John Christoffersen, October 2013).

Awareness of Global Suffering
At this stage in human evolution, it is nearly unfathomable that we could be on the brink of extinction, if not in the midst of terrible and unimaginable suffering. Even with technological advancements in medicine, food production and water purification cannot sustain a fast approaching 9 billion people. If 9 billion people consumed like western developed nations we would require 5 planets. The fact there is so much human suffering and mortality from dehydration and starvation is unacceptable. Over population is an extremely challenging problem, contributing to these serious issues. Poverty of basic physical needs, emotional and psychological impoverishment, illiteracy, poor education and lack of health care for millions of people is tragic. Western society is rich beyond imagination and has the knowledge, wealth, and power to eliminate it. Western society, however, does not have the collective will. Yes, there are many organizations trying to help, but it is simply not enough. Unfortunately, too many people close their eyes and pretend it is not happening. This is a defense mechanism and it works, but if our species is to continue to thrive into the next few centuries more of us need to be aware are be moved to action

Passion for Learning
Continuing with the idea of life-long learning, developing a passion for learning, exploring your world and the vastness of available knowledge, I will provide a few ideas to get you started. Think for a moment about a basic college calendar with hundreds of course and program offerings. Here is a short list of major programs of study:

Accounting and Taxes,
Business Administration and Marketing,
Economics and Statistics,
Electrical and Mechanical Engineering,
Nursing,
Architecture and drafting,
Computer programming and systems analysis,
Biology and the Sciences,
Art and Graphic design,
Law, Sociology, Psychology, Geography,
Philosophy and History, Political Science,
Media Arts and Music, Religion and Medicine…

Each of these major topics may have upwards of 50 to 100 specific course offerings, drilling down to allow us to discover the smallest detail of information on a topic available. Every detail and concept that was developed and thought of by somebody in the recent past and compiled in an organized fashion is brought to you in these courses. I find it fascinating that our libraries hold so much information yet we are still writing and publishing 50,000 to 100,000 books per year in North America. Another 100,000 books go unpublished and unread. Therefore, there continues to be a passion to understand and compile information regardless of how much information is currently available.

I once picked up a book, while a student at University, entitled 10,000 Ideas for Term Papers, Projects, Reports, and Speeches, by Kathryn Lamm. A few examples from the History section gave me a newfound respect for the vastness of knowledge we may never have considered. Here is a wonderful saying that I learned from a trainer in a past job:

SOME THINGS
Some things you know you know;
Some things you think you know,
And some things you don't know you don't know!

Think about this for a moment and I know in my heart you will grasp its profound significance to human arrogance, prejudice and dogma. My point is that we only know what we know and often we think we know something and it turns out to be incorrect. We really do not have a full understanding of many things and even more often, we do not even know what we do not know! Medicine is a good example. To illustrate this, we visit our doctor, describe our cold and flu like symptoms, an examination is done and a prescription is written. We are told to take the medication 3 times each day for 10 days on an empty stomach. Most of us do not have an understanding of virology and pharmacology so we simply accept the diagnosis and prescription and go on our way. The depth of knowledge the doctor must have is a culmination of 8 years of intensive study of the human immune system, physiology, biology, chemistry, medicine and even mathematics and statistical analysis as the foundation for his recommendation and prescription. All we know is that the pill will make the cold go away. We do not know how it works and we do not even know what questions to ask (i.e. some things we do not know we do not know) about this seemingly magic pill. The reality is that this pill is also the culmination of years and years of research and testing for effectiveness in a lab and controlled studies. It is the result of thousands of person-hours of learning!

Continuous Pursuits
I have written about Western Societies endless obsession with achievement and success. Remember there is nothing inherently wrong with goals or being successful. Challenging yourself and striving to obtain a coveted medal or trophy in a sporting event or a prestigious law or medical degree or that high paying promotion at work is not a bad thing. However, we seem to strive endlessly and mindlessly for more and better results, more money with no real understanding of why we are compelled to do so. What is the underlying belief or desire to achieve more? Western society needs to take a deep breath and ask why am I doing this. Is this really making me happy? Is it making a better life for children, family or community? Is this bringing us pleasure? How am I contributing to

my community, the less fortunate, and the world at large? These are questions all but a very few are asking.

Thich Nhat Hanh teaches us about Buddhism and the life and philosophy of the Buddha who lived 2500 years ago in India (Hanh, 1998). Thich Nhat Hanh tells us, "of a story in Zen circles about a man and a horse. The horse is galloping quickly, and it appears that the man on the horse is going somewhere important. Another man standing alongside the road, shouts, "Where are you going?" and the man on the horse shouts back, "I don't know! Ask the horse!" This is also our story. We are riding the horse, we do not know where we are going, and we cannot stop. The horse is our habit energy pulling us along, and we are powerless. We are always running from event to event without slowing the pace and asking why. We struggle all the time, even during our sleep...." Work at figuring out where you want to go, then, you can be the one holding the reins of your destiny.

If this is your story, you are not alone. I would recommend one of the following several solutions: First solution is to physically and mentally relax by practicing yoga or some other relaxation technique. The Relaxation Response is a favorite for anybody wanting to learn how to reduce anxiety from daily life (Benson, 1975). Many local Colleges or Universities offer courses for stress management or yoga. Secondly, if your group benefits allow for it, take advantage of the annual allotted visits to a massage therapist. Thirdly, take advantage of counselors every year. Regardless of whether the counselor is a Psychologist, Social worker or Pastor you will benefit with a better understanding of where you are headed. You may be thrilled to discover you are right on track to meet your goals and aspirations or you may sadly discover that you're are going in the wrong direction and need a change. Knowledge and awareness of self is the key to happiness.

Coping with difficult people is probably one of the biggest on the job stressors. Dealing with irrational customers, co-workers and supervisors will test our people skills to the maximum every day. Taking these situations home with you at the end of the day is not something you want to do. I know firsthand it will affect and infect everyone you love, including your friends, family, and neighbors.

A wonderful exploration into understanding difficult people and learning techniques and methods for coping with them is available. Robert Bramson and his colleagues conduct an in depth study of difficult people (Bramson, 1981) in the work place, in the home and in our society. He categorizes them into several distinct categories. He describes them by their actions, reactions and communications. He further offers suggestions for dealing with them without burning bridges, losing your job or getting punched in the nose. Refuse to let these people get in the way of your pursuits and happiness.

Self-Determination vs. Self-Destruction

I often allude to the idea of success as the self-contrived delusion of modern society. Success for most of Western society means that with hard work and determination you can achieve material wealth, recognition, and status. Whether you are an executive with a large corporation, a lawyer, business owner, or professor you are viewed as being a success. Owning a large home, with 2 or 3 luxury vehicles in the driveway, a boat, cottage or second home will be viewed by others as being successful. However, is this success leading to joy and happiness in one's life or is it a contribution to society in some way? Material wealth and prestigious job titles in no way defines success. Although for many people, wealth and success are synonymous.

There are countless stories of very wealthy individuals that are miserable with their lives. Addicted to prescription drugs and alcohol, stressed, anxious and at the very worst suicidal. Or, is it the *millionaire next door* that is most successful? The millionaire next door is the one that saved a part of what he earned, every paycheck and put it into a conservative investment portfolio earning modest returns to see it balloon over the years. This unassuming group did not need a prestigious job title or letters behind their names to be successful or feel worthy. Nor did they have to work 60-hour weeks to achieve their success. They simply worked average jobs for average incomes, and never spent or lived beyond their means.

Contentment seems to be the word that best describes this group. Rather than constant striving for more, they worked hard to reach a comfortable position in society and settled in. This group never felt there was something missing from their lives. Neither was this group driven for the sweet smell of success and recognition. Much of the fruits of success are fleeting, temporary, and then beginning all over again. Sadly, when the reward is not granted due to falling short of the goal, self-destruction ensues. The desire to achieve can be so strong it overcomes all sense of what will truly bring happiness. The next goal or project begins and further suffering, stress, and feelings of worthlessness are sure to follow. Having the desire to achieve a goal is noble, but without understanding why you want to achieve that goal, is destructive.

The best example of this kind of running without knowing where you are headed are those that want to make more money by making more sales, becoming a lawyer, doctor, a business executive or entrepreneur of any discipline. Here is a short monologue with a young want to be lawyer;

"Ok, why would you want to be a lawyer for example? Many lawyers are overworked, stressed out, frustrated with the system. What good can come of becoming a lawyer?"

"Well, a lawyer makes a good income and can convict dangerous criminals to protect society and uphold the law.

"Yes, but what does that do for you? Does this enhance the happiness in your life? Working from 7am to 10pm certainly won't make your spouse very happy and what about the moments you have missed with your children? So, why would you want to be a lawyer? Or other high stress occupation?

The answer: *Because I feel good when I am contributing to society. Yes!* Now this is what I am getting at. We need to look within and drill down a little deeper to understand why we are doing the things we do. Awareness is step one.

Lifestyle
I spoke of the power we have to pilot our own destiny. This is an essential piece to have health, wealth and meaning in our lives. We can choose to live in pursuit of wealth, success and recognition or we can choose to have a more balanced lifestyle. I want to clarify that neither path is inherently good or bad. Rather, should we not

ask how does our particular path contribute to our world and provide us with a deep sense of happiness and gratification? If your path has led you to stress and despair, you are probably in need of a deeper understanding of yourself. Along the path to your goals and pursuits you must be planning for a day you will retire, at least to a slower pace. I discussed goal planning, investing and using the expertise of a Financial Planner who can help you retire in comfort, no matter what they might mean to you individually. In our society, earning an income is essential and saving a part of it for the future is a key to having the equation balance in the end.

Everything boils down to *lifestyle and quality of life*. It involves everything from where you live, how you live, what you do, who you are, the environment you choose to live in whether it is a rural setting, big city suburbs or downtown urban living. Assess whether you enjoy a busy leisure lifestyle including hobbies such as painting, pottery making, model building, or cake decorating for example. Alternatively, are you more of a sports enthusiast as well as enjoying tennis, curling, swimming, or going to the gym 4 times a week? Determine whether you enjoy being part of team, a church or part of a volunteer group for local charity or volunteer or other recreational organization that helps the community in various ways. Maybe you prefer more solitary type activities like painting, sculpting, or photography. Good health, friends, family, work, recreation, hobbies, self-improvement, learning, and traveling to exotic places are some of the many ways we can live each moment to its fullest. If we are not living each moment the way we innately desire, we are not living the way nature intended. Whatever the case may be, the point is to remain passionate, active throughout your life, take responsibility, and make a contribution. Life is for the living. Experience all that life is!

Live for Today! Plan for Tomorrow.

BIBLIOGRAPHY

Alford, Catherine. (2013) *What Wealthy Means Around the World.* www.FrugalRules.com.

Batra, R. (1988). *Surviving The Great Depression of 1990.* New York: Dell Publishing Group.

Benson, H. (1975). *The Relaxation Response.* New York: Avon Books.

Black, W. K. (2005). *The Best Way to Rob a Bank is to Own One: How Corporate Executives and Politicians Looted the S&L Industry.* University of Texas Press.

Bolles, R. N. (1995). *What Color Is Your Parachute? A Practical Manual for Job-Hunters & Career Changers.* Berkeley, California: Ten Speed Press.

Bramson, R. (1981). *Coping With Difficult People.* New York: Anchor Press/Doubleday.

Brown, W. H. (2006). Identifying Superior Active PortfolioManagement. *Journal of Investment Management,* 4 (4), 15-40.

Brown, W. H. (2006). The Right Answer to the Wrong Question: Identifying Superior Active Portfolio Management. *Journal of Investment Management,* 15 - 40.

Browne, H. (1989). *The Economic Time Bomb.* New York : St. Martin's Press.

Cadsby, T. (1999). *The Power of Index Funds.* Toronto: Stoddart Publishing.

Carnegie, D. (1948). *How to Stop Worrying and Start Living.* New York: Simon and Schuster.

Cassidy, John. (2013). *American Inequality in Six Charts.* The New Yorker.

CIFSC, (2016). *Retail Investment Fund Category Definitions.* Canadian Investment Funds Standards Committee.

Centers for Disease Control and Prevention, CDC. (2015). *Health, United States, 2015.*

CEREAL, Cividep India, SOMO. (2015). *Nokia Disconnected. A corporate history from a worker's perspective.* The Goodelectronics Network.

CIBC World Markets. (2007, June 18). *Canadian Leading Indicators.* Retrieved March 2009, from www.Research.CIBCWM.com. citation.

Cogan, M. (1993). *Optimal Sports Nutrition. Your Competitve Edge.* . New York: Advanced Research Press.

Covey, S. R. (1989). *The 7 Habits of Highly Effective People.* New York: Simon & Schuster Inc.

Credit Suisse. (2009). *Global Equity Strategy.* Credit Suisse.

Dyer, W. (1978). *Pulling Your Own Strings.* New York: Avon Books. The Hearst Corporation.

Dyer, W. (2001). *There's a Spiritual Solution to Every Problem.* New York: Harper Collins.

Dyer, W. (1985). *What Do You Really Want For Your Children?* New York, N.Y.: William Morrow and Company.

The Economist (2012). Muddled Models.

Emsbo-Mattingly, Lisa (2016). *Stock Ideas for the Late Cycle*. Fidelity Investment Management.

Forbes, S. (2009, January 26). *Intelligent Investing Transcript: Jeremy Grantham*. Retrieved March 12, 2009, from Forbes.

Forstater, M. (2003). *The TAO. Finding The Way of Balance*. New York, NY.: Penguin Books.

Frank, Robert, (2010). *The Perfect Salary for Happiness: $75,000*. The Wall Street Journal. Summarized a study about links between Money and Happiness, which analyzed Gallup surveys of $450,000 Americans in 2008 and 2009. September 7, 2010.

Frankl, V. (1973). *The Doctor & The Soul From Psychotherapy to Logotherapy*. New York: Vintage Books.

The Huffington Post. (2014). *Here Is The Income Level At Which Money Won't Make You Any Happier In Each State*. Huffington Post.com.

Garmaise Investment Technologies Inc. and Mackenzie Financial Corporation. (1996). Client Investor Profile. Canada.

Gelb, M. (1998). *How To Think Like Leonardo da Vinci. Seven Steps to Genius Every Day*. New York: Random House.

Graham, B. (1973). *The Intelligent Investor* (Revised Edition ed.). New York: Collins Business Essentials.

Graham, B. (1973). *The Intelligent Investor*. New York, New York: Collins Business Essentials.

Gross, B. (2009). *The Future of Investing: Evolution or Revolution*. Newport Beach, California: PIMCO.

Guthrie, L. (2009). *Individual Pension Plans and the Family Business*. Retrieved 2009, from Manulife Financial.

Hanh, T. N. (1998). *The Heart of the Buddha's Teachings: Transforming Suffering into Peace, Joy and Liberation.* Berkeley California: Parallax Press.

Hill, N. (1960). *Think and Grow Rich.* New York: Fawcett Crest. Horizions BetaPro ETFs. (2009). *Profit or Protect in Bull & BearMarkets.* Toronto: Horizons BETAPRO ETFs.

Howell, Kelly. (2016). *12 Habits of the Happiest People on Earth.* Brain Sync News Letter. Retrieved August 10, 2016, from Brain Sync.com

Investopedia. (2009, June). *Elliott Wave Theory.* Retrieved June 3, 2009, from Investopedia.com

Simpson, Stephen. Investopedia. (2016, June). *8. Macroeconomics: The Business Cycle.* Retrieved June 12, 2016, from Investopedia.com

James, E. S. (1994). *Simplify Tour Life.* New York: Hyperion.

Kiplinger, K. (1999). *World Boom Ahead; Why Business and Consumers Will Prosper.* Washington: Kiplinger Books.

Lee, B. (1999). *Bruce Lee, Artist of Life.* (J. Little, Ed.) Boston, MA: Tutle Publishing.

Lowe, J. (2002). *The Man Who Beats the S&P. Investing With Bill Miller.* Toronto: John Wiley & Sons Canada.
Mauldin, J. (2009, March 30). *Why Bother with Bonds?* Retrieved 2009, from Greenlight Advisor.

National Center for Health Statistics. Health, United States, (2015): *With Special Feature on Racial and Ethnic Health Disparities. Hyattsville, MD. 2016.*

National Bureau of Economic Research. (2008). *Business Cycle Expansions and Contractions.* Retrieved 2009, from nber.org/cycles.html.

OECD. (2008). *Household Savings Rates 1990 to 2008 Canada vs. US.* Retrieved July 14, 2009, from OECD.ORG/data.

PlanPlus Inc. (2009). *Client Information Summary.* Retrieved 2009, from PlanPlus.com.

Poyser, L. H. (2005). *Practitioner's Guide To Trusts, Estates and Trust Returns 2005-2006.* Toronto: Thomson Canada Limited.

Reeves, T. C. (1992). *A Question of Character. A Life of John F. Kennedy.* Rocklin, California: Prima Publishing.
Ro, Sam. (2013). *Dividends Were Responsible For 42% Of Stock Market Returns Since 1930* Businessinsider.com/ stock-returns-price-dividend- contribution-2013-1

Robbins, A. (1986). *Unlimited Power.* Columbine, New York: Ballantine Books.

Robbins, A. (1986). *Unlimited Power.* New York: Ballantine Books.

Schilit, H. M. (2002). *Financial Shenanigans 2nd edition.* New York: McGraw-Hill.

Siegel, J. (2009, October 6). *"Stocks for the Long Run" still holds in spite of the painfull selloff.* Retrieved October 6, 2009, from FT.Com.

Stanley, T. J. (2001). *The Millionaire Mind.* Kansas City, Missouri: Andrews McMeel Publishing.

Statistics Canada. (2014). *Survey of Financial Security, 2012.* Retrieved August 24, 2016, from www.statcan.gc.ca.

Statistics Canada.(2016). *National Balance Sheet Accounts, financial indicators, households and no-profit institutions serving households.* Retrieved July 4, 2016, from www.statcan.gc.ca.

Statistics Canada. (2009, March 2). *Gross Domestic Product.* Retrieved March 29, 2009, from www.statcan.gc.ca.

Statistics Canada. (2011). *National Occupational Classifications for Statistics*. Retrieved July 2016, from www.statcan.gc.ca.

Statistics Canada. (2007). *Survey of Financial Security 2005*. Retrieved 2008, from www.statcan.ca/Daily/.

Statistics Canada. (2012). *Leading causes of death, by sex*. Retrieved 2016, from www.statcan..gc.ca/tables.

Statistics Canada. (2012, May 12). *Health-adjusted life expectancy by sex*. Retrieved July 2016 from www.statcan.gc.ca.

Stephen Soreff, M. (2006, September 28). *Suicide*. Retrieved 2008, from www.emedicine.com
The Globe and Mail. (2009, June 29). *Victims lash out at Madoff*. Retrieved June 29, 2009, from globeinvestor.com.

Thomas J. Stanley, P. (2001). *The Millionaire Mind*. Kansas City: Andrews McMeel Publishing.

Thorton, Grant (2015). *The Tax Planning Guide 2015-2016*. Retrieved September 21, 2016, from www.taxplanningguide.ca

Turner, G. (1996). *2015: After the Boom, How to Prosper Through the Coming Retirement Crisis*. Toronto: Key Porter Books.

Turner, G. (1996). *2015: After the Boom, How to Prosper Through the Coming Retirement Crisis*. Toronto: Key Porter Books.

Wiggin, W. B. (2006). *Empire of Debt: The Rise of an Epic Financial Crisis*. Hoboken, New Jersey: John Wiley & Sons.

Wilson, B., Gwen, B., & Bullis, N. J. (2003). *The Family Trust Guide*.

Toronto: The Canadian Institute of Chartered Accountants.

Printed in the United States
By Bookmasters